'Avant-garde' Art Groups in China, 1979–1989

'Avant-garde' Art Groups in China, 1979-1989
The Stars–The Northern Art Group–
The Pond Association–Xiamen Dada
A Critical Polylogue

Paul Gladston

intellect Bristol, UK / Chicago, USA

ShanghART
香 格 纳 画 廊

www.shanghartgallery.com

Publication supported by the
ShanghART Gallery

First published in the UK in 2013 by
Intellect, The Mill, Parnall Road, Fishponds, Bristol, BS16 3JG, UK

First published in the USA in 2013 by
Intellect, The University of Chicago Press, 1427 E. 60th Street,
Chicago, IL 60637, USA

A catalogue record for this book is available from the
British Library.

Cover designer: Ellen Thomas
Cover image: Members of the Northern Art Group
   in 1987 – courtesy of Shu Qun
Copy-editor: MPS Technologies
Production manager: Bethan Ball
Typesetting: Planman Technologies

Print ISBN: 978-1-84150-715-6
ePDF ISBN: 978-1-78320-052-8
ePub ISBN: 978-1-78320-053-5

Printed and bound by Bell & Bain, UK

Contents

Acknowledgements

Above all, I would like to thank the artists who participated in the making of this book for their enormous generosity and patience. I would also like to thank Lorenz Helbling and Laura Zhou of the ShanghART Gallery in Shanghai and Johnson Chang (Chang Tsong-zung) of the Hanart TZ Gallery in Hong Kong who assisted in contacting some of the artists whose thoughts, impressions and recollections are represented here, as well as the Asia Art Archive for providing some of the images included in this book. Thanks are also due to my former research assistant Xu Sujing for her work in transcribing and translating the conversations contained in this book and to my PhD student Yao Yung-Wen for her assistance in checking the factual accuracy of the artists' statements. In addition, I would like to express my gratitude to the University of Nottingham and the University of Nottingham Ningbo, China, for providing research funding and a period of study leave in support of this project. Finally, I would like to thank Keith Wallace at *Yishu* for giving me a platform for my early writings on contemporary Chinese art.

About the Author

Paul Gladston is Associate Professor of Culture, Film and Media and Director of the Centre for Contemporary East-Asian Cultural Studies (CEACS) at the University of Nottingham (United Kingdom). Between 2005 and 2010, he was inaugural Head of the Department of International Communications and Director of the Institute for Comparative Cultural Studies at the University of Nottingham Ningbo, China. He has written extensively on contemporary Chinese art with particular reference to the concerns of critical theory. His book-length publications include *Art History after Deconstruction* (2005), *China and Other Spaces* (2009), *Contemporary Art in Shanghai: Conversations with Seven Chinese Artists* (2011) and *Contemporary Chinese Art and Criticality* (2012), a special edition of the *Journal of Visual Art Practice*, co-edited with Katie Hill.

Dr. Paul Gladston
The University of Nottingham, Trent Building, University Park, Nottingham, NG7 2RD, UK
E-mail: paul.gladston@nottingham.ac.uk

Introduction

This book focuses on four of the most significant 'avant-garde' art groups active within the People's Republic of China (PRC) between 1979 and 1989: the Stars (*Xingxing* 星星), the Northern Art Group (*Beifang yishu qunti* 北方艺术群体), the Pond Association (*Chi she* 池社) and Xiamen Dada (*Xiamen Dada* 厦门达达). By the mid-1980s, scores of similar self-organized groups had come together (Gao 2007a: back cover notes)—many in little more than name only—as part of the liberalization of society that had begun to take place within the PRC following the death of Mao Zedong 毛泽东 (1893–1976), in 1976, and the acceptance of Deng Xiaoping 邓小平's (1904–1997) programme of Reform and Opening (*Gaige kaifang* 改革开放) at the XI Central Committee of the Chinese Communist Party (CCP), in December 1978. These 'avant-garde' groups were an enormously important part of the development of contemporary art in China during the ten-year period from 1979 to 1989. They offered a collective as well as protective platform for artistic practices, which diverged markedly from the established conventions of Maoist socialist-realism, by combining aspects of indigenous Chinese cultural thought and practice (both modern and traditional) with images, attitudes and techniques appropriated from Western(ized) modernist and postmodernist art. In 1989, public actions by all 'avant-garde' art groups in China were suspended as part of the conservative crackdown that followed the Tian'anmen protests of the same year, thereby effectively drawing a line under a period of widespread collectivism within China's 'avant-garde' art world. By that time, most of the groups in question, many of which were only loosely organized, had in any case already drifted apart not least because of an increasing sense of individualism among their members brought about in large part by China's post-Maoist liberalization.

In spite of their importance, published writings about 'avant-garde' art groups active within China during the late 1970s and 1980s have, up to now, been extremely limited in scope, confined for the most part to relatively brief passages contained within narrative histories tracing the wider development of contemporary Chinese art (e.g. Lü and Yi 1991; Köppel-Yang 2003; Erickson 2005; Gao 2005; Berghuis 2006), biographical studies of contemporary Chinese artists (Smith 2005), related anthologies of documentary sources (Wu 2010) and texts posted on websites. Moreover, much of what has been written has tended to rely heavily on contemporaneous accounts of the activities of the groups in question and to accept those accounts more or less at face value, thereby perpetuating numerous factual inaccuracies. Absent from the literature are more focused critical readings based on detailed research involving the critical triangulation of a variety of primary and secondary sources. This book is an attempt to present a series of such critical readings accompanied by transcripts of in-depth conversations with artists who were formerly members of 'avant-garde' art groups during the period in question; it also presents an introductory essay contextualizing the development of 'avant-garde' art in China.

One of the methodological challenges presented by the use of conversations as a means of gathering and presenting data is that interviewees may not always be able to recall past events accurately. Moreover, the accounts of interviewees may be subject to the effects of 'reconstructive memory'; that is to say, conscious or unconscious attempts to reframe the significance of past events. Reconstructive memory stems almost invariably from a desire on the part of interviewees to present their past actions and, perhaps, those of others in a favourable light. Within the particular context of the PRC, where there are continuing governmental restrictions on freedom of speech and action, it is also important to recognize that artists speaking 'on the record' may choose consciously or unconsciously to temper their accounts for fear of government reprisals and, perhaps, to cover the tracks of their own previous political indiscretions. To lessen the effect of these potentially distorting factors, much care has been taken to cross-reference what was said by the artists with information gleaned from other sources. Furthermore, artists involved in the conversations were often asked to respond to follow-up questions both as a means of clarifying initially vague responses and, where possible, to resolve/explain discrepancies between their accounts and those contained in existing documentary sources.

The conversations, whose edited transcripts are presented here, were conducted within the PRC between 2006 and 2010 in English and Mandarin Chinese with the assistance of a native speaking Chinese interpreter. They were recorded digitally *in situ* before being translated and transcribed into English. As anyone familiar with the making of transcriptions of recorded conversations will readily acknowledge, recorded speech is often repetitious, contradictory, elliptical and grammatically incorrect. As a consequence, transcriptions of recorded speech more often than not require careful editing so that they can be made comprehensible while adhering as closely as possible to the traces of what was actually said. The transcripts presented here should therefore be seen, like most other published conversations, not as verbatim records but as considered constructs after the fact.

No amount of careful translation, editing or footnoting will, however, negate entirely the slippages of understanding that take place as a result of the translation of meaning from one cultural/linguistic context to another. Not only is the translation of meaning from one cultural/linguistic context to another subject to problematic absences of conceptual/ idiomatic equivalence between differing language systems, but, as post-structuralist accounts of linguistic signification have shown (e.g. Derrida 1972; Ulmer 1985 [1983]; Bhabha 1994), linguistic utterances/acts of signification are also subject to the continual possibility of deconstructive re-motivation (that is to say, the generation of supplementary understandings of their significance) as a result of changed circumstances of time and place in a manner broadly analogous to the dislocating effects of the Western avant-garde's artistic pairing of collage-montage. Consequently, the transcripts of conversations presented here should be thought of not simply as constructs but as constructs whose meaning has been and is still open to re-motivation through transformative acts of translation/(re-)reading. As such, they arguably share in the conspicuously uncertain significance of the 'avant-garde' artworks upon which they, in part, reflect, which are themselves—as assemblages of the traces of Chinese and non-Chinese cultural elements—both products of and subject to the refractive effects of cultural translation. By extension, the same could be said of the readings and translations of other sources contained in this book.

As Richard Whittaker indicates in the introduction to his book *The Conversations: Interviews with Sixteen Contemporary Artists* (Whittaker 2008: 7–8)—to which this present publication is strongly indebted[1]—a key reason for conducting conversations with artists as means of elucidating the significance of artworks is that they provide accounts of the lived experience of art-making that have the potential to extend or even contradict what has been said and written by others (i.e. art historians and critics) working outside the prevailing conditions of artistic practice. The use of conversations for that purpose here is, however, by no means intended as a privileging of the voice of the artist over the 'corrupted' writing of others. Rather, it is envisaged as a means of adding to and intervening critically upon other written accounts in a manner commensurate with the pervasively deconstructive effects of linguistic signification/translation highlighted earlier in this introduction.

The decision to adopt this particular analytical format draws directly on the work of two other critical writers. The first of these is Jacques Derrida whose radical collage-text *Glas* (Derrida 1974) juxtaposes writings by the poet and playwright Jean Genet and the philosopher G.W.F. Hegel as a deconstructive means of opening up each to the positioning of the other while internally dividing and questioning the authority of both. The second is the intercultural philosopher Franz Martin Wimmer who has argued that, in order to go beyond the rash universalism or relativistic particularism of philosophical thinking conducted from a single cultural point of view, it is necessary to engage critically with other cultural perspectives in the form of a polylogue or 'dialogue of many' (Wimmer 2004). In the case of both of these writers, there is a desire to challenge supposedly authoritative truth claims by entering into an unsettling interaction between differing intellectual/cultural outlooks. In adopting a similarly multi-voiced approach here, it is hoped that the subject of 'avant-garde' art in China, which is open to interpretation from often starkly contrasting Chinese and non-Chinese perspectives, will exceed the limitations of any single cultural purview.

As the various texts assembled here show, the significance of 'avant-garde' art in China between 1979 and 1989 is both complex and uncertain. While 'avant-garde' artists in China during the late 1970s and 1980s may appear from a Western perspective to have been involved in a more or less straightforward appropriation of attitudes and techniques associated with Western(ized) modernism and postmodernism as part of the opening-up and reform of Chinese society after the death of Mao, those outside influences were invariably subject to reworking in relation to not only the localized demands of the indigenous Chinese art world but also the persistent influence of earlier Chinese translations of Western(ized) cultural thought and practice. The product of this reworking is a shifting and complexly intersecting fabric of artistic grafting that resists any single interpretative perspective. Consequently, while it is possible to interpret 'avant-garde' art in China between 1979 and 1989 as a manifestation of China's post-Maoist modernity, it is equally possible to view that art as a reaffirmation of a specifically Chinese sense of cultural identity, both in resistance to the supposedly deracinating effects of Western(ized) modernity and as a progressive response to the widespread destruction of traditional Chinese culture that took place within the PRC as part of the Cultural Revolution during the late 1960s and early 1970s.

It would, however, be a mistake to think that Chinese 'avant-garde' artists were fully conscious or in control of this complex process of cultural grafting. As the conversations presented here show, many of the members of the groups in question were and continue to be disinterested in the theoretical significances of the processes involved in their practice as artists, preferring instead (as artists often do) to concentrate on practical issues related to making art and the aesthetic aspects of self-expression. What is more, where members of the groups in question did engage in intellectual analysis of their practice, this often led to stances that to a contemporary Western audience may seem either unduly individualistic and/or elitist. Here, it is important to recognize two significant factors: first, that while Chinese 'avant-garde' art has often been interpreted in Western(ized) contexts as an expression of political dissidence on the part of its makers, such simplistic readings underestimate the drive of Chinese 'avant-garde' artists of the late 1970s and 1980s to do simply as they pleased without the burden of the constant engagement with political ideology that had dominated the Maoist period; and second, the lack of any significant formalized training within China during the 1970s and 1980s in Western(ized) interpretations of the practical and theoretical implications of 'avant-garde' art-making (not least the deconstructive potential of collage-montage). Against this background, it is not surprising to find in the conversations published here constant reconstructive reversions to a more familiar localized cultural territory associated with China's immediate communist past as well as its extended traditions. The result is a densely compacted palimpsest of possible meanings that points continually away from established Western(ized) art theory along corridors of thought without obvious cultural direction or end.

To explore that significance more fully, it is necessary to contextualize Chinese 'avant-garde' art groups and associations of the late 1970s and 1980s in relation to not only the immediate circumstances of their coming together after 1979 but also the wider development of modern and contemporary art within China since the early twentieth century. The essay that follows this introduction is an attempt to situate 'avant-garde' art in China during the late 1970s and 1980s in relation to that extended historical context. By contextualizing Chinese 'avant-garde' art groups and associations of the late 1970s and 1980s in this way, it is possible to see that the cultural outlook of artists associated with those groups was, while very much of its time, strongly informed by traces of the attitudes and preoccupations of earlier generations of modern Chinese artists as part of China's post-imperial modernization.

Note on Chinese names and terms: Chinese names are presented throughout this book in the order traditional to Chinese culture with family names preceding given names. Chinese names and specialist terms are given in pinyin (the Romanized version of Mandarin Chinese) and Mandarin Chinese. Chinese terms in pinyin and Mandarin are accompanied by English translations throughout.

Note

1   Other influences on the format of the present publication include an at times highly unsettling conversation between the writer Gordon Burn (1948–2009)—author of *Somebody's Husband, Somebody's Son* (1984)—and Gilbert and George conducted in 1978 (Burn 2009: 126–139) as well as those between the critic David Sylvester (1924–2001) and Francis Bacon (1909–1992) conducted during the 1960s and 1970s (Sylvester 1987; 1980).

China's Post-Maoist 'Avant-garde' in Context: Modern and Contemporary Art in China, 1911–2011

Modernist and realist art in China, 1911–1949

Western modes of pictorial representation, including the use of perspective geometry, *chiascuro* and the technique of oil painting on canvas, are known to have entered China during the early seventeenth century through the teachings of Jesuit missionaries including Giuseppe Castiglioni (1688–1766) (known in China as Lang Shining 郎世宁), who taught artists in the court of the Qianlong Emperor (r. 1735–1799) (Clunas 1997:78–80). The impact of these Western modes of representation on the work of indigenous Chinese artists resulted in culturally mixed forms of picture-making that brought together the technical objectivity of Western illusionism with traditional Chinese styles and techniques, involving more obviously subjective renderings of pattern and form while excluding more troubling Western subject matter such as the Crucifixion (Clunas 1997: 129–130).

In spite of this established connection between China and the West, recognizably modern forms of visual art conspicuously resistant to tradition produced by Chinese nationals did not begin to appear within China until the first half of the twentieth century, between the Xinhai Revolution (Xinhai Geming 辛亥革命) of 1911—which led to the abdication of Puyi 溥仪(1906–1967), China's last emperor, and the establishment of republican rule under the provisional leadership of Sun Yat-sen 孙逸仙 (1866–1925) in 1912—and the beginning of the Second Sino–Japanese War in 1937.

At the end of the nineteenth and the beginning of the twentieth century, there was a growing perception within Chinese society that China had become an economically, technologically, militarily and politically-backward state whose adherence to traditional Confucian cultural values, as part of feudal dynastic rule, had not only prevented it from developing materially alongside Europe, North America and Japan but also supported the perpetuation of huge and shameful social inequalities among the Chinese people. In response, educated Chinese began to travel extensively in Europe (particularly France and Germany), North America, South East Asia and Japan seeking to familiarize themselves with modern Western(ized) culture. On returning to China, many of these educated Chinese went on to play a significant role in the modernization of Chinese society by promoting practices and ways of thinking that departed radically from China's established cultural traditions.

The main rallying point for cultural change within China during the early decades of the twentieth century was the New Culture Movement (*Xin wenhua yundong* 新文化运动), which first began to coalesce in the wake of calls for social, political and cultural change issued in, among other places, the newly founded journal *New Youth* (also known as *La Jeunnesse*), shortly after the establishment of republican rule in 1912. The movement gained national prominence following a wave of student protests on 4 May 1919 initiated in response to the unfavourable terms forced upon China at the Versailles Peace Conference of the same year. As Lynn Pan has indicated, the events of 4 May 1919 led to a cultural upsurge across China known as the May Fourth Movement (*Wusi yundong* 五四运动) that has been widely interpreted as 'the start of the social revolution to which the Chinese Communist Party would eventually lay claim' (Pan 2008: 48–49).

In spite of its nationwide impact, the New Culture Movement was far from being unified in its outlook and aims. While some of those who associated themselves with the movement viewed the persistence of traditional Chinese cultural values as the principal impediment to China's modernization, others were reluctant to embrace Westernized modernity fully for fear of uprooting China's distinctive, civilization-specific identity. As a consequence, the New Culture Movement was divided between a fervent desire to assimilate Western ideas and practices that pointed towards the possibility of progressive sociocultural change—most notably, those associated with American pragmatism, Social Darwinism and Nietzschean thought (Shen 2009: 361–365)—and an equally fervent desire to reconcile Western(ized) modernity with aspects of China's long-standing cultural traditions.

Set against this wider background of national-cultural reform, modernization of the visual arts in China manifested itself in a number of ways. Of crucial importance was the establishment of art academies dedicated to the transmission of Western artistic values and techniques. Among the most important of these was the school that would come to be known as the Shanghai Painting and Art Institute (*Shanghai tuhua meishu yuan* 上海图画美术院, or *Shanghai Meizhuan* 上海美专). Within academies such as these, Chinese students were taught what were considered, in Europe and North America at the time, highly conventional techniques, such as drawing and painting directly from life models, the landscape and collections of still-life objects. In China, however, these techniques pointed towards the possibility of a radical overcoming of the perceived decadence of established Chinese pictorial tradition, or, if not that, at the very least a means of its productive renewal. Strongly indicative of this difference in cultural outlook is the Shanghai Painting and Art Institute's involvement in a major public scandal over its use of life models, which was widely perceived within a Chinese society traditionally unused to public depictions of the naked human form as nothing short of immoral (Pan 2008: 53–54).[1]

Alongside the establishment of art academies dedicated to the transmission of Western artistic values and techniques, there were also calls for the development of a new approach towards art-making within China, based strongly on the principles and values of Western realism. Among those who supported the development of such an approach was the highly influential educationalist and philosopher Cai Yuanpei 蔡元培 (1868–1940), who, in 1917, argued that aesthetic education in China should replace religion, and that Chinese artists should abandon their traditional emphasis on subjectivity—given definition by the Chinese aesthetic concept of *i-ching* 意境 (idea-realm) (Wang 1995: 23–26)[2]—in favour of Western objectivist attitudes and techniques (Pan 2008: 50).[3] This desire to see traditional Chinese subjectivity replaced by Western realism was shared by the painters Xu Beihong 徐悲鸿 (1895–1953) and Jiang Zhaoke 蒋兆和 (1904–1986), both of whom adopted what was considered, from a Western perspective at the time, an academic-realist approach towards painting that would later go on to inform the development of socialist-realist art within China under communism.

In addition to those who supported the adoption of Western realism, there were others openly receptive to the anti-realist/abstractionist tendencies of Western modernism. These include members of the Shanghai-based Storm Society (*Juelanshe* 决澜社), China's first identifiably 'modernist' art group, founded by the artists Ni Yide 倪贻德 (1902–1969) and Pang Xunqin 庞熏琹 (1906–1985) in 1931. In their manifesto, the Storm Society, many of whose members had been trained in modern Westernized art techniques in either Paris or Tokyo, announced a collective desire not only to repudiate the art of their immediate surroundings in China, which they characterized as 'mediocre, philistine, feeble-minded, shallow, decrepit and sickly,' but also to create their own 'world of intersecting colour, line and form,' following the example set by the Fauvist, Cubist, Dada and Surrealist movements in Europe (Pan 2008: 67–69). This stated desire to embrace the intellectual and stylistic innovations of early-twentieth-century European modernism, while evinced to some extent by the formal execution of artworks produced by members of the group, was, however, by no means fully realized. Paintings by Ni Yide, for example, remain strongly indebted to pre-Cubist stylistic approaches associated with Impressionism and post-Impressionism, while those of Pang Xunqin emulate the look of Cubism and Futurism but only in a schematic, stylistically superficial and spatially unsophisticated way.

Another early-twentieth-century Chinese artist who trained outside China (in Paris, Dijon and Germany) and who sought to align himself with Western modernism was Lin Fengmian 林风眠 (1900–1991). Lin's paintings of the 1930s are clearly indebted stylistically to European Fauvism and Expressionism. Unlike members of the Storm Society, however, Lin advocated formal innovation explicitly in support of the making of an 'art for people's life,' or, as the curator and art historian Gao Minglu 高名潞 has put it, an 'art that saw abstract and metaphysical forms as a way to express a kind of humanist concern' (Gao 2005: 46). Also of importance at this time were Chinese modernists, such as Sanyu (Chang Yu 常玉) (1901–1966) and Pan Yuliang 潘玉良 (1899–1977), who, after first studying abroad, had chosen to live and work outside China. These artists are the precursors of later generations of diasporic Chinese artists, including those who left China in the 1980s and 1990s in the face of continuing political suppression.

Supporters of Western modernism in early-twentieth-century China also include the French-educated art critic Fu Lei 傅雷 (1908–1966). While Fu recognized the quality and importance of Western modernist art, and in particular that of the work of Paul Cézanne, he also regarded the anti-realist/abstractionist tendencies of Western modernism as having been heavily foreshadowed by the subjectivism of traditional Chinese art. This historicizing vision of traditional Chinese art and Western modernism supported Fu's view that the late-nineteenth- and twentieth-century practitioner of traditional Chinese *shan-shui* 山水[4] painting, Huang Binhong 黄宾虹 (1865–1955), was, in fact, a modern as well as traditional master (Roberts 2010).

A variation on this culturally mixed outlook can be found in relation to the Lingnan School (*Lingnan Huapai* 岭南画派) of painters, active in Hangzhou during the 1930s, whose members produced paintings combining traditional Chinese techniques and modern subject matter. Consider here, for example, Gao Jianfu 高剑父's *Flying in the Rain* (*Zhong Fei Xing* 雨中飞行 Yu) (1932), which depicts biplanes flying over a typically rendered *shan-shui* landscape (Erickson 2005: 11).

From a Western perspective, much of the work produced by Chinese modernists of the early twentieth century would appear to have little or no critical content other than a formalist desire to move beyond traditional Chinese modes of artistic production. Indeed, apart from rare examples of collage-montage—among them an anonymously produced photo-collage titled *Standard Chinese* (1911) (Gao 2005: 47)—there is no significant evidence of artworks produced in China during the early twentieth century that share to any great extent the pervasively unsettling implications of early-twentieth-century avant-garde art in Europe and North America. Seen through the lens of a localized Chinese modernity, however, early-twentieth-century works of art produced in China that reference Western realism and modernism can be understood to carry specific connotations of ideological radicalism that exceed the merely formalistic. The appropriation of Western realist and modernist styles by Chinese painters was part of an increasingly intense debate about the direction of modernization: a debate that raged between radicals and conservatives within China during the 1920s and 1930s (Mackerras 2008: 5–6). As a result, artistic modernism and realism in China became strongly aligned with differing ideological positions: the former with liberal bourgeois-democratic reform and the latter with socialist-revolutionary change.

By the mid-1930s, however, the pursuit of modernist approaches towards artistic production within China had become increasingly difficult because of hardening attitudes on the political right and left. While those on the right continued to condemn Westernized formalist modernism as a focus for extreme and unwelcome radicalism, those on the left became increasingly entrenched in their ideological positions, resulting in a shift in allegiance towards more populist/realist forms of artistic production, such as those developed by the Chinese Modern Woodcut Print Movement as a means of highlighting instances of social injustice and deprivation in line with socialist and communist aesthetic principles (Tang 2008).

Shortly after the establishment of republican government under the leadership of Sun Yat-sen in 1912, China began to fragment into competing factions, some under the control of the republican government and some under that of local warlords. After Sun's death in 1925 leadership of the republican government was transferred to Chiang Kai-shek 蒋介石 (1887–1975), who, in 1926, led a military action, known as the Northern Expedition, intended to unify the country under his leadership as head of China's nationalist party, the *Kuomintang* 国民党 (KMT). In contrast to Sun, Chiang was a traditionalist and nationalist authoritarian who rejected social democracy. As a result, in 1927, a major split took place between the KMT and the CCP and this led to intermittent civil war. In 1937, after years of escalation, the KMT initiated another conflict with invading Japanese imperial forces, known as the Second Sino–Japanese War, which severely weakened the KMT's grip on power while increasing Chiang's national prominence as a war leader. During the Second Sino–Japanese War, the KMT and CCP entered into an uneasy and only partially successful truce in order to coordinate their efforts against invading Japanese forces. With the defeat of Japan in 1945, and following a failed US attempt to broker a national coalition government, the KMT and CCP resumed their civil conflict; this resulted in the setting up of the PRC under communist rule, and in the retreat of nationalist forces to Taiwan in 1949.

During the late 1930s and 1940s, artistic production within China became increasingly subject to the pervasively disruptive effects of these overlapping military struggles. Although there was a continuation of Westernized modernist tendencies within China well into the 1940s (through the work of the Modern Woodcut Print Movement as well as that of painters such as Huang Xinbo 黄新波 (1916–1980)), the orientation of these works was very much towards social-realist/expressionist modes of representation, similar to those found in Europe and North America at around the same time (e.g. the work of Diego Rivera) rather than the formal experimentation and anti-realism that characterized the work of the Western avant-gardes.

Maoist socialist-realism, 1949–1976

In May 1942, Mao Zedong—who had by then achieved almost total dominance of the CCP, as leader of its simultaneous armed struggles with the KMT and occupying Japanese forces—convened a forum on literature and the arts at the CCP's headquarters in Yan'an in the northern Chinese province of Shaanxi.[5] In this forum, Mao gave his now famous 'Yan'an Talks on Literature and the Arts' (*Zai Yan'an wenyi zuotanhui shang de jianghua* 在延安文艺座谈会上的讲话) during which he argued that there is no art detached from or independent of politics and that a truly revolutionary Chinese art should be used to represent and promote the view of the masses; that is to say, the workers, peasants, soldiers and urban petty bourgeoisie who made up the vast majority of China's population at the time (Mackerras 2008: 149–150). This vision of art as part of a larger 'revolutionary machine,' which was influenced strongly by the cultural policies of the Soviet Union as well as views put forward by Chinese Marxists during the May Fourth Movement of 1919, subsequently became the basis of an official directive issued by the CCP shortly after it came to power in 1949. This official directive required all artists working in the newly founded PRC not only to take the view of the masses but also to uphold the revolutionary aims of the CCP.[6]

From the early 1950s until the beginning of the Cultural Revolution (*Wuchan jieji wenhua da geming* 无产阶级文化大革命)[7] in 1966, the CCP's official directive on the role of art within the PRC was administered by two government bodies: the Ministry of Culture (*Wenhua bu* 文化部), which was answerable to the Civil Government via the State Council and took responsibility for the ideological direction of artistic production in the PRC; and the All-China Federation of Literary and Art Circles (*Zhonghua quanguo wenxue yishujie lianhehui* 中华全国文学艺术界联合会) as well as its various branches, including the Chinese Artists Association (*Zhongguo meishujia xiehui* 中国美术家协会), which were in practice an extension of the CCP's propaganda department and exercised direct control over all practical matters related to art education, art-making and public exhibitions, suppressing or censoring anything that might be perceived to depart, intentionally or otherwise, from the stated ideological position of the CCP.

During the Cultural Revolution, this complex administrative system came to be seen by Mao and his supporters as both reactionary and irredeemably corrupt, and, therefore, a blockage to any direct interpretation of Maoist thought. As a consequence, it was replaced by a 'pure model' of cultural production that for a while gave the Red Guards (*Hongwei bing* 红卫兵)—young leftist revolutionaries operating with Mao's approval outside the CCP's institutionalized bureaucratic system[8]—free rein to promote Maoist revolutionary thought through public forms of street propaganda and to denounce, violently attack and in many cases kill 'capitalist roaders' (*Zou zi pai* 走资派) perceived to be in opposition to Maoist ideology (including many established Chinese artists and cultural administrators) (Berghuis 2006: 41).[9] Among the focuses for cultural revolutionary action at this time were the 'Four Olds' (*Si jiu* 四旧)—old thought, old customs, old culture and old morals. The campaign to destroy the Four Olds began in Beijing on 20 August 1966, shortly after the launch of the Cultural Revolution (Spence 1999: 575).

As a result of the extreme civil disorder that ensued in the wake of the implementation of this 'pure' model of cultural production, Mao eventually agreed to 'send down' the Red Guards, along with others of their generation, to work in the countryside where they were made to confront the stark realities of materially impoverished rural life within the PRC (otherwise known as the Down to the Countryside Movement (*Shang shan xia xiang yundong* 上山下海运动 – literally 'up to the mountains and down to the villages movement')). This reversal of political direction, which also involved the continued closure of most of the PRC's institutions of higher education, did not, however, lead to the immediate reinstatement of organized bureaucratic control over the arts within the PRC. Instead, the ideological and practical administration of the arts remained with central government officials until the death of Mao in 1976, after which it was handed back to newly constituted versions of the government bodies that had administered the arts prior to the Cultural Revolution.

Despite the severe ideological and bureaucratic restrictions that were placed on freedom of artistic expression within the PRC from the early 1950s to the mid-1970s, it would be a mistake to see all of the art made within the PRC during that period simply as a passive and stylistically monolithic tool of government focused narrowly on revolutionary change. Included in Mao's 'Yan'an Talks' are two observations on the future of artistic production under communism that, during the years from 1949 to the beginning of the Cultural Revolution, gave room not only for a certain degree of professional agency but also for continuity with tradition as part of the making and exhibiting of art. The first of these is that while literature and art should always be seen as subordinate to politics, they 'in their turn exert a great influence on politics' (Mackerras 2008: 149). The second is that art in the service of the CCP should look towards the 'rich legacy and the good traditions in literature and art that have been handed down from past ages in China and foreign countries' and that these 'old forms' should be 'remoulded and infused with new content[…]in the service of the people' (Mackerras 2008: 150). Consequently, before the extreme resistance to outside cultural influences and the widespread denigration of traditional Chinese cultural thought and practice that took hold during the Cultural Revolution,[10] artistic production within the PRC was able to accommodate a range of contrasting approaches. These contrasting approaches include the Soviet-influenced socialist-realism that became a mainstay of revolutionary art within the PRC from the early 1950s through to the mid-1980s, more traditional Chinese styles of painting such as *shan-shui* and *shui-mo* 水墨[11] and aspects of Chinese folk art, which had been adapted or co-opted more or less successfully to the ideological requirements of the CCP. Moreover, during the same period, artists within the PRC were able to assert their professional standing as cultural interpreters/mediators of Maoist thought, through the central and municipal artists associations that had been set up to manage the practical direction of official artistic production in the PRC after 1949, and through the work units (*danwei* 单位) that were brought together by those associations to produce artworks at a grass-roots level, from the late 1950s onwards, as part of a wider move towards collectivization in the PRC—associated with the Great Leap Forward (*Dayuejin* 大跃进).[12]

It is also important to note that during the period from 1949 to 1966 numerous artworks were made within the PRC in outward conformity to the directives of the CCP while incorporating allegorically coded criticism of the consequences of communist rule. Consider here, for example, Fu Baoshi's highly selective pictorial response to a poem by Mao Zedong, *Heavy Rain Falls on Youyan* (*Youyan dayu luo youyan* 大雨落幽燕) (1961), which presents an allegorical though still discernibly negative commentary on the tragic events that took place in the wake of the Great Leap Forward (Clarke 2008: 287). During the same period there were also artists who chose to work under serious threat of official denunciation and punishment outside China's state-controlled system. These artists include Lin Fengmian, the veteran Chinese modernist of the New Culture Movement, who continued to make expressionistic landscape paintings from 1949 up until the early years of the Cultural Revolution, when, after sustained public criticism, he was left with no option but to destroy his work (Clarke 2008: 287), as well as members of the No Name Group (*Wuming huahui* 无名画会), who, from the early 1960s until the mid-1970s and in an understandably clandestine manner, produced formalist (impressionistic) still-life, portrait and landscape paintings that did not conform to the given norms of Chinese socialist-realism (Gao 2007b).[13]

As previously indicated, during the Cultural Revolution the official acceptance of formal diversity and professional interpretation/mediation, an approach that had informed the production and exhibition of art within the PRC prior to 1966, gave way to a 'pure model' of cultural production intended to bring artistic practices into a more direct revolutionary engagement with society. The adoption of this model led not only to a widespread dereliction and destruction of traditional and externally-influenced forms of artistic expression, but, in addition, a significant curtailing of professional agency among artists within the PRC. At the same time, the Cultural Revolution also enabled young art workers to develop a significant (though by no means always welcome) public profile through their involvement in the collective making of various forms of visual propaganda, including *dazibao* 大字报 (big character posters),[14] mural paintings, and mass-produced images of Mao Zedong.[15] Furthermore, some of the methods employed by artworkers during the Cultural Revolution, among them street performances and multimedia events, are similar in some respects to the anti-realist techniques used by the Western avant-gardes. While this similarity did not come about as a result of any direct intercultural exchange between the West and China, given the closed, anti-Western nature of Chinese society at the time, it is nevertheless possible to register a further diversification of the possibilities of revolutionary art within the PRC, beyond the use of socialist-realist and traditional Chinese modes of production.

'Modern' art in China, 1976–1989

Following the death of Mao and the ending of the Cultural Revolution in 1976, the PRC entered a period of significant political uncertainty that, for a time—and most intensely during the brief moment of liberalization, known as the Beijing Spring (*Beijing zhi chun* 北京之春)[16] of 1977 to 1978—saw increasing public opposition to the established policies of the CCP. During this period there was not only a reinstatement of the institutional structures that had been used to govern the ideological and practical direction of artistic production within the PRC prior to 1966, but also a mass reopening of higher-education institutions, including many of the PRC's fine art academies and craft colleges.

Another significant change of political direction that strongly influenced the production and public exhibition of art within the PRC at this time was the confirmation of Deng Xiaoping's so-called policy of 'Reform and Opening' at the Third Plenary Session of the XI Central Committee of the Chinese Communist Party in December 1978 (an event that effectively secured Deng's leadership of the CCP over Mao's designated successor Hua Guofeng 华国锋 (1921–2008)). At this session, Deng, a one-time ally of Mao who had recently been reinstated to a position of power within the CCP after a number of years in political exile, sought to move beyond the transitional uncertainties of the Beijing Spring by proposing the adoption, by the CCP, of a series of related policies and directives, including the 'Four Modernizations,' (*Si ge xian dai hua* 四个现代化) the 'Two Hundreds' (*Shuangbai* 双百) directive and the 'Liberate Your Thinking and Search for the Truth in the Facts' (*Jiefang sixiang shishi qiu shi* 解放思想实事求是)[17] directive; the combination of which was intended to bring about a significant liberalization of party thinking, allowing for the formal rehabilitation of intellectuals and the opening up of space for entrepreneurial activity outside the previously all-pervasive ideological reach of the CCP. Accompanying these shifts in economic and social policy, there was also an official directive, further supported by Deng's 'Congratulatory Message to the Fourth Congress of Chinese Writers and Artists' (*Zai Zhongguo wenxue yishu gongzuozhe di si ci daibiao daihui shang de zhuci* 在中国文学艺术工作者第四次代表大会上的祝词) on 30 October 1979.[18] This directive attempted to draw a line under the 'irrational' personality cult surrounding Mao during the Cultural Revolution by calling upon artists to praise 'the masses of workers, farmers and soldiers, the Party and the old generation of revolutionaries rather than celebrating single personalities' (Köppel-Yang 2003: 76).

Crucially, while official administrative bodies such the Chinese Artists Association gave their public support to the directives handed down at the Third Plenary Session of the XI Central Committee, unlike the period from 1949 to the beginning of the Cultural Revolution, they made no attempt to supplement those directives with concrete administrative programmes of their own. Consequently, while directives issued at the Third Plenary Session of the XI Central Committee can be understood to have opened up space for artists to move beyond the established ideological outlook of the Cultural Revolution, there was no clear indication, from the official bodies responsible for the administration of cultural production within the PRC, of any corresponding initiatives or campaigns to which artists might be expected to contribute in practical terms.

As numerous commentators have pointed out, paradoxically this lack of administrative clarity allowed the CCP to maintain and even strengthen its control over developments in the cultural sphere (Köppel-Yang 2003: 45–47). Not only did the 'vague directives' of the PRC's cultural bureaucrats compel artists to exercise self-discipline in relation to their activities, for fear of the possibility of official disapprobation—a situation exacerbated by previous reversals of ideological direction in the PRC, such as that associated with Mao's One Hundred Flowers Bloom Campaign (*Baihua yundong* 百花运动)[19] of the 1950s, where those who had taken up Mao's invitation to criticize the CCP were denounced and in numerous cases violently punished—they also left considerable scope for the CCP to retighten ideological limits, particularly if the outcomes of Deng's reforms were perceived to threaten social stability or the political authority of the party in any way (Köppel-Yang 2003: 45–47).

Also of significance at this time is the emergence of calls, within official debates surrounding Deng Xiaoping's economic and social reforms, for an accompanying redefinition of modern Chinese culture. Such calls, which were strongly influenced by Deng's own use of the slogans 'Let One Hundred Flowers Bloom' (*Baihua qifang* 百花齐放) and 'Liberate Your Thinking' (*Jiefang sixiang* 解放思想), involved a renewed interest in a movement of cultural enlightenment (*Qimeng yudong* 启蒙运动), which was first brought into play during the 1920s and 1930s by China's modernizing New Culture and May Fourth movements. This renewal of interest saw the emergence, at the end of the 1970s, of a widely felt climate of 'humanist enthusiasm' (*Renwen reqing* 人文热情) within the PRC that would for the next ten years, with varying degrees of intensity, overwrite the profound sense of alienation experienced by the Chinese population as a result of the Cultural Revolution, thereby encouraging active participation in the CCP's centrally driven programme of reform.

In response to the directives issued at the Third Plenary Session of the XI Central Committee, as well as the emerging climate of humanist enthusiasm, towards the very end of the 1970s numerous semi-official art groups began to come together within the PRC to support the production and exhibition of artworks that departed openly from the established norms of artistic production during the Cultural Revolution. In the case of most of these groups, including the Oil Painting Research Association (*Youhua yanjiu hui* 油画研究会), who mounted a public exhibition of their work in Zhongshan Park in Beijing in February 1979, this departure was primarily a formalistic one that involved the production of academic-realist, impressionistic, post-impressionistic, expressionistic or semi-abstract artworks, sometimes incorporating the somewhat contentious representation of nude figures, that had little or no obvious social or political content; an understandably cautious approach given the vague directives issued by the CCP's cultural bureaucracy.

At the same time, China's recently reopened art academies began to produce a new cohort of graduates who opted to work within the PRC's official system of artistic production while responding to the CCP's call to depart from the established norms of pictorial representation during the Cultural Revolution. Two of the best known of the artists belonging to this generation are Cheng Conglin 程丛林 (b.1954) and Luo Zhongli 罗中立 (b.1948), who, as graduates of the Sichuan Academy of Fine Arts in Chongqing, became the focus for what came to be known as the Sichuan School of Painting (*Sichuan huapai* 四川画派). Paintings produced by these artists during the late 1970s and early 1980s are notable not only for their depiction of ordinary individuals and individual life experiences but in addition their decidedly subjectivist signification of human feeling. In the case of paintings by Cheng Conglin, such as *Snow on a Certain Day in a Certain Month in 1968* (*1968 nian mou yue mou ri, xue* 1968年某月某日, 雪) (1979), these departures from established pictorial convention became the basis for a poetically-charged reappraisal of the traumatic events of the Cultural Revolution, often referred to as 'Scar Art' (*Shanghen yishu* 伤痕艺术)—echoing a similar tendency within Chinese literary circles at that time, known as 'Scar Literature' (*Shanghen wenxue* 伤痕文学)—where the expression of individual feeling could be understood as part of a lived human response to the actuality of material events, rather than as an escape into bourgeois subjectivity. In the case of paintings by Luo Zhongli, such as his celebrated work *Father* (*Fuqin* 父亲) (1979), they became the basis for representations of the life of ordinary people, and in particular that of China's rural ethnic groups, subtly critical of the effectiveness of the socially inclusive policies of the CCP; an approach that came to be known, alongside comparable work by other artists, as 'Rural Realism' (*Xiangtu xieshi zhuyi* 乡土写实主义).

Although subject to a degree of official criticism at the time of their initial reception, Scar[20] and rural realist paintings were quickly reinterpreted as being in accordance with the directive supported by Deng at the Congress of Chinese Writers and Artists, which called for artists to praise the masses and revolutionary groups rather than single personalities. This view was confirmed by the awarding of first prize to Luo Zhongli's painting *Father* at the Second National Exhibition of Young Art (*Di'er jie qingnian meishu zuopin zhan* 第二届青年美术作品展) in 1980 and the subsequent acquisition of the painting by the permanent collection of the National Art Museum in Beijing.

During the immediate aftermath of the Cultural Revolution, official directives relating to the production and exhibition of art within the PRC can therefore be understood to have accommodated official, as well as semi-official, departures from established Maoist thought. However, given the existence of similar departures, both within and outside the PRC's official system of artistic production prior to 1976—in the case of formalist ways of working, those relating to the clandestine work of unofficial artists, such as those belonging to the No Name Group, and in the case of discernibly critical forms of realism, those that had taken place in a highly coded manner as part of China's official artistic mainstream—semi-official and official departures from artistic orthodoxy at the end of the 1970s and beginning of the 1980s should not be interpreted as an abrupt historical breaking with convention. Instead, they are perhaps better viewed as a politically mediated, moment of redefinition and disclosure where artistic tendencies that had hitherto been seen as beyond the ideological pale were allowed to enter into full public view.

Besides the production of artworks by artists of official and semi-official standing, the period immediately after the confirmation of Deng's reforms saw the production and exhibition of distinctly unofficial forms of art, which have since been interpreted as the starting point for the development of avant-garde, experimental and museum-based forms of art within the PRC since 1979, otherwise known in anglophone contexts as 'contemporary Chinese art.'[21] Within the existing literature on the subject (including that published within and outside the PRC), there is a generally held view that the development of contemporary Chinese art was initiated by artists belonging to a group known as the Stars , who, in Beijing, towards the end of September 1979, were the first to stage an unofficial public exhibition of artworks inside the PRC that not only did not conform to the CCP's then continuing requirement that all art should take the view of the masses and be entirely subservient to the political aims of the party (Hou 2002: 75), but also, in some cases at least, presented thinly veiled criticism of Mao and the CCP. Indeed, following the closure of their unofficial exhibition by local police after only two days, the Stars became the first artists within the PRC to oppose established CCP directives on the production and exhibition of art by mounting a protest march through the streets of Beijing calling for freedom of expression and the right to show their work officially in public. This action preceded the staging of two official exhibitions of the work of the Stars: one at the Huafang Studio (*Huafang zhi* 画舫斋) in Beijing in late 1979 and the other at the National Art Museum (*Zhongguo meishu guan* 中国美术馆) in Beijing in 1980.

The Stars' perceived status as the initiators of contemporary Chinese art therefore rests not simply on the group's apparent transgression of established limits on the production and exhibiting of art within the PRC but also on the public and ostensibly provocative manner in which that transgression took place. It is important to note, however, that this seemingly open transgression of established ideological limits on the part of the Stars was not, in fact, diametrically opposed to the views of the leadership of the CCP at the time who, under the direct influence of Deng Xiaoping, had sought to distance themselves from the preceding period of communist rule under Mao Zedong—primarily by supporting the climate of 'humanist enthusiasm' that had developed within the PRC as the result of a critical response, on the part of CCP intellectuals, to the profoundly destructive events of the Cultural Revolution. Furthermore, the actions of the Stars took place in close proximity to the events of the Beijing Spring and, in particular, to the public calls for freedom of expression associated with the PRC's nascent Democracy Movement (*Zhongguo minzhu yundong* 中国民主运动) and the emergence of the phenomenon known as the Democracy Wall (*Xidan minzhu qiang* 西单民主墙).[22] The actions of the Stars should not, therefore—alongside those of progressive semi-official and official art groups within the PRC at that time—be seen as an outright breaking with political orthodoxy, but as one strongly aligned with existing governmental and non-governmental moves towards the relaxing of existing ideological restrictions within the PRC. What is more, given that the Stars' unofficial exhibition was a response to official rejection of their ambition to stage a government-supported exhibition of their work in the prestigious National Art Museum in Beijing, the actions of the group should not be viewed simply as a collective attempt to transgress established ideological limits. Instead they might also be considered as a calculated bid for acceptance by the state within an emerging context of reform.

In response to repeated and increasingly strident challenges to its authority, under Deng's leadership in late 1979, the CCP initiated a series of political campaigns aimed at quelling public criticism of its policies. As a result of these campaigns—which included a government crackdown on the Democracy Movement and the Democracy Wall from March to December 1979, the Campaign against Bourgeois Liberalism (*Zichan jieji ziyou hua* 资产阶级自由化) of 1981 and the Anti-Spiritual Pollution Campaign (*Fan jingshen wuran yundong* 反精神污染运动) of October 1983 to February 1984—between 1981 and 1984 all unofficial public activities within the PRC were (in principle) suspended, including those associated with the production and exhibition of art.

With the abrupt ending of the Anti-Spiritual Pollution Campaign, in February 1984, a new situation developed within the PRC in which many of the prevailing restrictions on the production and exhibition of art outside the country's state-controlled system were effectively curtailed. While the CCP did not actually revoke the long-established Maoist directive that art produced and exhibited within the PRC should reflect the view of the masses and serve the revolutionary aims of the party, a tacit understanding was nevertheless established, again through the issuing of vague governmental directives. This understanding was that the unofficial production and exhibition of art outside the PRC's state-controlled system would be tolerated as long as those activities did not undermine the integrity of the PRC or the authority of the CCP. Consequently, a state of affairs developed—which still exists within the PRC today—that gives considerable scope for freedom of artistic expression while continuing to uphold generalized and ultimately mobile discursive boundaries on that freedom, requiring persistent self-reflection and self-discipline on the part of those who make and exhibit art within the PRC.

Also of significance here is the long shadow cast over Chinese society during the 1980s by the events of the Cultural Revolution. During the Cultural Revolution, individuals and groups perceived to be in opposition to Maoist ideology were subjected to violent and often protracted forms of castigation (*pipan* 批判) that required those on the receiving end to admit their misdemeanours and to publicly criticize themselves. Within the climate of humanist enthusiasm that emerged after the death of Mao, all forms of criticism (*piping* 批评) were consequently cast in a negative light, making any direct opposition to CCP doubly difficult.

In response to the qualified freedoms that developed after the ending of the Anti-Spiritual Pollution Campaign, a new generation of artists emerged, who opted to work openly outside the PRC's state-controlled system. Unlike the Stars at the time of their unofficial exhibition, however, this new generation, which came to be known as the 1985 New Wave (*Bawu xinchao meishu yundong* 八五新潮美术运动), no longer found itself in apparent opposition to established government directives. Furthermore, the work of this new generation took place at a time of increasing optimism within the PRC about the possibility of social progress associated with the climate of humanist enthusiasm that had developed during the period immediately following the death of Mao and the ending of the Cultural Revolution and that had persisted, more or less intact, despite the Campaign against Bourgeois Liberalism and the Anti-Spiritual Pollution Campaign of 1981 to 1984.

Within this climate of optimism, artists belonging to the 1985 New Wave were strongly empowered to develop artistic techniques and critical thinking that departed markedly from the socialist-realist cultural discourses upheld officially within the PRC after 1949—a state of affairs that, as the art critics Lü Peng 吕澎 and Yi Dan 易丹 make clear (Lü and Yi 1991:2–4), can be understood as a revival of the modernizing 'cultural revolution' initiated by the May Fourth Movement in 1919. What is more, as a consequence of the effects of Deng's policy of Reform and Opening, the development of this new approach towards art-making—that was widely referred to within the PRC at the time as *Zhongguo xiandai yishu* 中国现代艺术 (Chinese modern art)—was able to proceed with the benefit of a renewed openness to outside cultural influences mediated by a range of established and newly founded magazines and periodicals, including *Meishu zazhi* 美术杂志 (*Art*), *Jiangsu huakan* 江苏画刊 (*Jiangsu Pictorial*) and *Zhongguo meishu bao* 中国美术报 (*Fine Arts in China*).

As such, it is possible to differentiate the work of the 1985 New Wave and that of subsequent generations of contemporary Chinese artists not only from official socialist-realist art produced within the PRC after 1949 but also from two official/semi-official genres of contemporary Chinese art, which from the late 1970s onwards have occupied an increasingly important position within the PRC's cultural mainstream: modern variations on traditional Chinese *shan-shui* ink and brush painting known as *Guo hua* 国画 (National Painting); and institutionally acceptable forms of realism and abstraction sometimes referred to (somewhat confusingly) as 'Chinese Modern Art' (Sullivan 2001) in English.

While artists who produce artworks associated with these genres have almost invariably been influenced by aspects of Western visual art, that influence has been limited almost entirely, in the case of *Guo hua* and institutionally-acceptable forms of abstraction, to a perceived affinity between the explicit brushwork of Western Expressionism/Abstract Expressionism and that of traditional Chinese painting, and in the case of institutionally-acceptable forms of realism to the persistence, within Chinese art schools, of academic (socialist-realist) teaching methods imported from the Soviet Union in the 1950s. Consequently, both can be seen to diverge strongly from the more critical tendencies exhibited by contemporary Chinese art through their adherence to a rather less challenging formalism/aestheticism.

Also of importance during the 1980s were conferences and symposia that brought artists and critics together from across the PRC. These include the first Huangshan Symposium (*Huangshan huiyi* 黄山会议) held in Anhui Province in April 1985, during which over 70 artists and critics met to discuss trends in Western and Chinese art and to call for greater freedom of artistic and critical expression within the PRC; the Zhuhai Symposium (*Zhuhai huiyi* 珠海会议) of August 1986, where the idea of a national exhibition of modern art that would lead to the staging of the major retrospective China/Avant-Garde (*Xiandai meishu dazhan* 现代美术大展) was first proposed; and the second Huangshan Symposium of November 1988, which set out to reorientate the 1985 movement in preparation for the staging of China/Avant-Garde the following year (Köppel-Yang 2003: 55–56).

As a consequence of these publications and meetings, artists belonging to the 1985 New Wave were able to challenge established artistic norms within the PRC through the self-conscious appropriation/translation of images, styles and techniques associated with Western modernism and postmodernism, and, in particular, the Western avant-gardes' and post-avant-garde's critically disjunctive use of various forms of collage-montage (Köppel-Yang 2003: 20–25; Hou 2002: 75); a move which led to the first performances, installations and works of video art produced within the PRC.

At the same time, a great deal of the work produced by the 1985 New Wave was informed strongly by a desire to combine Western techniques and attitudes with aspects of traditional Chinese cultural thought and practice. Examples of this tendency include installation works by Gu Wenda 谷文达 and Xu Bing 徐冰, such as Gu's *Mysthos of Lost Dynasties—Form c: Pseudo-seal Scripture in Calligraphy Copybook Format* (*Shenhua yishi de wangchao- wei zhuanshu linmob benshi* 神话.遗失的王朝-伪篆书临摹本式) (1983–1987) and Xu's *A Book from the Sky* (Tianshu 天书) (1988), which incorporate techniques used in the production of traditional Chinese calligraphy, as well as conceptual works produced by the artist Huang Yongping 黄永砅, such as *Big Roulette* (*Da zhuanpan* 大转盘) (1987), which involve the combination of avant-garde collage-montage and automatist techniques with traditional Chinese divinatory practices.

As the art historian David Clarke has indicated, this desire to bring together outside cultural influences with indigenous Chinese thinking and practice—which was also a salient feature of modern art produced in China during the early twentieth century[23]— can be seen as a reaction to the 'seeming unavoidability of the inherited visual tradition in China and the difficulty of simply denying or discarding [that tradition] to achieve modernity without risking some kind of felt deracination' as well as 'the difficulty of simply continuing to produce the kind of art that had been made in quite different pre-modern cultural circumstances' (Clarke 2008: 274). It is therefore possible to view the work of the 1985 New Wave—and the work of subsequent generations of contemporary Chinese artists who have built on that work—not simply as variations on pre-existing Western models but as simultaneously modernizing and culturally resistant assemblages of Western and Chinese influences.

It is also important to note that the combining of Western and Chinese cultural influences by the artists of the 1985 New Wave is, as has been previously indicated here, part of an extended history of cultural interaction and exchange between the West and China that can be traced back at least as far as the sixteenth century. This history not only encompasses the assimilation/translation of Western cultural influences by China (oil painting and geometric perspective prior to the twentieth century, European and North American modernism during the early twentieth century (as amply demonstrated by the pre-war architecture of Shanghai) and Soviet socialist-realism during the Maoist period) but also the assimilation/ translation of Chinese cultural influences by the West, including those informing the development of chinoiserie in Europe during the eighteenth and early nineteenth centuries and the activities of the historical and neo avant-gardes during the early to mid-twentieth century (e.g. automatist techniques adopted by European Dadaists and Surrealists) (Choucha 1991: 39). In light of which it becomes possible to view contemporary Chinese art as part of a genealogy of multidirectional cultural re-contextualizations and re-motivations that effectively deconstruct the notion that there is any sort of categorical distinction between the visual culture of China and that of the West and, what is more, that contemporary Chinese art is simply a belated extension of Western modernism/postmodernism.

In addition to the appropriation of images, techniques and attitudes associated with Western modernism and postmodernism, and the reworking of traditional Chinese modes of art-making, the 1985 New Wave is also notable for its critical reworking of official imagery culled from the time of the Cultural Revolution. Among the exponents of this reworking are the artists Wang Guangyi 王广义, Yu Youhan 余友涵 and Wu Shanzhuan 吴山专, who in different ways sought to intervene with the authority of official modes of visual communication used during the Cultural Revolution by bringing those modes together with images and techniques culled from Western art and capitalist society, which ran counter to the direction of Maoist thought; a move that also had the effect of intervening with the authority of the Western elements incorporated into the work. Consider here, for example, Wu's performance-installation *This Afternoon No Water* (*Jintian xiawu ting shui* 今天下午停水*) (1988), which incorporates deliberately ambiguous *dazibao*-like assemblages accompanied by an equally ambiguous Red Guard–like megaphone-assisted declamation.

This critical treatment of official imagery from the Cultural Revolution was accompanied, towards the end of the 1980s, by an emerging discontent among some members of the 1985 New Wave about the humanist enthusiasm that had emerged within the PRC during the late 1970s. Significant markers of this emerging discontent include Geng Jianyi 耿建翌's multiple depiction of disingenuous laughter in *The Second State* (*Di'er zhuangtai* 第二状态) (1987–1988)—a prototype for the cynical realist paintings and sculptures of Fang Lijun 方力钧, Yue Minjun 岳敏君 and others that would emerge within the PRC during the early 1990s—and Wang Guangyi's call to 'Liquidate Humanist Enthusiasm' (*Qingli ren wen reqing* 清理人文热情) at the Second Huangshan symposium in November 1988 (Köppel-Yang 2003: 152)—a discursive prefiguring of the artist's later development of the critical and distinctly anti-humanistic genre of painting known as Political Pop (*Zhengzhi bopu* 政治波普).

In February 1989, the activities of the 1985 New Wave culminated in a major, officially sanctioned exhibition of modern art at the National Art Museum in Beijing known in English as 'China/Avant-Garde,' which included a wide range of works of art produced within the PRC outside the country's state-controlled system during the preceding decade. The exhibition was, however, short lived, first being closed down temporarily by government officials after the firing of a gunshot during an unscheduled performance, by the artists Xiao Lu 肖鲁 and Tang Song 唐宋, of what is known as the *Pistol Shot Event* (*Qiangji shijian* 枪击事件), and then completely after telephoned bomb threats.

A few months later all public activities related to the 1985 New Wave were suspended as a result of the conservative crackdown on society that followed the Tian'anmen killings of 4 June 1989.

'Contemporary' art in China, 1989–2011

When artists began to work openly again outside the PRC's state-controlled system during the early 1990s as a result of the waning of the post-Tian'anmen crackdown, they did so under very different circumstances from those that had prevailed within the PRC during the second half of the 1980s. Not only had many of the artists associated with 1985 New Wave chosen to leave the PRC in the aftermath of the Tian'anmen killings, but those that had stayed found themselves subject to a pervasive climate of uncertainty with regard to the intentions of the CCP. As a consequence, art produced unofficially within the PRC during the 1990s began to reflect a growing sense of doubt at odds with the underlying optimism of the 1980s. This state of affairs was marked not only by the emergence of the contemporary Chinese art movements, known as Cynical Realism (*Wanshi xianshi zhuyi* 玩世现实主义) and Political Pop, with their respective presentations of disingenuously upbeat and sceptically disengaged views of what was by then an increasingly market-driven society within the PRC, but also, as the curator and art historian Wu Hung 巫鸿 has indicated, by a change in the terminology used to refer to unofficial art within the PRC away from the term *Zhongguo xiandai yishu* 中国现代艺术 (Chinese modern art) to *Zhongguo dangdai yishu* 中国当代艺术 (Chinese contemporary art) (Wu 2008: 12–16). As Wu makes clear, this abandoning of the adjective 'modern' in favour of 'contemporary' can be understood to have signalled a growing disaffinity between unofficial art produced within the PRC and the supposedly progressive economic and social reforms initiated by the CCP (Wu 2008a: 291–292).

It is also important to note that 'contemporary' art produced by Chinese nationals within the PRC and abroad during this period began to depart in many instances from the established modes of production—principally painting, sculpture and printmaking—that had dominated unofficial Chinese art-making during the 1980s through the experimental use of video, performance, installation and site-specific approaches. Furthermore, during the early 1990s, many makers of contemporary art within the PRC, including those associated with the movement known as Apartment Art, (*Gongyu yishu* 公寓艺术) chose to produce and exhibit their work away from public view, both as a way of avoiding official censure and of creating distance between themselves and the CCP. Examples of this clandestine art include performances by Song Dong 宋冬 (b.1966), such as *A Kettle of Boiling Water* (*Yihu kaishui* 一壶开水) (1995) (where the artist walked along a side street pouring boiling water from a kettle), which were distinctly ephemeral, had no audience and exist now only in the form of documentary photographs.

While this retreat from the public gaze was an understandable reaction to the immediate circumstances of the conservative crackdown on society and culture that took place in the wake of the Tian'anmen killings, it can also be interpreted as a modern expression of China's traditional *literati* culture. The *literati* 文人, were a class of amateur (in the Western eighteenth-century sense of the word) artist-intellectuals who acted as government officials throughout the period of dynastic rule within China, taking on responsibility for maintaining social order/harmony in accordance with conceptions of filial piety set out in the writings of Confucius 孔子 (551–479 BCE). At times, this responsibility led members of the *literati*, as a matter of personal conscience, to oppose what they saw as inappropriate aspects of imperial policy. This opposition, which ran the risk of violent retribution or exile, often took the form of a deliberate withdrawal from public life. It is therefore possible to link the withdrawal of artists from society within the PRC after 1989 to a much longer tradition of opposition to authority predating China's entry into modernity during the early years of the twentieth century.

Also of importance in this regard is the work of Chinese women artists and artists of sexual difference, who, from a decidedly marginalized position within a still strongly patriarchal/ homophobic Chinese society, began to produce work that provided an incisive critical foil to the repressive, homogenizing tendencies of the Chinese communist state and its increasing entanglement with Western capitalism's connective economic narrative; examples of which include performances by the 'transgender' artist Fen-ma Liuming 芬-马六明 (b. 1969) as well as installations by Lin Tianmiao 林天苗 (b. 1961).

In addition to the emergence of inward-looking cynical and anti-humanist attitudes among contemporary artists within the PRC during the early 1990s, there was also an increasing outward-looking engagement with the international art world. Beginning with the international survey show 'Magiciens de la Terre' at the Pompidou Centre and the Grand Halle de la Villette in Paris in 1989, works of contemporary art produced within the PRC and by Chinese artists who had left China during the 1980s and 1990s became a regular feature of exhibitions worldwide, prompting a surge of interest in Chinese art on the international art market. Partly through this engagement with international curatorship and the international art market, Chinese makers of contemporary art also became more closely involved with the theoretical concerns of internationalized postmodernism and, in particular, issues related to post-colonialism.

This involvement should not, however, be seen as entirely congruent with the pluralistic, multiculturalist and politically correct attitudes conventionally associated with postmodernism and post-colonialism in an international context. While the work of contemporary Chinese artists was both presented and interpreted outside the PRC during the late 1980s and 1990s as a contribution to the international debate associated with postmodernism and post-colonialism at exhibitions such as Magiciens de la Terre, for many contemporary Chinese artists and critics of the 1990s, who continued to share in the historical reluctance of the Chinese to assimilate Western modernity on its own terms, postmodernism and post-colonialism presented themselves simply as new manifestations of Western cultural imperialism aimed at undermining the particularity of China's national-cultural identity. In light of this, Chinese artists and critics sought to adopt a range of practical and theoretical strategies with the intention of critically reworking and/or countering the influence of Westernized international postmodernism and post-colonialism.

A key example of this theoretical and practical reworking is Hou Hanru 侯瀚如's alignment of the conceptual indeterminacy of deconstructive postmodernism and post-colonialism with the irrationalism of traditional Chinese geomantic divinatory practices associated with *Feng shui* 风水 and the *I Ching* 易经 (*The Book of Changes*) (Hou 2002: 61–62, 174); a move which seeks to undermine the international dominance of Western(ized) postmodernism and post-colonialism by asserting the historical primacy of Chinese tradition (in a manner not unlike Fu Lei's valorization of Chinese tradition underlying his assessment of the work of Huang Binhong during the early twentieth century).

More recently—following the staging of a number of highly challenging exhibitions within the PRC, including 'Post-sense Sensibility: Alien Bodies and Delusion' (*Houganxing: yixing yu wangxiang* 后感性: . 异形与妄想) in Beijing in 1999 and 'Fuck Off—Uncooperative Stance' (whose title in Mandarin Chinese *Buhezuo fangshi* 不合作方式 can be translated literally as 'Ways of Non-Cooperation') in Shanghai in 2000 (Ai and Feng 2000), which incorporated works involving real and simulated acts of violence to animal and human bodies[24]—contemporary Chinese art has taken a noticeable turn away from the decidedly resistant attitudes of the 1990s towards far less obviously critical/transgressive modes of working. To some extent this turn can be interpreted as a response to a directive issued by the Chinese Ministry of Culture in 2001 calling for an end to 'All Performances and Bloody, Brutal Displays of Obscenity in the Name of Art' (Wu 2010: 276–277); the first such directive to be issued within the PRC since 1979. More importantly, however, it can also be seen to be part of an increasing institutionalization of contemporary Chinese art both within and outside the PRC since the latter half of the 1990s; one that has seen the staging of major travelling exhibitions of contemporary Chinese art, including 'Inside Out: New Chinese Art' (1998–2000) and 'The Wall: Reshaping Contemporary Chinese Art' (2005–2006), as well as a growing number of international biennales and triennials sited in Chinese cities such as Shanghai (The Shanghai Biennale [*Shanghai shuangnianzhan* 上海双年展]) and Guangzhou (the Guangzhou Triennial [*Guangzhou sannianzhan* 广州三年展]). Moreover, it can also be viewed as symptomatic of government attempts to promote a socially constructive creative industries sector within the PRC. As the critic and curator Wu Hung has indicated, this institutionalization of contemporary Chinese art can be understood to have been facilitated by a well-established international network of Chinese artists and critics who are now able to move more or less freely between the PRC and other nation-states and who are consequently well placed to mediate the production and reception of contemporary Chinese art in relation to differing social, economic, cultural and political contexts within and outside the PRC (Wu 2008a: 301–303).

Among some younger artists, this move away from openly critical/transgressive modes of art-making has led to a highly introspective engagement with questions of the self as well as narrowly focused assertions of localized cultural identity. Examples of the former include the work of the Beijing-based artists Song Kun 宋琨 (Gladston 2008c: 111–120) and of the latter the work of the Shanghai-based duo Birdhead 鸟头 (Song Tao (b.1979) and Ji Weiyu (b.1980) (Gladston 2007: 183–195).

Here it is also important to note that contemporary Chinese art of the 1990s and beyond has been produced and exhibited in relation to an increasing climate of nationalism within the PRC—as so amply demonstrated by the symbolism of the opening ceremony of the Beijing Olympics in 2008—which has accompanied the country's prodigious economic growth of the last two decades. While this climate of nationalism has been tempered to some degree by the CCP—who are eager to avoid any internal instability as well as outward impressions of imperialistic ambition—more widely within the PRC it has acted as a focus for a new modern sense of Chinese cultural identity; one that underpins the recent emergence of highly exceptionalist readings of contemporary Chinese art by critics such as Gao Minglu, Fan Di'an 范迪安, Wang Lin 王林 and Zhu Qingshen 朱青生(Shao 2012).

'Avant-garde' art groups in China, 1979–1989

One of the defining features of the development of 'modern' art within the PRC during the late 1970s and 1980s is the coalescing of artists into groups and associations. From the inception of contemporary Chinese art during the two-year period, immediately following the confirmation of Deng Xiaoping's programme of economic and social reforms at the Third Plenary Session of the XI Central Committee of the Chinese Communist Party in December 1978, through to the conservative crackdown that took place in the aftermath of the Tian'anmen killings of 4 June 1989, over 100 of these groups and associations were formed in different locations throughout the PRC (Gao 2007a: back cover notes). Some of these groups had clearly defined organizational structures and collectively agreed aims, some came together rather more loosely, perhaps only for a single meeting or exhibition, and some existed in name only. As the curator and historian of contemporary Chinese art Gao Minglu has indicated, groups and associations of this sort fulfilled an important role not only as forums within which artists could share ideas and stimulate one another's creative ambitions at a time when the possibilities and parameters of unofficial art-making in China had yet to be established, but also as protective cells shielding artists wedded to the pursuit of individual creativity from the normative expectations of a society that, at the time, remained strongly under the collectivizing influence of Maoist thought (Köppel-Yang 2003: 58–59).

As such, these groups can be understood to have occupied a position similar to that ascribed to Western avant-garde groups and movements insofar as they served as a locus for the envisioning of forward-looking cultural change. Indeed, in the PRC, the adjectives *xiandai* and *dangdai* used as part of the terms *Zhongguo xiandai yishu* and *Zhongguo dangdai yishu* are widely seen as synonymous with the term *qianwei* 前卫(Wu 2008: 16), which, as Martina Köppel-Yang points out, signifies a state of merging with and semiotically opposing established social, political and cultural norms (Köppel-Yang 2003: 35–37), broadly commensurate with the meaning of the English term 'avant-garde.'

It would, however, be a mistake to align art groups active within the PRC during the late 1970s and 1980s directly with a Westernized understanding of the term 'avant-garde.' While the Western avant-gardes are widely acknowledged to have sought a blurring of the boundary between art and life as a way to bring about a critical reworking of the latter along the more playful lines of the former (Bürger 1984 [1974]), this is by no means straightforwardly the case in relation to the work of 'avant-garde' art groups within the PRC during the late 1970s and 1980s. Here, it is important to acknowledge that the emergence of *qianwei* ('avant-garde') art within the PRC, during the late 1970s and 1980s, involved the necessary reconstruction of a relatively autonomous sphere of artistic self-expression as a move away from the party-dominated and distinctly non-autonomous socialist-realism and street propaganda of the Maoist period. Consequently, while the term *qianwei* signifies an oppositional stance towards established convention broadly consonant with that of the Western historical avant-gardes, the general trajectory of 'avant-garde' art within the PRC after 1979 can be seen to run, as the philosopher Zhenming Zhai 翟振明 has argued, more or less contrary to the Western historical avant-gardes' desire to negate artistic autonomy as part of a critical sublation of art within everyday praxis (Gladston 2011a). What is more, in seeking to rebuild a relatively autonomous aesthetic sphere after the ravages of the Maoist period, many of those involved in the activities of 'avant-garde' art groups within the PRC, during the late 1970s and 1980s, were actively involved in revisiting and reworking aspects of traditional Chinese cultural thought and practice. It is therefore necessary to make a distinction between *qianwei* forms of art within the PRC since 1979 and the Western avant-gardes on the basis that the former can be understood to go against the grain of the latter's intentions by actively seeking to reinstate autonomous cultural practice and tradition as part of its opposition to established social, political and cultural norms.

That said, it would also be a mistake to assume that 'avant-garde' art produced within the PRC during the 1980s was entirely successful in setting itself apart from the established interests of the state. In spite of the progressive liberalization of many aspects of Chinese culture and society after 1979—including the effective freeing of artists from any direct responsibility to serve the interests of the masses and the revolutionary aims of the CCP—within the PRC during the late 1970s and 1980s artists were still subject to significant restrictions with regard to open public criticism of the CCP as well as anything that might be perceived to threaten the integrity of the Chinese nation-state. Consequently, while 'avant-garde' art groups occupied a position of relative freedom from ideological government intervention, they and their members were nevertheless strongly discouraged from using their art as a platform for anti-authoritarian criticism by the constant threat of state violence.

During the 1980s, 'avant-garde' art groups within the PRC were also subject to the limiting effects of the CCP's chosen way of doing governmental business after the death of Mao, which following the ending of the Anti-Spiritual Pollution Campaign in 1984, tended strongly, as previously indicated, towards the handing down of vague rather than explicit directives on individual and collective behaviour; this resulted in making space for greater social freedoms while at the same time instilling a pervasively controlling (panoptical) sense of self-surveillance/self-discipline throughout Chinese society with respect to imprecise boundaries of social acceptability. Moreover, while 'avant-garde' art within the PRC during the late 1970s and 1980s most certainly did act as a vehicle for sociopolitical critique, its part in the opening up of a relatively autonomous cultural-artistic sphere after the ending of the Cultural Revolution can also be seen to be very much in keeping with Deng's modernizing program of economic and social reforms and the associated clearing of 'depoliticized' space for entrepreneurial activity. To which extent, 'avant-garde' art produced within the PRC during the 1970s and 1980s made itself very much party to the political/ideological aims of the CCP.

It would also be wrong to assume that all artists involved in the production of 'avant-garde' art within the PRC during the late 1970s and 1980s were in direct opposition to governmental authority. Consider here, for example, statements made by the artist Yu Youhan—who along with Wang Guangyi, was one of the progenitors of the Chinese art movement known as Political Pop—in which Yu discusses his intentions in making a series of paintings incorporating images of Mao Zedong made at the end of the 1980s and beginning of the 1990s:

When I painted the Mao series, though I cherished the Maoist period, I also held more reflective and critical feelings about that period too. So, some paintings, which may appear to be a form of bohemian realist art, didn't express optimistic feelings at all. Instead, they were trying to reveal feelings about the betrayal of socialism. I think the Mao series of Pop paintings should belong to the history of China's folk or historical paintings. In these paintings, the background colours are very bright. But, if you look carefully, there are unstable elements in the background suggesting that disaster may take place at any time. As for my feelings towards Mao, though I no longer admire him as I used to during the Cultural Revolution, I don't think we should deny him totally. And I don't think Western propaganda about Mao is right either. I think every leader would like to lead their country toward a better future. (Gladston 2011b: 32)

As numerous commentators, including Köppel-Yang (2003: 152–161), have suggested, it is possible to view the appropriation of images of Mao by contemporary Chinese artists as part of the making of Political Pop as a covertly counter-authoritarian gesture. Nevertheless, as the statement above shows, Yu's own intentions in doing so would appear to be far less than straightforward.

'Avant-garde' art produced within the PRC during the 1970s and 1980s can therefore be understood to have occupied a highly indeterminate position in relation to the prevailing sociopolitical/economic mainstream; one in which it can be seen to have shuttled continually— like Western(ized) postmodernist art but under somewhat different sociopolitical and economic circumstances—between resistance to and complicity with established authority. It is therefore necessary to qualify perceptions of the use of 'avant-garde' tactics within the PRC insofar as *qianwei* art produced within the PRC can be seen not only to upend the negative anti-autonomous tendencies of the Western historical avant-gardes, but also to share in postmodernism's somewhat indeterminate positioning in relation to established authority.

As the following accounts of the activities of four of the most prominent 'avant-garde' art groups active within the PRC between 1979 and 1989 show, this indeterminate positioning is not simply a matter of theoretical speculation. Rather, it is something that was very much lived out in the everyday.

Notes

1   In China, pictorial depictions of the naked human form were traditionally confined to private collections of erotica.
2   The term *i-ching* refers to the notion that a work of art should not simply represent appearances but should also give form to the artist's subjective experience of the world. This approach is understood as having the potential to engender an empathetic sense of the artist's felt relationship with nature on the part of the viewer of the work of art.
3   Cai also supported progress in the arts and had a strong interest in European modernism. During a visit to Europe between 1907 and 1911, he met Picasso and bought a number of Cubist paintings.
4   *Shan-shui* (literally, 'mountains and water') is a traditional style of Chinese landscape painting involving the use of ink and brush on rice paper or silk to depict natural scenes incorporating

mountains, rivers, streams, waterfalls and lakes. *Shan-shui* first emerged as a distinct painterly style during the Liu Song dynasty (刘宋王朝 *Liu Song Wangchao*) (420–479) and is understood to embody a traditional Daoist belief in the desirability of a close interrelationship between human beings and nature associated with the aesthetic concept of *i-ching*.

5   The Yan'an conference on literature and the arts was part of the *Yan'an Zhenfeng Yundong* 延安整风运动 (Yan'an Rectification Movement), a campaign in Yan'an and surrounding CCP-controlled areas, conducted between 1942 and 1944, through which Mao sought to confirm his position as sole leader of the CCP and impose his own version of Marxist-Leninism. The campaign involved an attempt to rid the CCP of the intellectual influence of the May Fourth Movement. Over 10,000 individuals were killed as a result.

6   This official directive has never been formally rescinded and therefore continues to provide an ideological boundary for the production and public exhibition of works of art within the PRC.

7   The Cultural Revolution (*Wuchan jieji wenhua da geming*; literally, 'The Great Proletarian Cultural Revolution') was a period of widespread political, cultural and social upheaval that took place in the PRC between 1966 and Mao Zedong's death in 1976. During the early years of the Cultural Revolution (between 1966 and 1969), young leftist revolutionaries known as Red Guards mounted attacks on individuals and institutions perceived to be in opposition to established Maoist thought. The circumstances that led to the launching of the Cultural Revolution are contested: some argue that students responded to calls from Mao for renewed class struggle, and others say that Mao himself responded to spontaneous student action. There is, however, general agreement that the Cultural Revolution enabled Mao to regain power following his marginalization within the CCP after the disastrous events of the Great Leap Forward.

8   The Red Guards were a revolutionary mass movement of young people that, between 1966 and 1969, played a central role in the events of the Cultural Revolution. They rooted out and violently combated what they saw as counter-revolutionary and elitist activities at all levels of Chinese society. Shortly after the Red Guards coming together, in 1966, the movement broke up into different factions with 'radicals' adopting an uncompromisingly critical attitude towards established power, aside from Mao himself, and 'rebels' who attempted to protect party structures from direct attack by the Red Guards. This led to violent confrontation between radical and rebel groups until Mao Zedong intervened to disband the latter in 1967, giving radicals free rein to pursue their revolutionary aims. Following violent intervention by the People's Liberation Army (and with Mao's agreement), in 1969 the Red Guards were disbanded in an attempt to curb the extreme civil disorder that had ensued as a result of their actions.

9   The number of deaths resulting from the events of the Cultural Revolution is unverified but may well be in excess of one million.

10   During the Cultural Revolution, practitioners of traditional Chinese ink and brush painting such as Li Keran 李可染 (1907–1989) and Pan Tianshou 潘天寿 (1897–1971), who had previously been revered as masters, were publicly denounced as bourgeois counter-revolutionaries. While some of these artists responded by adapting their work to the representation of revolutionary themes, others had their work included in touring

exhibitions of 'black painting' that were held up to public ridicule throughout the PRC. At this time, many senior practitioners of traditional Chinese painting were imprisoned and forced to re-educate themselves in Maoist thought. Artists who wished to make paintings outside the PRC's state-controlled system using modern Western-influenced techniques were also persecuted and forced to pursue their artistic aims in secret.

11   The term *shui-mo* refers broadly to the traditional Chinese technique of ink and brush painting on paper. It is also used to refer more specifically to forms of Chinese ink and brush painting that make use of colour as well as Chinese ink and brush painting involving the depiction of human figures.

12   The Great Leap Forward was an economic and social plan put forward by the CCP during the late 1950s. It aimed to transform the PRC's largely traditional agrarian economy into one based on collectivist forms of agricultural and industrial production. The plan, which was implemented between 1958 and 1961, heavily disrupted agricultural production within the PRC. This disruption coincided with extreme weather conditions, in 1959 and 1960, bringing about a widespread famine, which resulted in the death of tens of millions of people (estimates range between 18 and 45 million). The disastrous events of the Great Leap Forward lead to open criticism of Mao and his marginalization within the CCP.

13   The No Name Group, whose leading members became active as artists outside the CCP's state-controlled system during the early 1960s, was the first unofficial art group to emerge after the founding of the PRC. The group set itself apart from the official ideology of socialist-realism by painting still-lifes, portraits and landscapes that emphasized formalist aesthetics over social content. The group staged a significant public exhibition of its work in the PRC in 1979.

14   *Dazibao* (big character posters—literally, 'big character reports') are handwritten, wall-mounted posters with large-scale Chinese characters that were used historically in China as a form of popular communication and protest. In modern times, *dazibao* have been supplemented by fragments of text taken from newspapers as well as printed reports and photographic images. During the Cultural Revolution, *dazibao* were produced as a means of communicating political directives and of denouncing individuals and groups perceived to be in opposition to established Maoist thinking. *Dazibao* were also used as a means of public protest during the Democracy Wall Movement.

15   In one instance, a publishing house is reported as having produced over 900 million reproductions of a painting of Mao in support of a government campaign (Erickson 2005: 13).

16   The Beijing Spring was a brief period of liberalization that took place within the PRC during 1977 and 1978. The term 'Beijing Spring' refers to a similar period of liberalization within Czechoslovakia during 1968, known as the 'Prague Spring.' During the Beijing Spring, the Chinese people were able to criticize the government of the PRC more freely than had previously been the case under Maoist rule. Much of the criticism voiced at this time was directed towards the events of the Cultural Revolution and the behaviour of government officials.

17   The Four Modernizations policy called for the modernization of technology, education, agriculture and the military. The Two Hundreds directive, which takes its name from the slogan 'Let one hundred flowers bloom and one hundred schools contend,' called for greater

diversity of thought and public debate as part of the process of reform, effectively reviving a similar campaign initiated by Mao Zedong in 1956. The Liberate Your Thinking and Search for the Truth in the Facts directive sought to promote experimental research and the discussion of subject-specific questions rather than purely ideological ones.

18   The Fourth Congress of Chinese Writers and Artists took place in Beijing between 30 October and 16 November 1979. As part of the reporting of the Congress, public statements were issued calling on artists to 'Emancipate Thought and Encourage Literary and Artistic Democracy.'

19   The One Hundred Flowers Bloom Campaign was a CCP campaign, during 1956 and 1957, which encouraged Chinese citizens to express their views on matters of national government policy openly. The campaign was launched under the slogan: 'Letting a hundred flowers bloom and a hundred schools of thought contend is the policy for promoting progress in the arts and sciences and a flourishing socialist culture in our land.' The campaign was eventually brought to an end after soliciting comments highly critical of CCP policy. Many of those who had voiced criticism of the party were severely punished. Some commentators have interpreted the One Hundred Flowers Bloom Campaign as a calculated attempt by Mao Zedong to flush out and crush dissent within the PRC, although this is by no means certain. The campaign was followed by a reassertion of orthodox Maoist ideology.

20   Such paintings were criticized in some official quarters as 'inadequately realistic' (Köppel-Yang 2003: 88–90).

21   The term 'contemporary Chinese art' is now used widely within an anglophone context to denote avant-garde, experimental and museum-based forms of art produced as part of the liberalization of culture that has taken place within the PRC since the death of Mao Zedong and the ending of the Cultural Revolution in 1976. The use of this term extends not only to scholarly texts but also to an ever-growing body of magazine and newspaper articles, exhibition catalogues, tourist guides and market surveys aimed at popular audiences eager to learn more about the development of culture in the PRC during the post-Maoist period. For writers in Mandarin Chinese (*putonghau* 普通话), the corresponding term is *Zhongguo dangdai yishu* 中国当代艺术, which is often translated literally into English, in the Mandarin-speaking context, as 'Chinese contemporary art' (e.g. Zhang 2008: 4).

22   The Democracy Wall was a large brick wall running along Xidan Street (*Xidan jie* 西单街) in the Xicheng district (西城区 *Xicheng qu*) of Beijing onto which members of the general public, including individuals belonging to the Chinese Democracy Movement, posted texts, posters, images and *dazibao* critical of government policy. The wall, which first came into use in December 1978, was initially tolerated by officials, who wished to secure Deng Xiaoping's grip on power by encouraging criticism of previous governmental failures. As a result of sustained criticism of the prevailing political order, the CCP initiated a crackdown on the Democracy Movement in March 1979. This not only led to the arrest of the leader of the Democracy Movement, Wei Jinsheng 魏京生, who was later sentenced to 15 years in prison, but also, in December 1979, to the removal of the Democracy Wall from Xidan Street to Ritan Park (*Ritan gongyuan* 日坛公园), where public access was strictly monitored. Shortly afterwards, during the same month, the wall was closed down completely as part of a government campaign to end public opposition to socialism. According to Gao Minglu,

some painters, including a number who would go on to join the Stars, used the Democracy Wall as a place to display their 'modern works' publicly prior to the Stars' first unofficial exhibition. Gao also suggests that the Stars' decision to mount their work on railings close to the National Art Gallery in Beijing may have been influenced by the use of *dazibao* during the Cultural Revolution and as part of the Democracy Wall Movement (Gao 2005: 64). Zhu Zhu states that a member of the Stars, Yin Guangzhong, curated an exhibition of artworks titled 'Exhibition of Five Guizhou Youths'(*Guiyang wu qingnian huazhan* 贵阳五青年画展) at the Democracy Wall prior to the Stars' unofficial exhibition (Zhu 2007a: 22).

23 For a more detailed discussion of attempts to reconcile Western(ized) modernity with aspects of China's established cultural traditions as part of the development of modern art in China during the early twentieth century, see Danzker (2004:18–72).

24 See Gladston (2009: 92–104).

THE STARS — THE NORTHERN ART GROUP — THE POND ASSOCIATION — XIAMEN DADA

The Stars (*Xingxing* 星星)

The Stars group was formed as a result of the actions of two mature students at the Beijing Workers' Cultural Centre (*Beijing gongren wehhua* 北京工人文化), Ma Desheng 马德升 and Huang Rui 黄锐. They, encouraged by views solicited from fellow students and teachers at the centre, including the artist and teacher He Baoshen 何宝森, approached government officials requesting permission to stage an exhibition of experimental art alongside China's 'Fifth National Art Exhibition' (*Di wu jie quanguo meizhan* 第五届全国美展) at the National Art Museum in Beijing during September 1979.

Ma and Huang's request was turned down on the grounds that there would be no space available within the museum to house such an exhibition—a predictable outcome given the then established government policy that those exhibiting art publicly within the PRC should first gain officially approved political status and give proof of long-standing conformity to nationally codified aesthetic principles, neither of which could be claimed by Ma and Huang. Undaunted, Ma and Huang requested access to an alternative exhibition space. This request was also turned down.

In response, Ma and Huang set about organizing an unofficial exhibition of the work of 23 largely self-taught artists, including Zhong Ahcheng 钟阿城, Bo Yun 薄云, Qu Leilei 曲磊磊, Yan Li 李岩, Li Shuang 李爽, Wang Keping 王克平, Gan Shaocheng 甘少成, Yang Yiping 杨益平, Mao Lizi 毛栗子, Ai Weiwei 艾未未 and Chen Yansheng 陈延生, which was staged outdoors in public space to the east of the National Museum in Beijing on 27 and 28 September 1979 with the title 'Exhibition of the Stars' (*Xingxing meizhan* 星星美展).[1] Works exhibited in the exhibition, many of which were hung on street-side railings adjacent to the National Museum, included paintings, prints and wooden sculptures often produced in a distinctly amateurish manner at odds with the academic conventions of Soviet-influenced socialist-realism within the PRC. As the critic Li Xianting 栗宪庭 writing in a contemporaneous article makes clear, works included in the Stars' exhibition can be divided into two categories: 'those that delved into life, and those that explored form' (Li 2010: 11). This division of interests is also suggested by the preface to the Stars' exhibition written by Huang Rui which states that while works by the Stars speak to the group's 'individual ideals,' the group also wished to give their artistic 'harvest back to the land, and to the people' (Huang Rui 2010: 7–8) (Plate 1).

Berghuis suggests indirectly that the Stars' decision to mount an unofficial outdoor exhibition may have been influenced by performance installations titled *Plastic Bag Happenings in China* (*Zhongguo jiaodai ke binlin* 中国胶袋客宾临), staged by the Hong Kong artist Kwok Mang-ho 郭孟浩, outdoors in Beijing and surrounding areas in the autumn of 1979, which, he claims, were witnessed by Huang Rui. However, the chronological relationship of the Stars' unofficial outdoor exhibition to the staging of Kwok's performance installations is unclear. A more likely precedent for the Stars' unofficial exhibition is the staging of outdoor exhibitions by semi-official art groups within the PRC in the months preceding that of the Stars. These include an exhibition of the work of the Oil Painting Research Association (*Youhua yanjiu hui* 油画研究会), which was held in Zhongshan Park (*Zhongshan gongyuan* 中山公园) in Beijing in February 1979, some seven months before the Stars' first exhibition, and the Painting Exhibition of the Twelve (*Shi'er ren huazhan* 十二人画展), which was held outdoors in Shanghai in 1978 (Köppel-Yang 2003: 59).

The unofficial outdoor exhibition of the work of the Stars attracted considerable public attention and was closed down on the orders of the Dongcheng Public Security Bureau (*Dongcheng gonganju* 东城公安局) after only two days, on the morning of 29 September.[2] According to an account by Xu Wenli 徐文立, Liu Qing 刘青 and others, titled 'A Letter to the People' 一封信给人, which was posted publicly in Beijing in October 1979, the Dongcheng Public Security Bureau mobilized 'nearly one hundred policemen' who 'seized all of the exhibited works [by the Stars] left in the care of the National Gallery.' The letter also claims that, in addition to the police, there was a 'group of unidentified people who gathered together in an organized way to cause a commotion and to harass and abuse the exhibition's personnel' and that this unidentified group 'made trouble with foreign reporters for no reason' (Xu and Liu 2010: 8).

Immediately following the closure of the Stars' outdoor exhibition, Ma and Huang were taken to a local police station where government officials explained the reasons for their decision: first, that, as organizers of the Stars' exhibition, Ma and Huang had not received legally required permission from municipal and national artists associations, the Public Security Bureau and the Cultural Branch of the Beijing Municipal Government; second, that the event broke newly issued restrictions on unofficial public display known as the 'Six Announcements'; and third, that growing interest in the exhibition posed a serious threat to public order (a significant concern to the authorities in Beijing at the time because of continuing public unrest associated with the PRC's burgeoning Democracy Movement).

On the same day, Huang turned to his friends Bei Dao 北岛 and Mang Ke 芒克, founding editors of the literary magazine *Jintian* 今天 (*Today*), for advice on what action might be taken in protest against the closure of the Stars' outdoor exhibition. As a result of Huang's discussions with Bei and Mang, the Stars became a focus of interest for Liu Qing and Xu Wenli, founders of the underground political magazine *April 5th Forum* (*Siwu luntan* 四五论坛)—the title of which refers to public protests in Beijing following the death of China's long-serving Premier Zhou Enlai 周恩来 (1898–1976) on 5 April 1976—who viewed the decision of the Dongcheng Security Bureau to close down the group's exhibition as unconstitutional and were concerned that jurisdiction over public exhibitions of art might begin to shift dangerously away from recognized government bodies to the police. In light of these concerns, Liu and Xu encouraged the Stars to demand a public apology from the Dongcheng Public Security Bureau with a deadline of 9.00am on 1 August.

In response, Ma and Huang posted two copies of a letter of public protest, one at the Democracy Wall at Xidan Street in Beijing and another at the site of the Stars' outdoor exhibition next to the National Museum. According to Xu and Qing's 'A Letter to the People,' Ma and Huang's letter of public protest called on the Beijing Municipal Government (*Beijing shi zhengfu* 北京市政府) to 'redress' the Dongcheng Bureau's 'mistaken behaviour' (Xu and Liu 2010: 8–9). Ma and Huang's letter was also taken by hand to the Confidential Communications Office (*Jiyao tongxun shi* 机要通讯室) of the Beijing Municipal Committee. During the following day, police reacted by posting their own public notices at the site of the exhibition stating that it had been taken down solely in order to safeguard public order.

Soon after the closure of their outdoor exhibition, members of the Stars were also invited to attend a meeting at the National Museum in Beijing by Liu Xun, Head of the Beijing Municipal Artists Association (*Beijing shi meishujia xiehui* 北京市美术家协会). Liu, who had been imprisoned for ten years as a result of his denunciation as a 'rightist' in 1957 and who may well have sympathized with the stand taken by the Stars, announced to the group that their exhibition would be restaged officially in mid-October 1979 at the Huafang Studio (*Huafang zhai* 画舫斋) in Beihai Park (*Beihai gongyuan* 北海公园), just north of the Forbidden City in Beijing. Consequently, some members of the Stars moved their work from the National Gallery, where it had been kept under protection on the instructions of Liu Xun, to the Huafang Studio in preparation for their forthcoming exhibition there.

Despite Liu Xun's conciliatory offer and with no response to Ma and Huang's open letter having been received from the Beijing Municipal Committee, eight of the Stars[3] then took part in a public protest against the closure of their exhibition. The protest, which had been jointly organized by Huang Rui, Bei Dao, Mang Ke, Liu Qing and Xu Wenli, began at 9.15am on 1 October with speeches at the Democracy Wall in Xidan recounting the aims of the Stars and their grievances against the Dongcheng Bureau. These speeches were then followed by a rain-sodden march through the streets of Beijing to the offices of the Beijing Municipal Committee (Plate 2).

During the march, which attracted the attention of foreign journalists gathered to report on the PRC's National Day celebrations in Beijing on the same day, somewhere between 700 and 1000 participants took to the streets of Beijing preceded by red banners emblazoned with the slogans 'March to Uphold the Constitution' and 'Political Democracy – Artistic Freedom!' ('*Yao yishu ziyou, yao zhengzhi minzhu*' 要艺术自由, 要政治民主).[4] At Liubukuo (六部口), the protesters encountered a police picket-line that prevented them from marching further along Chang'an Avenue (*Chang'an Jie* 长安街). Published accounts of what happened next differ. According to Zhu Zhu, the appearance of the police caused all but a very few of the protesters to disperse into Beijing's side streets (Zhu 2007a: 25–26). However, Xu and Liu's 'A Letter to the People' states that the protesters were simply diverted and carried on in an orderly fashion to their destination (Xu and Liu 2010: 10). Both Liu Qing and Xu Wenli were later arrested and imprisoned for three years as a direct consequence of their involvement in the planning of the Stars' public protest (Berghuis 2008: 45–46). By contrast, none of Stars who took part in the protest were detained or imprisoned by the authorities.

Following their protest, the Stars were allowed to restage their first exhibition at the Huafang Studio in Beihai Park, not as initially promised in mid-October 1979, but instead between 23 November and 2 December of the same year.[5] In the summer of 1980, the Stars Painters Association (*Xingxing huahui* 星星画会) was formally recognized by the Chinese authorities (although it could not register officially because of its continued standing as an autonomous group). With the support of another one-time 'rightist' Jiang Feng 江丰, Chairman of the Chinese Artists Association, the group was eventually allowed to stage a second official exhibition of its work at the National Gallery in Beijing, between 24 and 30 August 1980. This exhibition, which was the first by an independent art group to be held in a major state-run institution within the PRC since 1949, reportedly attracted an audience of between 80,000 and 200,000 and significantly polarized public and critical opinion (Plates 3 and 4).[6]

The Stars were subsequently refused permission to mount any further exhibitions of their work because of the onset of the Campaign against Bourgeois Liberalism in 1981. Over the course of the next few years most of the core members of the Stars left to pursue their artistic and literary ambitions outside the PRC.

In light of the public protest surrounding their first unofficial outdoor exhibition, many commentators have characterized the Stars as socially and politically motivated artists who deliberately sought to challenge the authority of the CCP by openly transgressing established ideological limits on the production and public display of art within the PRC (e.g. Erickson 2005: 16). What is more, many of those same commentators have further characterized the supposedly transgressive actions of the Stars as a definitive starting point for the progressive liberalization of the visual arts within the PRC, running alongside the social and economic reforms initiated by the adoption of Deng's policy of Reform and Opening (Köppel-Yang 2003: 194). These views have been further bolstered by assertions that the seemingly radical anti-authoritarian stance taken by the Stars was strongly influenced by the active participation of many of its members in the events of the Cultural Revolution (see Berghuis 2008: 40–41), and that artworks produced by some members of the Stars present thinly veiled criticism of Mao Zedong and the CCP—most notably in this regard wooden sculptures by Wang Keping, including *Idol* (*Ouxiang* 偶像), *Long, Long Life!* (*Wanwan sui!* 万万岁), *Breathing* (*Huxi* 呼吸) and *Silence* (*Chenmo* 沉默) (Köppel-Yang 2003: 124–130) (Plate 5).

There are, however, significant grounds for qualifying these views. While it should not be denied that the actions of the Stars presented a major challenge to established cultural orthodoxy within the PRC and that the group ran a significant risk of punishment by the state as a result of its actions, it is by no means clear that the long-standing ideological restrictions on individual freedom of expression that the Stars are supposed to have transgressed were, in fact, still unequivocally in place at the end of 1979. Although Deng's policy of Reform and

Opening makes no specific provision for the production and display of visual art outside the socialist-realist discourses established by Mao during the 1940s, it does call explicitly for the opening-up of space for social and economic activity away from the previously all-pervasive ideological purview of the CCP as well as the rehabilitation of free-thinking intellectuals and experts as a necessary catalyst of social and political reform (a major inversion of the PRC's social hierarchy under Mao, which placed the interests of workers, soldiers and peasants above those of the bourgeoisie, petty bourgeoisie and intelligentsia).

Moreover, before their first unofficial exhibition, not only were the Stars already immersed in an existing climate of political liberalization and protest associated with the Beijing Spring and the Democracy Wall Movement, most also enjoyed a relatively privileged and politically informed social standing as children of high-ranking government cadres (*ganbu* 干部), intellectuals and army officers. Without this combination of a major shift in government policy, the emergence of a conspicuous non-governmental resistance to political authoritarianism and their relatively privileged social status, it seems unlikely that the Stars would have been in a position to depart in such a public manner as they did from established political directives on the role of art within the PRC. The actions of the Stars are therefore open to interpretation, not as a decisive breaking with established convention but as a performative manifestation of attitudes and practices already prefigured (if not explicitly legitimized) as part of the PRC's newly emerging discursive landscape after the Cultural Revolution.

It is possible to go further in this regard by drawing attention to precedents for the activities of the Stars within the indigenous art world of the PRC prior to 1979. As Gao Minglu has indicated, from the early 1960s through to the late 1970s, artists associated with the No Name Group of painters were already engaged in the organized making and display of artworks outside the PRC's state-controlled system; albeit in a semi-clandestine manner and without the explicit promotion of social or political content (Gao 2007b). In addition to this, there were also numerous public exhibitions by semi-official Chinese art groups, similar in format to that of the Stars that took place prior to September 1979.

What is more, it is also possible to see the use of allegory and symbolism by some members of the Stars—for example, in relation to works by Yan Li (Plate 6), Ma Desheng (Plate 7), Huang Rui, Wang Keping and Qu Leilei (Plate 8)—as similar in its critical intent to the use of comparably elliptical forms of visual language used as part of the Chinese Modern Woodcut Movement (*Zhongguo xinxing banhua yundong* 中国新兴版画运动) of the 1930s (Tang 2008) and the making of socialist-realist art during the Maoist period (examples of which can be interpreted as presenting coded criticism of Mao and the policies of the CCP) (Clarke 2008: 287). Indeed, that connection with the past is strongly corroborated by members of the Stars speaking in a published conversation with Li Xianting published in the journal *Meishu zazhi (Art)* in 1980 (Li 1980). In this published conversation, Wang Keping, Ma Desheng, Huang Rui and Qu Leilei all seek to present their work as a critical response to the events of the Cultural Revolution and the actions of the Gang of Four (*Siren bang* 四人帮) and to draw attention to the influence on their work of early-twentieth-century

Western and Chinese modernism, including works by Picasso, Käthe Kollwitz and members of the Chinese Modern Woodcut Movement.

In addition, most of the core members of the Stars belonged to educated families who had occupied positions of high status within Chinese society prior to 1949 (a situation that effectively disqualified almost all of the Stars from participation in the activities of 'radical' Red Guards during the Cultural Revolution).[7] As a consequence, they were exposed as part of their early education to attitudes and practices associated with China's long-standing *literati* traditions that look towards a subjective, spontaneous and somewhat amateurish engagement with the making of art. As the conversations with Yan Li and Qu Leilei included here show, the Stars' challenge to prevailing limits on the production and exhibition of art within Chinese society at the end of the 1970s can thus be understood to stem not just from a desire for modernizing social progress but also to achieve that progress, in part at least, through a return to established Chinese cultural values and, in particular, the reinstatement of the position of China's historically free-thinking *literati* culture.

Furthermore, it is important to note that the Stars had no clearly stated collective political agenda outside a general resistance to restrictions on freedom of personal expression (the politicization of events following the closure of the Stars' unofficial outdoor exhibition having come about largely through the intervention of the political activists Xu Wenli and Liu Qing). While it could be argued that reluctance on the part of the Stars to adopt an explicitly stated political position and, consequently, to make artworks with unambiguously political content simply reflects the persistence of tight restrictions on freedom of speech still in place within the PRC at the end of the 1970s, as the conversations presented here also indicate, the Stars would appear to have chosen to have made a conscious distinction between the functions of art and politics as a way of resisting continuing entanglement with the restrictive effects of the immanent politicization of life within the PRC; a choice that can be understood to have manifested itself both in relation to an aversion on the part of many of the Stars to any sort of formal institutionalized artistic training and the decision of most of the group not to take part in the protest march on 1 October 1979.

Conversations with members of the Stars

Yan Li (b. 1954)[8]

Paul Gladston: When and under what circumstances did the Stars[9] first come together as a group?

Yan Li: The Stars first came together as a group in 1979. This was shortly after the period known as the Beijing Spring when Chinese society became more open following the death of Mao Zedong and the ending of the Cultural Revolution. At that time, people felt the need to speak out rather than keeping their thoughts and feelings to themselves. The Stars' first exhibition took place on 27 and 28 September 1979. We exhibited our work in the open air, mounting it on iron railings in a park to the east of the National Art Museum in Beijing, but eventually the police stopped us as we didn't have official permission. We then staged a protest march on National Day, 1 October 1979, objecting to the closure of our exhibition. At the time of our first exhibition, there was a phenomenon known as the Democracy Wall, which had started at Xidan Street in Beijing in December 1978. This phenomenon came about because there were certain problems that couldn't be solved at a local level after the ending of the Cultural Revolution; so people travelled to Beijing from all over China to try to find higher government officials who would help them to solve these problems. But, they didn't know where to find the higher government officials in Beijing. So, they wrote notes and posted them on a wall at Xidan Street hoping that the government officials would read them. That's why it was called the Democracy Wall—the people were able to make their views and concerns known to the government in a public way. Our protest march started at the Democracy Wall and proceeded along Chang-an avenue past Tian'anmen Square before finally ending up at the building that housed the Party Committee of the City of Beijing. During our protest march, we called for freedom of expression and an opportunity to exhibit our work in public. The strange thing was that our protest succeeded. After a couple of months we were given permission to restage our first exhibition at the Huafang Studio inside Beihai Park. We were then allowed to stage a second, official exhibition of our work at the National Art Museum in Beijing during late August and September 1980.

PG: When and under what circumstances did the Stars stop working together as a group?

YL: Towards the end of 1980 the group was banned. We weren't allowed to stage any further exhibitions of our work during 1981. From then on, members of the Stars went abroad one by one. Some got student visas, some got visiting scholarships and some were married to foreign people. From late 1981 to 1986, ten important members of the group went abroad, to places such as America, France, Japan and the United Kingdom. Officially, all members of the Stars group were banned from exhibiting in China between the end of 1980 and early 1984.

PG: Why were the Stars and other groups banned between late 1980 and 1984? And how did the Stars know that they had been banned?

YL: There was a crackdown by the government on all areas of civil society, beginning with the suppression of the Democracy Movement in early 1978. Eventually, all journals and organizations in civil society were banned. In the middle of 1981, the Stars applied to hold exhibitions at a number of official venues, but we were refused by all of them.

PG: The Stars' first unofficial exhibition and the group's subsequent protest march can be understood to have presented a significant challenge to established government directives on the role of art within the PRC. Although Deng Xiaoping's opening and reform policy had been approved by the CCP in December 1978, there was no specific provision within that policy for the making and display of art outside the PRC's official state-controlled system. In September 1979, what were the likely consequences for anyone making or publicly displaying art that did not have official government approval?

YL: At the time, we still had to work within tight government restrictions. We had to do things step by step, trying to push the existing boundaries back little by little. If they, the government, went backwards, we would go forwards. If the government went forwards, we would go backwards. In China, during the 1970s and early 1980s, it was like that all the time. It was very difficult. We couldn't predict what would happen and we were worried that the police might come for us any time. Sometimes, the police would knock at your door and ask you to go to the police station. They would ask you questions and then release you. After one month, the police would come again. Most people would just answer the questions broadly.

PG: When the police took you away for questioning, did they hurt you or physically intimidate you in any way, or did they just ask questions?

YL: Well, they would ask questions like 'You met some foreigner last week, what did you talk about?' They might insult you verbally, but, in my experience, there was no actual physical violence. For members of groups who talked about political issues in China, there was a very real danger they might be sent to jail.

PG: During the late 1970s and early 1980s, did you feel that the Chinese government was not sure what should happen as a result of Deng's reforms…that it was not entirely in control of events? Did you also sense reluctance on the part of government officials to implement Deng's reforms? After all, China's history during the revolutionary period from 1949 onwards had seen numerous reversals of political direction and consequential reversals of individual fortune, not least in relation to the One Hundred Flowers Bloom Campaign of the mid- to late 1950s.

YL: Yes. One of the problems was that government officials were frightened of doing things that might be perceived as being against the party line…people didn't want to take risks, or they might not be fully aware of central government policy. From time to time, central government may have adopted a more relaxed attitude towards freedom of expression, but local government officials often upheld established restrictions for fear of the consequences of getting things wrong. Sometimes it was the other way around. Local government officials would be liberal, but central government might not think the same way. And there's another interesting phenomenon in China: if the government bans an artwork—for instance, in 1995, my literary work was banned by government officials—it's an entirely open-ended thing. They would never indicate if or when the ban had been lifted. In 1999, after four years, one of my friends who works as a publisher decided to publish my work in China, and it was successfully published without government permission. None of this was new, of course. China had a long history of censorship even before communism.

PG: Did the Stars do any work together as a group after 1981?

YL: Yes, we held retrospective exhibitions in Hong Kong, Japan and Beijing. The Hong Kong exhibition was held at the Hanart TZ Gallery to celebrate the tenth anniversary of the Stars in 1989.[10] We also held small shows in Tokyo to celebrate our fifteenth anniversary and our twentieth anniversary.[11] The latest exhibition was held in Beijing in 2007. I contacted members of the group one by one. By then, most of our works had been bought by foreign people. Many people in China had heard of our group's name, but hadn't seen our work. I thought we needed to hurry, because the amount being paid for modern Chinese art on the international art market had increased significantly. In 2006 and 2007, many of the artists belonging to the Stars sold their artworks. I contacted everyone in the group in the middle of 2006 and asked them not to sell all of the work they still had because I needed some of it for the Beijing exhibition. After one and a half years, we held the show at the Today Art Museum in Beijing.[12] Some people are trying to mount an exhibition of our work at the National Art Museum in Beijing this year...in 2009. But I'm not sure whether it will work out or not.[13]

PG: 2009 is also the twentieth anniversary of the China/Avant-Garde exhibition.[14] Recently, there was an attempt to stage a series of public talks at the opening of a retrospective in Beijing about the China/Avant-Garde exhibition, but the authorities intervened to stop the talks going ahead on the grounds that the organizers, who included Gao Minglu, had not secured official permission.[15] The fact that 2009 is also the sixtieth anniversary of the founding of the PRC as well as the twentieth anniversary of the Tian'anmen protests almost certainly influenced the decision of the authorities to prevent the talks planned by the organizers of the China/Avant-Garde retrospective from going ahead. The Chinese government is still quick to ban or curtail any public event that might be seen as a challenge to public order, especially during times of national celebration or on the anniversary of sensitive historical events.

YL: Yes, I know. We would also like to have an anniversary show this year, but it's not so promising.

PG: Who were the core members of the Stars?

YL: There were 11 core members of the group who got together and worked together. There were writers as well as painters and sculptors. Apart from me, they included Ma Desheng, Zhong Ahcheng, Bo Yun, Qu Leilei, Huang Rui, Li Shuang, Wang Keping, Gan Shaocheng, Yang Yiping and Mao Lizi. In addition to these core members, there were others who were associated more loosely with the activities of the group, such as Ai Weiwei and Chen Yansheng 陈延生.[16] At the time, the composers Tan Dun 谭盾, Qu Xiaosong 瞿小松, Ye Xiaogang 叶小纲[17] and a woman writer and musician called Liu Suola 刘索拉 were also among my friends, although none of them were actual members of the Stars.

PG: Was there an agreed hierarchy within the group?

YL: No, we were friends and equals. We didn't want to appoint anyone as the leader of the group because if we got into trouble there wouldn't be any single person who could be held responsible. We faced all the problems together.

PG: How did the Stars arrive at collective action? Other contemporary Chinese art groups and associations of the late 1970s and 1980s, such as the Northern Art Group, formed organizing committees that can be understood to have mirrored organizational structures within the CCP.

YL: We were actually against those kinds of structures. We just formed the group organically. We were quite idealistic and we still are.

PG: Did you have any personal ambitions during your time with the Stars?

YL: I always wanted to publish a literary magazine inside mainland China. I went to New York on a student visa in 1985 and stayed there for more than 15 years. When I was living in New York, I was part of a group of Chinese musicians, writers, artists and film directors which got together almost every week to hold parties. In 1987, I started a poetry magazine in New York called *First Line*. I collected together literary works that couldn't be published within mainland China. I published them in New York and then tried to send them back to mainland China for more than seven years.

PG: So, you were forced to pursue your personal literary ambitions outside the PRC?

YL: Yes, from 1985 to 2000. But those of us who were in exile continued to write poems using our first language, which is like an organ inside our bodies. I can't use a second language to express myself. Where's the market for these poems? Here in China, of course. That's why I now prefer to stay here to write and publish my work.

PG: Were there any disputes among the members of the Stars?

YL: If there were any arguments, they were only about small things. Everyone knew that the government was very strong and that we might be in danger of imprisonment if we said or did anything against the government. So we needed each other's company; we needed to comfort one another. Consequently, there weren't any strong arguments or conflicts.

PG: When you disagreed with one another, what did you disagree about? Can you be specific?

YL: Well, it's hard to say. We had to trust each very strongly because we might be in danger at anytime. Even if one of us was caught by the police, we wouldn't say anything.

PG: Did personal ambitions conflict in any way with the collective aims of the group? It seems to me that the Stars' position was somewhat contradictory? You shared a desire for individual freedom of expression, but sought to pursue that freedom as a group. At the time, were you aware of having to negotiate between the collectivism of the group and your personal ambitions as artists?

YL: We say we are good men first before becoming good artists. We would like to write good poems because we would like to correct our behaviour.

PG: That sounds very much like a traditional Chinese attitude towards the role of culture: the notion of culture as a means of personal transformation, self-betterment or elevation (*wenhua* 文化) (Louie 2008: 14–19). At the time, during the late 1970s and early 1980s, did you see the activities of the Stars as having some sort of relationship to traditional Chinese culture?

YL: Yes, there is a connection. We learned good things from our tradition.

PG: Could you be more specific? What exactly did you learn?

YL: There may have been an unconscious influence. My grandfather was a traditional Chinese doctor. I think, looking back, that he influenced me to a large extent. My grandfather, Yan Cangshan, was not only a doctor, he was, like other members of his profession, also good at painting, calligraphy, playing music and writing poetry. Our family had a collection of traditional Chinese paintings and calligraphies. So I saw traditional Chinese painting, calligraphy and poetry quite often when I was a child (Li 2008: 5–45). My great, great-grandfather, Yan Xiaojiang, was a painter during the Qing dynasty. Personally, I don't like using traditional Chinese painting techniques though, because they don't match with the representation of modern things.

PG: Most of the Stars were sons and daughters of high-ranking government cadres,[18] army officers or intellectuals (Chen 1987: 327). What sort of bearing did these connections to the higher echelons of Chinese society have on the activities of the Stars?

YL: Because children of intellectuals get more education and influence from their families, they are more sensitive to matters of morality and conscience. Thus, their reactions are more intense. The Cultural Revolution hit the people with independent thinking harder: as for the rest, it was mutual revenge between conflicting officials. Mao Zedong presided over this cruel spectacle. In 1968, I spent some time living with my parents in a party dormitory in Beijing—this gave me insight into social connections within the CCP. After the Communist Revolution in 1949, people came from all over China to work for the CCP. As a result, the life of Beijing became very diverse. People from different places were able to get together and to share their thoughts.

PG: Were any of the Stars members of the Red Guards during the Cultural Revolution? At least one commentator has implied strongly that at least some of the Stars were Red Guards and that this influenced the group's desire to pursue radical cultural change.[19]

YL: Personally, I was never a member of the Red Guards. I was from a privileged family background and therefore considered unsuitable. This was the same for almost all of the Stars. I went to the countryside during the Cultural Revolution, but only briefly and certainly not because I had been a Red Guard. My parents were disillusioned party officials and were sent down to the countryside because of their views. I went to the countryside at one point to accompany them.

PG: Did you take part in any unofficial art-making activities before you joined the Stars?

YL: Yes. During the Cultural Revolution there were literary groups who got together to read Chinese translations of Western books and exchanged these books even though they were banned. Most group members were between 14 and 24 years old. In 1970, I met some poets who had started writing underground poems, including Bei Dao and Mang Ke. I started writing my own poems in 1973 when I was 19 years old. We kept in touch and exchanged our works until 1978. Between 1977 and 1980, there were numerous unofficial groups in Beijing, including political groups associated with the publications *Beijing Spring* (*Beijing zhi chun* 北京之春) and *Fertile Ground* (*Wo tu* 沃土). These groups had good relations with one another, just like brothers and sisters. However, they were all banned at the end of 1980. There was also a literary magazine called *Today*, which was organized by Bei Dao and Mang Ke. Some of the Stars contributed poetry and/or illustrations to *Today*; about half a dozen, I think. Like me, they all liked the arts and making art. They included Ma Desheng, Qu Leilei, Huang Rui, Gan Shaocheng, Zhong Ahcheng.

PG: Could you give specific examples of the translated versions of Western books that you were reading during the Cultural Revolution?

YL: Victor Hugo's novel about the terror during the French Revolution, *Ninety-Three*, which was first published in China in 1963, banned during the Cultural Revolution and then published again in China in 1978; also a book by Balzac, another work of French literature. We read many translated books from Britain, Russia, France, America, etc. At that time, it was illegal to read these books. But we secretly swapped the books we had. As I said before,

I was working in a factory from 1970. I lived on-site at the factory as part of the work unit[20] to which I had been assigned. The factory had a library next to where I stayed, which had previously been for the benefit of the workers but which was locked during the Cultural Revolution. I broke in and took some of the books. I still have some of them. At that time, there was an attempt to erase all old style, reactionary culture. That's why some libraries locked the books away while others burned them.

PG: Did you have access to any Western books that had been published during the twentieth-century?

YL: Yes, but most were from America, such as Jack London. There were also examples of revolutionary literature from the Soviet Union—books by Joseph Brodsky, for example.

PG: What sort of influence did the Western books that you read in translation during the Cultural Revolution have on your work as an artist?

YL: The books that were available to us had all been translated before the Cultural Revolution. All of them, including translated Western books, had been subject to official screening from 1949 through to the 1960s. This screening severely limited the number of books available to us. It also meant that most of the books available to us from outside China were from the Soviet Union. The influence of the books I read was actually quite limited. Mostly what I got from them was heartfelt feelings of freedom and humanity.

PG: Some commentators have argued that the Stars' first unofficial exhibition marks the beginning of the development of contemporary Chinese art—that is to say, of modern Chinese art produced outside the PRC's state-controlled system (Zhu 2007a). The curator and art historian Gao Minglu has sought to question this reading by drawing attention to the work of the No Name Group, whose leading members began to produce modern art unofficially within the PRC during the early 1960s. As Martina Köppel-Yang has indicated, there were also public exhibitions of the work of semi-official art groups and associations in the PRC similar in content to those of the Stars that were staged prior to the Stars' first unofficial exhibition; for example, the exhibition of the work of the Oil Painting Research Association, which was held in Zhongshan Park in Beijing in February 1979, some seven months before the Stars' first unofficial exhibition, and the Painting Exhibition of the Twelve, which was held in Shanghai in 1978. In short, there were historical precedents for the activities of the Stars.

YL: Yes, but the groups you mentioned were producing impressionistic landscapes, portraits and still-life paintings that emphasized form rather than social content. I think the Stars were the first group to do something different. We were more socially and politically oriented, I would say.

PG: Could you be more specific? In what ways was the work of the Stars more socially and politically oriented than that of other unofficial and semi-official Chinese art groups?

YL: Our aim was to gain freedom of expression for artists and writers.

PG: The Stars' first unofficial exhibition and the group's subsequent protest march could be interpreted as attempts to achieve those aims; but what about the paintings, drawings, sculptures and poems that you produced? Did you see your artworks as having a specifically critical function in relation to society and politics? Some members of the Stars, including you, Ma Desheng, Qu Leilei and Wang Keping, produced artworks whose significance is either allegorical or highly ambiguous. For example, one of your own paintings, *Home* (*Jia* 家), which was shown at the second official exhibition of the work of the Stars in 1980, can be read either as a domestic scene with washing hung out to dry on a line outside two adjoining houses, or as an embracing couple; a metaphor perhaps for your views on freedom of expression. Was allegory and ambiguity of meaning used simply as a way of avoiding official censure, or, like Western avant-garde and postmodernist artists, did you use it to demonstrate the inherent uncertainty of linguistic signification and, therefore, to undermine—that is to say, deconstruct—conventional representations of reality (Owens 1980a: 67–86; 1980b: 59–80).

YL: We had to be ambiguous because we always had to consider the risks…because all of us have only one chance at life. So, sometimes I had to destroy some of my works. As for using allegory and ambiguity in the way you describe it…yes, we did use it in that way.[21] But, at the time, we didn't have any direct knowledge of the Western avant-gardes.

PG: In formal terms, many of your own paintings of the late 1970s and early 1980s strongly resemble paintings by Western avant-garde artists of the early twentieth century—in particular those produced by the Surrealists. Something similar could be said of sculptures by Wang Keping and of drawings by Qu Leilei. Given that you didn't have any direct knowledge of the Western avant-gardes, how do you account for these resemblances?

YL: Humanity! Personally, I never think about Western culture or Eastern culture. Human beings share a lot of things and have a lot in common.

PG: A renewed interest in humanism—'humanist enthusiasm,' as it was known at the time— is certainly an important aspect of the development of contemporary Chinese art within the PRC during the late 1970s and 1980s. As part of this renewed interest in humanism, did the Stars have more focused concerns related to human values and issues of human dignity? Did the group have specific views on differences in sexuality or ethnicity, for example? Did they have a feminist agenda?

YL: I think people have different experiences and that they influence one another.

PG: Did the Stars have an agreed political position or ideological point of view?

YL: Under the circumstances in China at that time, any behaviour that strove for independent selfhood was seen as a bid for political power. In fact, any exhibition presented to the public was judged to include political factors, and the exhibitions that were allowed to take place were considered to be approved political behaviour. At the end of the 1970s in China, there was, as you just mentioned, a general return to humanistic ways of thinking in opposition to the prolonged distortion of human nature that had taken place during the Cultural Revolution. In making this kind of effort, there will always be a few people who charge to the front and face greater risk. But, the socialist government in China now overwrites the idealism we had before by emphasizing the importance of economic development.

PG: As an individual, how did you see yourself politically during your time with the Stars? Was organized politics at all important to you?

YL: I'm not interested in organized politics. I'm an individualist, because it's the only way to get things done as an artist in China. If you are in a political group in China, then you belong to the government.[22] I want to do things spontaneously—according to natural law, which is above human law.[23]

PG: When the Stars exhibited their work publicly in 1979 and 1980, people who came to see those exhibitions were able to make written comments in 'guest books.' Some wrote in disapproval while others wrote in favour of what the group was doing (Zhu 2007a: 27; Köppel-Yang 2003: 127–129).[24] What was your impression at the time? What sort of public impact did the Stars have as a result of their exhibitions?

YL: Only a relatively small number of people saw our exhibitions in Beijing.[25] But the spiritual influence spread out.[26] A lot of older scholars and artists supported us.[27] And people wrote letters to each other, so people from other cities knew about us and they started their own groups in other places too.[28] In those days, letter writing was the principle means of communication between individuals living in different parts of China. At that time, the atmosphere was still very tight, but people were eager to express themselves. When they heard some people had started a group, they followed very quickly. Also, at that time, most people were materially very poor, so they weren't frightened of losing anything. That's why poetry and literature were really big things in China during the 1970s and early 1980s.

PG: The work of the Stars was criticized at the time of its initial showing for being ugly and, therefore, ideologically negative. The critic Gao Yan 高焰 referred to the work of Wang

Keping, for example, as exhibiting a 'black Western humour' contrary to the positive aesthetic values of socialist-realism (Köppel-Yang 2003: 127–130). Did the Stars have any particular views on the role of aesthetics in relation to their work?

YL: The world in China was grey when you opened the window during the 1970s, and I felt the need to make it more colourful. That's why I used a lot of bright colours in my painting. I thought my paintings were beautiful.

PG: So, you used beauty as a resistance to the visual impoverishment of your immediate surroundings…even as a means of intervening in and changing those surroundings?

YL: I didn't think that much at the time; most of the time the feelings came spontaneously.

PG: Most, if not all, of the members of the Stars were self-taught or largely self-taught as artists.[29] Was this simply because you didn't have access to formal training—although colleges and universities had reopened after the Cultural Revolution, the number of available places was severely limited—or was there an active desire on the part of the members of the Stars to detach themselves from the institutionalized socialist-realist techniques still favoured by the CCP at the time?

YL: At that time, one effectively became a tool of government by following China's institutionalized way of painting. If you had not been trained at art school you would be overlooked by the government.

PG: So, it wasn't just a question of lack of access to education, but of actively avoiding certain ways of working legitimized by the government…ways of working that coincided with established government ideology?[30]

YL: Yes. It was like that at the time. Now, young people have much more freedom and many more choices. That's why a lot of them don't care for politics that much. They don't feel they have anything much to resist.

PG: By holding their protest march on 1 October, were the Stars trying deliberately to attract the attention of the international media who were in Beijing to cover the official celebrations for National Day? (Köppel-Yang 2003: 127)

YL: By 1979, China had established diplomatic relations with the United States, so there were representatives of the Western media in Beijing at the time. There were some reports of our protest march by the Western media. There were no reports by the Chinese media. They didn't appear during the march.

PG: After the Stars held their protest march, two of the organizers of the march, Liu Qing and Xu Wenli, who edited the political magazine *April 5th Forum* (*Siwu yundong* 四五论坛) but who were not members of the Stars, were arrested and sent to jail. None of the Stars who took part in the march were arrested or sent to jail (Berghuis 2008: 46). Why was that?

YL: Artists in civil society were striving for personal rights of freedom of expression and the opening-up of public space for freedom of expression. Members of political organizations in civil society doubted the legitimacy of the authorities. Comparing the two, the latter had a tendency to get organized in order to subvert power. Thus, they were attacked more ruthlessly by the government. This is the way totalitarian governments always work. At the time, we were ready to be arrested and imprisoned. Nevertheless, we thought we had no choice but to take this course of action. Otherwise, as a person and as an artist, how could one find a way to move forward? Actually, Liu Qing and Xu Wenli were not arrested immediately after our protest march, but one month later on unrelated matters.

PG: Did the Stars get drawn into a position of open political confrontation with the authorities as a result of Liu Qing and Xu Wenli's involvement in the protest march on 1 October 1979, as some commentators have suggested?[31]

YL: No, it was a self-determined social role. One person cannot take on too many roles in life. One can only specialize in relation to one's own field. In other words, politicians will orient themselves directly towards politics, while artists are more concerned with the right to publish or publicly exhibit their work. If an artwork cannot be published or publicly exhibited, the content of that work simply goes no further. Thus, the first priority of the artist is to strive for the right to put his or her own work in the public eye.

PG: So, would it be right to say that the Stars were not aiming to contribute to the overthrow of the PRC's existing political order but simply to gain autonomy as cultural agents in relation to that existing order?

YL: Yes. After Mao Zedong passed away, most people thought that Chinese society would begin to function in a relatively normal manner. That is to say, quite a few people hoped to foist all of the blame for the Cultural Revolution on the Gang of Four[32] and even Mao Zedong, and then everyone could put down their burdens and achieve a rational, civilized social order. Initially, the Stars also entertained such a fantasy, but the actual facts were not that straightforward. This is because China's culture of governance for thousands of years has always been to have one supremely powerful person who says what goes. In China, our political system is that after one dynasty another dynasty comes—so one emperor after another. We say that anyone who wants to be the emperor has to kill the existing emperor first. Given this kind of cultural background, there was nothing the members of the Stars could do to radically change the existing political order in China.

PG: Besides the connection with the founders of *April 5th Forum*, did the activities of the Stars intersect directly with the activities of other political groups?

YL: Well, we knew that it would be really risky to discuss political issues directly, so we used more indirect means of expression, such as through painting, literature and poetry. That's why our poetry was called 'Misty Poetry' (*Menglong shi* 朦胧诗).

PG: Does Misty Poetry have a relationship to a longer Chinese tradition of aesthetic uncertainty and ambiguity, both in relation to poetry and painting.

YL: Principally, I think it has a relationship to the connections between people. I share things with my friends, and when I write things, I think about them. Or maybe, as I said before, there's an unconscious connection with tradition.[33]

PG: In the West, some commentators have described the Stars as political dissidents (Erickson 2005: 16). This description fits in conveniently with lingering Cold War notions of a dialectical opposition between capitalist and communist ideologies. Did the Stars see themselves as political dissidents?

YL: That's the easy way to see it. That's one kind of phenomenon. I think dissident behaviour is everywhere, even in America. Why would you say it's just in China? In America, they also have dissidents!

PG: I would like to suggest that your relationship with Chinese society and politics was a rather more complicated one than that suggested by the use of the term 'dissident.' There are certain things that you wanted to resist: principally, ideological restrictions on freedom of expression and the forced distancing of artists from active critical involvement in China's political and social life. And, by striving to gain freedom of expression, you ran a very real risk of losing your liberty, or worse, at a time of great social instability and political uncertainty. But, it seems to me that this resistance was against restrictions that Deng Xiaoping's reforms had, in principle at least, already overturned by setting the stage for the opening up of public spaces outside the all-pervasive influence of established party ideology. Consequently, your striving for freedom of expression should not be viewed as a dissident act *per se*, but as part of, by then, an ideologically legitimized movement to re-establish the relative autonomy of cultural life within the PRC, following on from the destructive events of the Cultural Revolution. What is more, many of you were the children of high-ranking government cadres, army officers or intellectuals, which meant that you were, to some extent at least, part of and conversant with China's prevailing power structures.

YL: At the level of civilization, of culture, I'm a poet, and, as such, I have to think a lot about socially related things. If you think these things are relevant to your work, then they become your things. I'm a human being first, then a poet. When I do visual things, I like to share them with other people. And I don't care what other people say to me or about me. I don't care about fame either. I just do my thing.

PG: The Cultural Revolution was, among other things, a deliberate attempt to interrupt the continuity of China's established cultural traditions. Were the Stars actively seeking to criticize the interruptive effects of the Cultural Revolution? Did your art, like Scar Literature and Scar Art, look towards an active re-evaluation of China's recent past? Moreover, did the Stars see themselves as being actively involved in the construction of a modern, more humane Chinese society following on from the damaging effects of the Cultural Revolution?

YL: Yes, we tried. My parents were committed underground members of the CCP before the revolution of 1949. They were intellectuals. My father, Yan Shijing, attended the American Christian School in Shanghai. He wrote and spoke English. He was a student of chemistry and wrote his final thesis in English. In 1951, my parents went to Beijing to work for the government as high-ranking cadres. After the revolution, the CCP recruited people from all over China to work for the Party in Beijing. I was born in Beijing in 1954, but after a time my parents sent me to live with my grandparents in Shanghai. During the Cultural Revolution my grandfather was visited by Red Guards six times; they took and destroyed everything he had, including his paintings, his books and other things he had collected. He was placed under house arrest between the end of 1967 and early 1968 and, after constant denunciation, committed suicide at the age of 70 in April 1968. Before that, he sent me back to my parents in Beijing. He said to me: 'I can't protect you anymore.' So I went to live with my parents for a time in Beijing. They were living in a party dormitory. After a time, my parents became very disillusioned. They were sent down to the countryside in Hunan Province in 1968 at the height of the Cultural Revolution. I stayed on in Beijing and lived alone as a 14-year-old boy running with a gang of other boys—chasing girls [laughs]. Each month I picked up money at the post office sent by my parents. I enrolled in high school, but there were no classes. Initially my parents were happy for me to live alone in Beijing because I still had rights of residency in the city on my official identity documentation and they thought that they might never be able to return to Beijing if I went to the countryside with them and lost these rights. Eventually, in 1969, I went to live with my parents in the countryside. One day, there was an announcement that five counter-revolutionaries were to be executed in public. I arrived late at the killing ground, which was on a slope with the prisoners being held at the bottom. The whole event was surrounded by a huge crowd of hundreds, maybe even thousands of people. I heard the gunshots when the prisoners were executed—usually prisoners were made to kneel down and they were shot in the back of the head at close range. The whole crowd surged forward, and then suddenly pulled back. I fought through the crowd to the bottom of the slope to look at what had happened. Those at the front of the crowd had stripped the executed prisoners of all of their clothing. The people in the countryside were so poor at that time that they would even steal the clothes of the dead. In 1970, I returned to Beijing to work in a factory because so many young people had been sent down to the countryside that there was a shortage of young workers. In 1970, my father was detained by the government. He was freed after four years, but was disabled as a result of the harsh conditions during his confinement. My father died in 1981. That's my background as an artist. We wanted to construct a modern, more humane Chinese society after all of that destruction.

PG: Did the Stars see themselves not only as being involved in the construction of a modern, more humane Chinese society but also, to some degree, in the renewal of traditional Chinese culture after the interruptive events of the Cultural Revolution?

YL: That's not so clear. If I want to reconstruct culture, first I have to have the right to do things freely; for instance, to freely set up my own publishing company. Personally, I feel that I have achieved something because I have published some of my books…though it's mostly been outside of China.

PG: What influence did the Stars have on your subsequent work as a painter and poet?

YL: Having gone through so many things, I feel my personality is getting stronger and I'm not afraid of anything. So, I feel that I can write what I like to write rather than feeling restricted.

PG: Poetry, literature and art have played a major role in China's redevelopment since the adoption of Deng Xiaoping's policy of opening-up and reform in December 1978. That said— most people in the PRC, including politicians, would still see China's cultural life as subordinate to the country's economic and social reforms. What is interesting, however, is that when there is a potentially challenging or disruptive cultural event, such as the China/Avant-Garde retrospective exhibition, the authorities usually get quite concerned; concerned enough to intervene…at least, that's the way it appears. Despite the overwhelming preoccupation with economic and social reform, there would still appear to be an underlying sensitivity on the part of the government with regard to the unsettling effects of cultural production. Do you think that is the case?

YL: Yes. As part of Chinese tradition, emperors and kings always saw poets, artists and writers as having the power to do both good things and bad things. They wouldn't even allow artists to do good things because such things should be seen to be done by the government. The problem we have in China at the moment is that we have had economic but not cultural reform. There are now a lot of freedoms in relation to the economy, but on the culture and media side only art galleries and museums are able to act with relative freedom—not broadcasting, not publishing—because galleries and museums present visual, not written material. The written word is still heavily proscribed by the government. That's why galleries continue to have a critical impact on the PRC.

Qu Leilei (b. 1951)[34]

Paul Gladston: The Stars are widely considered to be the first art group within China after the death of Mao Zedong to have exhibited its work unofficially in public. Were you involved in any unofficial art-making activities before you joined the Stars?

Qu Leilei: Art before the Stars…I should go back to a very early stage; probably back to my childhood. I like art purely because of personal desires and interests. I started learning how to make art at an early age, probably about six or seven years old. But it wasn't that serious. When I started learning Chinese characters, I learned how to use a brush. At the same time as I learned calligraphy I was copying traditional paintings. I tried to copy figure paintings, landscapes and calligraphy. It was a perfect period of time during my childhood because I concentrated on painting rather than doing other things. I remember painting during weekends or holidays. Some of the happiest moments of my childhood that I can think of now were those moments I saved pocket money and bought myself a new brush. For a long period of time I only had three brushes: two little 'white cloud' and one little 'red leather' which could be used for meticulous style painting. I was also very grateful to one of my primary school teachers, whose name was Tan Wanchun. He wasn't that famous but had learned from the great artist Qi Baishi 齐白石.[35] He was very skilful. I remember spending days learning to draw lines, doing observations of birds and flowers. I did lots of sketches. I not only did brush works but also pencil works. From the very beginning, I learned both Western and Chinese traditional styles and techniques, a mixture. I admired works by artists like Qi Baishi, Ren Bonian 任伯年[36] and also Xu Beihong.[37] I particularly liked Xu Beihong's nude paintings, which were still very rare in China at that time during the 1950s. Life drawing and nude paintings had been brought into China by artists of that generation from the beginning of twentieth century. It was only half a century since nude paintings had been brought into China from the West. There was a history of extraordinary erotic paintings in China. These paintings revealed the double moral standards of Chinese society historically. On the one hand, women were expected to be very restrained in public. However, on the other hand, there were many extremely erotic paintings shown in private, which I could appreciate from an artistic point of view. My early involvement in art has something to do with my family background. My mother and two of my sisters, whose names were Miaomiao and Cuicui, all worked in the medical field. My mother was born into a traditional intellectual family, and her grandfather and great-grandfather were both doctors. Her family had enormous book collections, which unfortunately were destroyed during war time. As for my father's side, the family of his generation was quite poor, but it was considered to be a family of heroes. For instance, my grandfather on my father's side was the leader of one of the peasant revolts of the time. Of course, the revolt didn't succeed and my grandfather died in a very sad situation. My paternal grandmother had ten children and my father was the youngest one and the only survivor. The rest of the children died at a young age. Both of my parents joined the Communist Party at the same time in 1938 in Shandong Province, but they didn't know each other at that time. And they were both promoted to be senior officials in the party later on.

PG: Your early involvement in art came about because of your mother's traditional intellectual family background?

QL: Yes. All of my uncles from my mother's side could paint, do calligraphy and play musical instruments. So I think I got the artistic influence from my mother's side, and my theoretical or rational outlook from my father's side. My father became a writer later on, and his books, including *Linhai xueyuan* 林海雪原 (*Linhai Academy*), became very popular during the 1950s and 1960s. My parents had very close relations with doctors, professors and writers. Since childhood, these people came to visit my parents and later on I realized all of them were very prestigious and well-known in their fields. Let's go a bit further here. My father's surname is Qu, which is very rare in China. We have a book in China that lists all of the Chinese surnames. It's called *Baijia xing* 百家姓 (*Hundred Family Surnames*).[38] During the Tang, Song, Ming and Qing dynasties, the surname Qu wasn't included in the book. Only in the 1950s, when *Xin baijia xing* 新百家姓 (*New Hundred Family Surnames*) was published, was the surname Qu included on the last page. My father tried to find out the history of our surname, but because of a lack of records, nothing could be proved. However, generation after generation the story was passed down orally through our family saying that my ancestors had been wiped out in history, though it wasn't clear when that happened. Historically, in China we had the *Zhulian jiu zu* 株连九族 (Nine Familial Exterminations) policy,[39] which was followed if someone offended the emperor. The whole family, no matter whether they were close or distant, would be killed. And it was said that the whole Qu family moved from Yunnan to Shandong during the Hongwu period of the Ming dynasty, which means we lived in Yunnan before the Ming dynasty. Yunnan was bordering with Tibet. So it was said that we might be Tibetans. Interestingly, a couple of times when I was in England people thought I was from Tibet. Even more interestingly, if we look at the evolution of the traditional Chinese character of '*qu*,' 曲 it has been conjectured that changes to the character '*qu*' also had something to do with the historical wiping out event. My mother's surname is Liu 刘, which is a very old surname in China. That's something about the history of my parents' family backgrounds.[40] Both my parents changed their names after they joined the CCP. Talking about names, in China, we believe that one's name affects one's fate. My given name is Lei, which consists of three stones. It seems to affect my fate because my life has been related to stones or rocks.

PG: When did your parents get married?

QL: They were married in 1946 in Mudanjiang, which is in Manchuria. Before the end of the war of liberation and the establishing of New China in 1949, they had to build

Dongbei genjudi 东北根据地 (literally, the North-Eastern Regional Base). This meant clearing away the power structures left over from the old warlords, the *Kuomintang* and the Japanese. It also meant the enacting of land reforms. That's why they were both in Manchuria. You may have heard of the *Yan'an zhengfeng yundong* 延安整风运动 (Yan'an Rectification Movement), when many brilliant communist soldiers were killed. This was learned from the Soviet Union…Stalin and his purification of the leadership of the Red Army. Killing good communist leaders affected China hugely later on. Apart from Yan'an, the killing of soldiers also took place in Shandong. This was the *Su tuo* 肃托 (Purge Trotsky) event of 1940 or 1941. At that time, the Japanese still occupied Shandong. My parents were both in Shandong. They were arrested by the Party as part of the *Su Tuo* event and placed in the same prison. They were among a very few who survived incarceration. The reason my mother was arrested was that she insisted on saying that she didn't do anything wrong and that she didn't know who Trotsky was. That's how my parents got to know each other. After they were cleared by the Party and got out of prison, they became friends and got married. They were in the *Renmin jiefangjun* 人民解放军 (People's Liberation Army)[41] again and the troops went from Shandong to Manchuria to prepare the liberation of Manchuria and the whole of China. Both of them had important roles in the army in Manchuria.

PG: When and where were you born?

QL: I was born in Qiqiha'er in 1951.

PG: When did your parents move from Manchuria to Beijing?

QL: To make a complicated story short, after the liberation my father started working in a railway factory in Shenyang. This was because the country needed to reconstruct its industry. At that time, production for the railways was separated into two factories: one was in Shenyang and the other was in Qiqiha'er. My father moved to be the party sectary and manager of the factory in Qiqiha'er. However, due to another career crisis, my father decided to write rather than leading party roles in the factory, and his books were quite successful. Later on, in 1955, my father started working in Beijing following an invitation by the first minister of the Department for Industry, Huang Jing 黄敬.

PG: So, you were about four years old when you arrived in Beijing.

QL: Yes. Right, I'm going to talk something about myself now. From being very young, I knew I was from a good family background. But I only got to know a lot of family stories much later on. From childhood I wasn't a good team player. I remember, I preferred to stay at home. My family's approach to education was very traditional. None of us were spoiled. None of us were sent to private school. And I often wore clothes handed down by my older brother and sister: I wore clothes and socks that had been mended. We hardly had any pocket money. So for a long period of time we had no idea about money or material life. It was only in the 1980s that I started having the concept of money. In my earlier life, I always faced three career choices: one was to become a doctor, one was to become a swimmer and one was to become a painter. The three professions looked quite different, but they all involved my personal interests. But the dreams of becoming a doctor or a swimmer were broken one after the other because of the Cultural Revolution.

PG: Could you say more about your early development as a painter?

QL: I kept painting no matter what kinds of situations I had to face. Before the Cultural Revolution, when I was in primary school, my paintings were shown in international children's exhibitions, and won awards from school. Most of my works then were in traditional Chinese styles, which included 'birds-flowers' style, *gong-bi* 工笔 and *xieyi* 写意.[42] I was hugely influenced by traditional Chinese aesthetics from a very young age. My mother used to teach us classical Chinese literature, poems and paintings at home. Sometimes my mother taught us Tang poems and, based on the meanings of the poems, my brother and I were asked to draw pictures. So I got to know from an early stage that 'there's a picture in a poem, and there's a poem in a picture' (*Shi zhong you hua, hua zhong you shi* 诗中有画，画中有诗).[43] This is one of the characteristics of traditional Chinese *literati* painting. I felt I learned more from my family education than my school education.

PG: So, you were conscious that you were being educated in the classical *literati* tradition?

QL: No, I wasn't aware of it at the time. I just enjoyed that way of education. Earlier I mentioned my primary school stage of education. Let's move on to the middle school stage. I should admit that I learned more about traditional Chinese culture from my family education. In school, we were educated more in the political ways of communism. In the 1960s, we didn't know anything about pop songs—for instance, the Beatles—what we cared about were political events such as the independence of African countries, the Vietnam War and anti-imperialism. However, no matter what the social background was like, I kept painting. I painted many images of Lei Feng 雷锋 and Wang Jie 王杰, who were role models set up by Mao Zedong.[44] Mao encouraged people throughout the whole country to learn from comrade Lei Feng—hence, the slogan *Xiang Lei Feng tongzhi xuexi* 向雷锋同志学习. Why? It was only later that I realized we were being brainwashed. The authorities at the time treated people as if they were robots; machines. We were encouraged to sacrifice our personal lives and interests for the communist ideology of the country...or more specifically, one man's ideology, which was the tragedy of China. If one looks at the celebration of the sixtieth anniversary of the founding of the People's Republic of China in 2009, it's clear that history has been twisted. The message passed on was because of Mao, China has now become strong and splendid. If one looks at Hu Jintao—who was wearing a Sun Yat-sen suit on that day similar to the one that Mao wore—it seemed to symbolize another superpower dictatorship.

It took me a long time to realize what humanity was and how to express my personal feelings. Yes, we were brought up with views that were one-sided. For a long period of time I had no idea at all what it was like for people from a poor family background. It was only later that I realized what terrible lives a lot poor people had led. Since I was from a good family background, I was convinced communism was successful in China.

PG: So there were two competing or contradictory threads running through your early life: a traditional Chinese upper-class cultural education and exposure to Maoist ideology.…

QL: They were not contradictory. They mingled together like art. Chairman Mao knew how to mingle Chinese Confucianism, communist ideology and fascism together. He once said, only when one studies ancient Chinese knowledge and civilization can one deal with Chinese issues or things. He spent years reading classical Chinese books. So, on the one hand, I accepted traditional Chinese culture and, on the other hand, I accepted communist education, which encouraged heroism. Also, we say: 'whoever wins the war gets the power.' (*Cheng zhe wei wang* 成者为王)[45]

PG: So, not only communism, but also Confucianism?

QL: Yes, it's a mixture. Come back to what I mentioned previously about Lei Feng and Wang Jie, whose portraits I painted a number of times. Both Lei Feng and Wang Jie were great soldiers who thought of others before themselves and were very loyal. Chairman Mao encouraged us to learn from them. So, at that time, everyone wanted to become a hero—which meant to restrain one's personal feelings, be hard-working, be loyal to the country and Mao, but also, it meant to be cruel to one's enemies.

PG: There seems to be another contradiction here; a personal one this time. The making of heroic images of Lei Feng and Wang Jie suggests that you wanted to show that you were a loyal student of Maoist ideology. At that same time you said earlier that you didn't particularly like the restrictions of communal life; that, as a child, you weren't a good 'team player.'

QL: Oh, that's before I went to primary school, when I hated to go to nursery. I became more sociable in primary school. I didn't feel my personalities to be contradictory. Saying that, I started reading a lot of translated versions of books of Western literature at a young age; books which weren't supposed to be read at that age.

PG: You joined the army in 1967 and you left in 1973. What happened after you left the army?

QL: I have to say a little bit more about my life before 1973. Before the Cultural Revolution, I mainly painted traditional Chinese paintings. However, that style of painting was forbidden during the Cultural Revolution. Instead, I used my calligraphy skills to do *dazibao* and communist propaganda paintings during the time of the Cultural Revolution.

PG: So, you made *dazibao* in support of the Cultural Revolution while you were still at school?

QL: Yes. But soon, I was accused of being against Madam Mao because I wrote some critical words about her as part of a *dazibao*. To escape the dangerous consequences of my actions, I joined the navy when I was 16. I remember a meeting between my father and some of his friends arranging for me to go into the navy. However, because of my parents, who were also accused during the Cultural Revolution, I didn't stay in the navy for long; only half a year. After that, I went to the countryside in Manchuria to become a barefoot doctor.

PG: Why did you write openly against Madam Mao?

QL: Because of anger. I thought the situation was wrong. I didn't think it was Chairman Mao's fault, but Madam Mao's. I was investigated by the Office of the People's Dictatorship (*Qunzhong zhuanzheng bangongshi* 群众专政办公室). To escape, I went to the countryside. I chose to do so rather than being sent down. I actually enjoyed the life there. However, my dream to become a good barefoot doctor was broken when I received a call indirectly from my parents asking me to go back to Beijing. I realized something might have happened at home. That was in 1968. When I went home, my parents had been liberated and got power again. So I was allowed to rejoin the military, the army this time, which was considered to be the best way to escape the dangerous atmosphere during the Cultural Revolution. It took me a while to adjust to life as a soldier. However, I did quite well in the army. I was working as part of a propaganda team. We criticized Einstein's theory of relativity even though we didn't know what it was. Everything seemed to be mad at that time.

PG: Why did you criticize the theory of relativity?

QL: Because it was from a capitalist country. When I was in the army, I didn't paint as much as I had before—but I started writing.

PG: What did you write about?

QL: I was asked to write something like reports, in a journalistic style. I became a Communist Party member after staying in the army for a while. During my time in the army, I had the opportunity to travel all over the country, and noticed what kind of life people led; I saw people beaten to death. I remember my teacher in middle school was severely tortured by Red Guards who were once my schoolmates. I remember seeing her dead body lying on a platform in the schoolyard and the breeze lifting her clothing to reveal the colour of the bruises on her skin. Another time I can't forget is when we travelled to Zhanjiang in Canton (Guangdong) Province. Once, I was washing my clothes by a river and by accident I saw a young girl, naked taking a shower opposite to me. At that time in Southern China, because of the hot weather, people there tended to take a shower several times a day. And because of the poor conditions at that time, some showering places didn't have proper doors. So that's the first time I saw a woman's naked body. I was so nervous that I actually ran away as quickly as possible pretending that I didn't see. However, I could never forget that moment. I think part of my artistic aspiration came from that.[46]

PG: Where you ever a member of the Red Guards?

QL: No, I wasn't. My brother was a Red Guard. The conditions to become a Red Guard were very complicated. Red Guards usually came from good family backgrounds. I was refused, but my brother was accepted.

PG: Did any members of the Stars belong to the Red Guards?

QL: Not really.

PG: When I interviewed Yan Li, he said at least one of the Stars was a Red Guard. Who might that have been?

QL: Probably, Wang Keping was for a short period of time. Coming back to what I was saying, I was promoted to be an officer in the army later on. However, due to my earlier criticism of Madam Mao, I was still under supervision. Because of the complicated situation at the time, my girlfriend left me, which made me reflect on what had gone wrong. And then there was the death of Lin Biao 林彪[47] in 1971, who was my father's boss and who was also considered to be the best student of Chairman Mao. It made me reflect even harder on the situation and was a turning point in the development of my thoughts. Because of my position, I had the advantage of reading books before they were burned, though these books were collected from intellectual families and were forbidden in public during the Cultural Revolution. After serious reflection on the situation, I told myself that the military route wasn't suitable for me. And then the social and political situation started changing too; for instance, the visit of Nixon in 1972 and the 'Four Modernizations.'[48] I became determined to make some sort of contribution to the modernization of the country. That's why I left the army in 1973.

PG: What did you do next?

QL: Only then did I begin to realize my personal interests. I came back to Beijing and by chance I started working as a lighting technician for Beijing Television (*Beijing dianshitai* 北京电视台), which is now called CCTV (China Central Television [*Zhongguo zhongyang dianshitai* 中国中央电视台]), mainly working on documentaries. Again, I had the opportunity to travel all over the country and to meet different kinds of people. However, apart from working as a technician in a TV station, I was also determined to be an artist. So I worked as a technician as a way of earning a living while painting in my spare time, which was my real interest. I gradually realized that traditional Chinese painting was not enough for me to express myself, so I exposed myself to Western art.

PG: Did you receive any formal training? Were you able to go to art college, for example?

QL: No, I didn't get any formal art training. But, since my parents had many friends who were artists, I learned from them sometimes. With help from my mother, I also had the opportunity to study life painting at the *Gong nong bing xueyuan* 工农兵学院 (Workers, Farmers and Soldiers School)[49] for a few months, which was very beneficial.

PG: So you had some formal training and that was towards the end of the Cultural Revolution during the mid-1970s?

QL: Yes. Let's move on to 1976, which was such a significant year for China and for myself too. 1976 was the year of the dragon. Zhou Enlai[50] and Zhu De 朱德[51] died in quick succession. Then there was the Tangshan earthquake,[52] in which thousands and thousands of people died. At Beijing Television we were asked to do a documentary about the earthquake in Tangshan. At night, when we had nothing to do, I took out a notebook to do line drawing.

PG: What was the subject of those drawings? Was it the aftermath of the earthquake?

QL: For instance, there were two lives (people), which were drawn onto a globe, a beautiful girl facing the globe dropping tears.

PG: So, they were symbolic drawings?

QL: Yes. And they came spontaneously from my imagination. That's the first time in my life I used painting or drawing to express my feelings. They were published in *Today* magazine later on. Some of the works shown in the first Stars group exhibition were also drawn during this period of time.

PG: And the style was more Westernized than traditional Chinese?

QL: Yes. But I also think practising line drawing was really a good combination of traditional Chinese painting and Western painting. Once I visited a famous artist to ask for suggestions about some of my works. The artist looked at my works for a while and said 'Picasso'. At the time, I didn't know who Picasso was.

PG: What influences did you take from Western art?

QL: After 1973, I learned a lot from Russian art.

PG: Apart from that, did you have any knowledge of the work of other Western artists?

QL: No, just Russian artists; until later, probably in 1975 or so. I went to visit a friend of mine, whose father was once the principal of Peking University. His father had a large book collection and I found French impressionist paintings on his book shelves. That's actually the first time I saw some paintings like that, which inspired me greatly. That's how I started doing oil paintings. Also, I started learning more about Western art history. I got ill in 1976 after the Tangshan earthquake and nearly died. And suddenly, the news broke out saying Mao had died.

PG: How did you feel about that? When Mao died, were there mixed emotions?

QL: When Zhou Enlai died, the authorities sent out spies to see who cried; and when Mao died, the authorities sent out spies to check who didn't cry. Another big event I'd like to mention is the April 5th Event in 1976, which was just before the death of Zhu De. This event was also known as the Tian'anmen Event, in which people from all over the country got together at Tian'anmen to remember Zhou Enlai and to protest against the Gang of Four and Mao. I got involved in this event too. It seemed that people tried to memorize the dead against the living. I saw many people using Zhou Enlai's portrait to cover up Mao's. And then Mao died and Deng Xiaoping got power, which opened up the country again. After that many magazines were published expressing new ideas. One of them was named *Tan suo* 探索 (*Explore*), which was edited by Wei Jinsheng. Another, edited by Bei Dao, was named *Jintian* (*Today*). There were some others like *Beijing zhi chun* (*Beijing Spring*), edited by Liu Jing and Xu Wenli.

PG: Did you have association with these magazines?

QL: Yes, we were all very close friends. The editor of *Explore* magazine was put into prison because of his belief in political modernization. He believed that without political reforms the country wouldn't become modernized. He was arrested in 1978 on the excuse of committing political crimes. Actually, his trial was recorded by me while I was working at Beijing TV. I gave the record to Liu Jing and Xu Wenli and they put it on the Democracy Wall at Xidan.

PG: So how did you get to know these people?

QL: I got to know them through other friends. One of them was Guo Lusheng 郭路生 (his pen name was *Shi zhi* 食指, which means 'index finger'), who was a friend of mine since childhood. He's also one of the pioneers of modern poetry in China. One of his poems named *Xiangxin weilai* 相信未来 ('Believe in the Future') was well-known at the time. Through Guo Lusheng I got to know Bei Dao and became deeply involved in *Today* magazine. I did some paintings for the magazine. That's how I got to know Huang Rui, Ma Desheng and Zhong Acheng, who were members of the Stars group.

PG: How did the Stars come together as a group?

QL: Huang Rui and Ma Desheng were discussing the staging of an exhibition and they asked me to participate.

PG: At that time in China there were semi-official art groups who were already beginning to show their work in public.

QL: Yes, one of the groups was called *Wu ming* (No Name Group). Quite a few groups did exhibitions then. All the arts, including literature, poems, music and paintings, started booming and were shown at the Democracy Wall. In the beginning, Deng Xiaoping supported free expression at the Democracy Wall. However, when he regained power he got rid of it because he couldn't accept people criticizing him. Let's get back to the Stars group. Huang Rui, Ma Desheng, Zhong Acheng and me invited some other friends to get involved, such as Wang Keping, who also worked at Beijing TV. And then Bo Yun and Yan Li joined. There were probably 12 core members. Ai Weiwei wasn't a major member at the time.

PG: Can I check some facts with you? There's no consistency within the existing literature with regard to the names of those who were members of the Stars. Yan Li gave me a list, which includes the names you've just mentioned. It also includes Li Shuang (Yan Li's girlfriend at the time), Shao Fei (Bei Dao's girlfriend), Geng Shaocheng, Yang Yiping and Mao Lizi. Would you agree with that list?

QL: That's right. As for Ai Weiwei, he wasn't a core member at first, but became more important later.

PG: How many people took part in the Stars' first official exhibition in Beihai Park?

QL: I think more than 30 people.

PG: So there was a core membership and others who were invited to exhibit? I've seen some of the works. Some were symbolic—surrealistic, for want of a better term—and others were more academic in the Western sense.

QL: Yes, that's right. Star members had different styles of painting, but we shared similar concepts and ideas. It wasn't a tight organization.

PG: What were the aims of the group? What were you trying to achieve?

QL: Personally, I think it was self-expression. I was born with an innocent mind but then brainwashed. It was only later that I learned how to express personal feelings and humanistic needs. That's what the function of art should be like. It's been said that the Stars group used Western techniques and forms to examine and reflect on Chinese life; I think it makes sense.

PG: Could you be more precise about the Western influences on the group?

QL: People have commented that it's Western, but they couldn't identify what kind of Western influence—Dada, or expressionist, they can't tell. We didn't have any formal academic training and we imitated reproductions of Western works.

PG: Some of the work by the Stars is similar in style to Western-influenced Chinese woodblock prints and paintings of the early twentieth century.

QL: That's right. Lu Xun 鲁迅[53] brought in wooden block prints in the early twentieth century, which strongly influenced Chinese art. Personally, I think I have been closely influenced by three artistic movements from the West: one is impressionism, one is expressionism and the other one is surrealism. Only when these three forms came together, could I express what I'd like to say. Another point I'd like to make is that art functioned in China from the time of Confucius until to Mao's time as a political tool. Confucius once said: '*Zhi yu dao, ju yu de, you yu yi*' 志于道, 据于德, 游于艺;'[54] and Mao once said 'art has to serve the revolution of the proletarian class.'[55] What the Stars group was trying to do was to break away from this traditional artistic purpose to serve politics and make art just for self-expression. This is the significance of the Stars group I think.

PG: Members of the No Name Group were making impressionistic/expressionistic paintings in China during the 1960s and 1970s and exhibited those paintings during the 1970s. In what ways, if any, did the activities of the Stars differ from those of the No Name Group?

QL: I think probably the quality of the artworks; and the other difference might be that we were more distant from the social-political background.

PG: Can we take that a little further? Some members of the No Name Group were making impressionistic paintings during the 1960s and 1970s. This was quite a challenge to established political ideology in China at the time, since it departed from the official CCP directive that art should reflect the reality of the mass of people. But it seems to me that, in contrast to the No Name Group, what some of you were doing in the Stars was to use allegory, poetic allusion and symbolism as an active way to undermine the authority of official representations of reality. If we look at Western art, allegory and symbolism have been used as ways of questioning reality and the way reality is represented. So, instead of saying simply, this is reality and this is how reality should be represented—which is a Maoist way of doing things, you were perhaps setting out to question what counts as reality, and how reality might be represented?

QL: Yes, that's right. During our exhibitions, I heard people commenting that they had never seen anything like our artworks, which expressed the life of the people of that generation. If we look at the history of China, it looks very glorious. But behind the glorious surface, there were prices to pay: the death of thousands of people.

PG: You were challenging the official representation of reality by offering another point of view?

QL: Yes. I felt I had the responsibility to do that.

PG: Earlier you touched on the Confucian view that art has the potential to influence society for the better, that it can be used to promote social order, learning and responsibility. It seems to me that the use of art as a way of challenging established views of reality is more Daoist in tone. Within a present day mainland Chinese cultural context, deconstructivist thought and practice has been compared to the classical Daoist philosopher Zhuangzi 庄子's opposition to rigid Confucian notions of social order and etiquette associated with the term *Li-Jiao* 礼教. During the pre-Qin period (third century BCE), Zhuangzi criticized Confucian notions of rigid social order on the grounds that they alienated society from nature and, therefore, from a spontaneous achievement of social harmony. Zhuangzi also argued that conceptual oppositions signified by language were rigid and arbitrary and therefore pointed away from natural conceptions of value which were less clearly defined in accordance with the Daoist conception of an interactive reciprocation between the otherwise opposing forces of *yin* and *yang* (e.g. Yang [2008]). Did the Stars align themselves selfconsciously with Daoist thinking in any way?

QL: Within traditional Chinese culture there are three main branches of philosophy: Confucianism, Daoism and Buddhism, which are understood to complement one another. We say, *Jin zhe jianji tianxia*, 进则兼济天下 which means 'when people are successful they get more involved with political responsibilities,' and *Tui zhe dushan qishen*, 退则独善其身 which means 'if people lose power, they can still cultivate themselves.'[56] Aesthetically, traditional Chinese landscape paintings were more influenced by Daoism.

PG: Can you unpack that a little? Do you mean that the Stars upheld the traditional Chinese idea of a complementary relationship between Confucian, Daoist and Buddhist thinking?

QL: As for my own works, it took me a long time to find myself. And then when I found myself, I went beyond what I had been taught. I was standing at the height of a humanistic perspective; one concerning people's living conditions and thus began looking for the significance of life. For me, good artworks should contain these elements. At the moment it seems that there are no agreed standards by which to judge good artworks. When I was talking to some young artists at the Venice Biennale, they said they couldn't be bothered about good art or bad art. For them, there's no line for doing good art or bad art.

PG: So, in your view, good art has some kind of moral responsibility?

QL: Yes, there should be a line there to judge good art or bad art. To be honest, the most important thing relating to the Stars' show in 1979 was the action of putting our works on the Democracy Wall. The action itself was more significant than the artworks. China needed changes. So we did it and started a change.

PG: In 1979 and 1980, when you were engaging with the idea of humanism, were you also attempting to consciously reassert aspects of traditional Chinese thought and practice?

QL: Not as much as nowadays.

PG: Can we explore the intentions of the Stars group in a little more detail? Most members of the Stars were from intellectual family backgrounds and from families that had political power.

QL: Yes, that's true. I know Wang Keping's father was the chairperson of the Tianjin Literature and Art Association (*Tianjin wenxue yishu jie lianhehui* 天津文学艺术界联合会), and Zhong Acheng's father was a well-known film critic.

PG: Despite your family backgrounds, did you see yourselves as contributing to an attempt to overthrow the established political system in China? What was in your mind at the time?

QL: Most of us didn't want to be politicians. We wanted to be artists who could paint what we'd like to paint and express freely what we thought. But inevitably, we got involved in political movements to some extent.

PG: During the Maoist period, the established social order in China was supposedly overturned. Mao sought to elevate the social position of soldiers, workers and peasants while relegating intellectuals. Given that most members of the Stars group came from intellectual backgrounds, were you attempting self-consciously to reassert the position of intellectuals in Chinese public life? Deng Xiaoping's reforms had already signalled the return of intellectuals to mainstream political life before the Stars held their first exhibition and the group's subsequent protest march. So there was already a propitious context for what you were doing. Arguably, what you were doing was to occupy space already opened up by Deng's reforms rather than carving that space out entirely for yourselves in a straightforward resistance to governmental authority.

QL: Yes. After 1979, I worked as an art director at Beijing TV. I took the entrance examination of the Central Academy of Art in Beijing, but I didn't get in, though I was placed number four in the examination. I left China in 1985 to go to England.

PG: When you went to England and other countries later on, did you become aware of differences between artworks produced by the Stars and contemporary art produced outside China?

QL: Yes, they were quite different. When I first arrived in England, I didn't like the contemporary artworks there. I prefer classical Western art. From 1985 to 1989 was another period of transition in my life. I was crazy about Western art before I went to England, but when I was in England I started looking at traditional Chinese art again and started adopting traditional Chinese techniques again. I tried different styles of traditional Chinese art, including landscape paintings. I also became clearer about what kind of artist I'd like to be. I became chairman of an association called the British-Chinese Painting Association (*Yingguo Zhongguo shuhua jia xiehui* 英国中国书画家会). I tried a lot of different styles. When the Tian'anmen Massacre happened in 1989, I turned suddenly to the origin; to what kind of man I'd like to be, to what kind of artist I'd like to be. From then on, it's clearer. I spent five years doing a project called 'The Sun in My Dream, the First Half of My Life (*Meng zhong de tai yang, wo de ban sheng* 梦中的太阳—我的半生).' Then I made some artworks related to comparing different cultures, which was called 'Here and Now: Facing the New Century.' From 2006 onwards, I calmed down a bit and did something more aesthetic related to the beauty of human bodies. I dealt with ink and brush and shadow and light, which never happened in Chinese art history before. I tried to compare ancient Chinese masters and to find the ways that we are better than them. I know my calligraphy and line drawing is not as good as them, but they didn't know human anatomy. Also, they didn't know light and shadow—*chiascuro*—which is the soul of Western art. From that point of view, I think I lead to another direction for Chinese ink and brush painting—opened a new possibility.

PG: I see contemporary Chinese art as strongly aestheticized. Even an artist like Huang Yongping, who's making work that's approximately Dadaist, has a tendency towards aestheticism it seems to me. Avant-garde Western art has been critical of established aesthetics, developing the idea of an anti-aesthetic—take the work of Marcel Duchamp and Dada as well as certain forms of post-war conceptualism and performance, for example. During your time in the Stars, were you conscious of retaining an aesthetic dimension to your work contrary to the intentions of the Western avant-gardes?

QL: We didn't know really. We didn't know much.

PG: Did you think about aesthetics at all?

QL: Not really. I always think I'm quite classical.

Notes

1   According to Köppel-Yang, the Stars' first unofficial exhibition included 140 works by 23 artists (Köppel-Yang 2003: 60). Gao Minglu offers a slightly different account, stating that the Stars' first unofficial exhibition included over 150 works by 23 artists. Gao also dates the beginning of the Stars' first unofficial exhibition incorrectly to 26 September 1979 (Gao 2005: 64). Berghuis states that the Stars' unofficial exhibition involved 23 participants (Berghuis 2008: 40). Zhu Zhu states, with reference to a recollection by Wang Keping, that the Stars' first exhibition was made up of over 150 artworks including 'oil paintings, inkbrush paintings, pen drawings, woodcuts and wooden statues' and that some of the statues were 'placed on the ground' while some of the paintings 'were hung on trees'. Zhu also states that poems by contributors to *Jintian* (*Today*) magazine were hung next to the paintings (Zhu 2007a: 25).

2   According to Erickson, on the day after the opening of the Stars' unofficial exhibition, the police first tried to arrest the group, but later backed down when the participating artists 'insisted on the guarantee of artistic freedom afforded by the Chinese constitution.' Erickson also asserts that on the following day the police effectively closed down the exhibition by denying the Stars access to the exhibition site as well as to the place where their works had been stored overnight. Furthermore, Erickson claims that the police sent minor criminals to harass the Stars (Erickson 2005: 16). This account accords largely with that of Xu and Qing (2010). Berghuis states that the police started to remove the Stars' work from the site of their unofficial exhibition on the morning of 28 September 1979 (Berghuis 2008: 43). Zhu Zhu claims, with reference to a recollection by Wang Keping, that there was a stand-off between the police and the Stars on the morning of the second day of their first exhibition, but that the exhibition nevertheless continued into the afternoon. Zhu also claims that, on the morning of 29 September, the place where the Stars work had been stored overnight was closed off by police and that the Beijing Public Works Bureau posted a notice at the site of Stars' exhibition banning its continuation (Zhu 2007a: 25).

3   Berghuis states that immediately after the closure of the Stars' unofficial exhibition on 28 September, only three of the participating artists wanted to join the protest march, but that by the following day this number had grown to eight (Berghuis 2008: 46). Zhu Zhu also states that eight of the 23 artists who had participated in the Stars' first exhibition took part in the subsequent protest march (Zhu 2007a: 25).

4   According to Erickson, participants in the Stars' protest march carried a banner inscribed with the slogan 'We Demand Artistic Freedom' (Erickson 2005: 16).

5   According to Berghuis, the exhibition attracted approximately 200,000 visitors (Berghuis 2008: 226).

6   Published accounts of the Stars' exhibitions vary. According to Köppel-Yang, the Stars only held two public exhibitions during 1979–1980: the first, unofficially in a park adjacent to the National Art Gallery in Beijing in September 1979; and the second, officially inside the gallery during August 1980 with the title 'Exhibition of the Stars' (*Xingxing meizhan* 星星美展). This account omits the Stars' first official exhibition at the Huafang Studio in Beihai Park. Köppel-Yang also states that the official exhibition of the work of the Stars at the National Art Gallery in Beijing was only open for seven days (Köppel-Yang 2003: 60, 127). Accounts by Andrews and Gao also omit to mention the Stars' exhibition at the Huafang Studio (Andrews 1994: 397–398; Gao 2005: 64). Berghuis's account of the Stars' exhibitions (which draws heavily on an unpublished MA thesis by Fok Siu Har, a student at the University of Hong Kong), agrees in large part with the one put forward here by Yan Li (Berghuis 2008: 40–46). The Stars' second official exhibition at the National Art Gallery in Beijing opened on 24 August 1980. The exhibition, which was scheduled originally to run for three weeks, was extended for a further two weeks because of extraordinary public interest.

7   The only core member of the Stars known to have been a Red Guard is Wang Keping.

8   This is an edited version of a conversation recorded at Yan Li's home in Shanghai on 15 February 2009.

9   According to Andrews, the name *Xingxing* makes reference to the title of an article by Mao Zedong written in 1930, titled 'A Tiny Spark Can Set the Steppes Ablaze' (Andrews 1994: 43, 396).

10 This exhibition, titled 'The Stars: Ten Years', subsequently travelled to the Festival d'Automne de Paris (Chang 1989).

11 The twentieth-anniversary exhibition of the Stars, 'Xingxing Group Show', was held at the Tokyo Gallery, Japan in 1999.

12 This exhibition, titled 'Origin Point—Stars Group Retrospective Exhibition', was held at the Today Art Museum in Beijing between 18 and 28 November 2007. An English language description of the exhibition posted on the website of the Today Art Museum reads: '"Stars Group" dated from the end of the 1970's to the beginning of the 1980's could be considered the first real art movement of the Modernism since the Culture Revolution in China, it doesn't only carry the art value of a turning point, but also marks the political scene of the society of a special period of the history. This exhibition collects almost a hundred works created before 1985 by the members of Stars Group, on one hand, they show the art movement of that special period of time and review this movement standing on the contemporary angle of view, search for some deeper meaning of the history and the society; On the other hand, by discussing over "Stars Group" again, these works question the development of contemporary art with a historical gesture, reflect the origin and the metropolitan territory of Chinese art of nowadays' [sic] (Anon. http://www.todayartmuseum.com).

13 This exhibition did not take place.

14 The title of the China/Avant-Garde exhibition in Mandarin Chinese is *Xiandai meishu dazhan* 现代美术大展 ('A Grand Exhibition of Modern Art').

15   The '20th Anniversary Celebration of the Chinese Modern Art Exhibition' opened at the National Agriculture Exhibition Centre, the Wall Art Museum and the Today Art Museum in Beijing on 5 February 2009. The exhibition was largely made up of documents, photographs, videos and correspondence relating to the China/Avant-Garde exhibition of 1989 that had been collected together by its organizers during the previous two decades. The exhibition's opening ceremony, which included a series of public talks, was cancelled as a result of police intervention on the evening before it was scheduled to take place. The police reportedly intervened on the grounds that the event had not been properly registered with the authorities. According to a statement posted on the Internet at the Artinfo website, 'The acts of censorship [relating to the exhibition] indicate a wariness and sensitivity on the part of the Chinese government as the 20th anniversary of the Tiananmen Square protests approaches.' The same website also reports Gao Minglu, the exhibition's chief organizer, as saying, 'I'm not disappointed for the exhibit, I'm disappointed because our system is still so out of date, still so conservative…It's been 20 years and it's still the same' (Anon. http://www.artinfo.com).

16   According to Köppel-Yang, the 'hard core' of the Stars consisted of seven members: Zhong Ahcheng, Ma Desheng, Wang Keping, Huang Rui, Qu Leilei, Ai Weiwei and Li Shuang (Köppel-Yang 2003: 60). Berghuis states that important participants in the Stars unofficial exhibition included Ma Desheng, Huang Rui, He Baoshen, Ai Weiwei, Li Shuang, Qu Leilei, Shao Fei, Wang Keping, Wang Luyan, Yan Li, Yin Guangzhong, Zhao Gang and Zhong Ancheng (Berghuis 2008: 40). Zhu Zhu also states that Ai Weiwei was an important member of the Stars (Zhu 2007a: 21 and 23).

17   Tan Dun (b. 1957) is an internationally acclaimed composer of contemporary classical music. Among his works is *The Map*, a large-scale multimedia music event, first staged in the PRC in November 2003. See *Tan Dun* (2004), *The Map*, Berlin: Deutsche Grammophon. He is also the composer of film scores for *Crouching Tiger, Hidden Dragon* and *Hero*. Qu Xiaosong (b. 1952) is a composer of contemporary classical music. His works include the operas *Oedipus* (1993) and *The Death of Oedipus* (1994) as well as the chamber opera *The Test* (2004). Ye Xiaogang (b. 1955) is a composer of contemporary classical music. His work includes the *Great Wall Symphony* (2002).

18   The CCP and government cadre system within the PRC is broadly equivalent to the civil service in other national contexts. A cadre is a full-time public official responsible for managing the implementation of an aspect of party or government policy.

19   Berghuis suggests that the stance taken by Stars was directly influenced by their participation in the activities of the Cultural Revolution, incorrectly implying that most had been members of the Red Guards (Berghuis 2008: 40–41). Zhu Zhu states (incorrectly) that Qu Leilei was 'a "red guard" who travelled about forging revolutionary ties' (Zhu 2007a: 23).

20   *Danwei* (work unit) is the name commonly given to a place of work in the PRC. Although the term was first used as part of the collectivization of working practices and the setting up of state-owned enterprises during the revolutionary period between 1949 and 1976, it still retains a degree of currency within the PRC of the early twenty-first century. Before the onset of Deng Xiaoping's reforms, *danwei* acted as the operational front line in the implementation of party policy and therefore sat at the base of an extended party hierarchy.

As such, *danwei* not only were sites of work but also provided the workers who were attached to them with housing, shops, medical facilities, canteens and other public services. Workers were usually assigned to a *danwei* for life and required their work unit's permission to carry out actions such as getting married, having children and travelling. Workers who did not comply with the wishes of the *danwei* could be punished by having their pay, status or living conditions downgraded.

21 According to Köppel-Yang, it is possible to read *Idol*, one of the sculptural works by Wang Keping exhibited at the Exhibition of the Stars, as an allegory that 'not only reveals the mechanisms of political propaganda, but also…the sensibility with which the Chinese people react to such propaganda, and the fact that it's repertory of signs actually had infiltrated the collective unconscious' (Köppel-Yang 2003: 122).

22 As literary scholar and philosopher Wang Keping (not to be confused with the Stars member of the same name) has indicated, a detachment from 'social bonds and involvements' is strongly characteristic of traditional Chinese Daoist thinking (Wang 2009: 3). A similar form of renunciation, especially of involvement in organized politics, is also strongly characteristic of European Dada (Bigsby 1978: 17–18).

23 Yan Li's comment here is indicative of a traditional Chinese cultural preference for spontaneity and naturalness associated with the term *ziran* (literally, 'what is so of itself') (Zhang 2002: 162–169).

24 A facsimile of an article titled 'An Exhibition which Twice Took Beijing by Storm' taken from an unnamed source and posted on the Stars' official website, cites a number of comments taken from the guest books at the Stars' exhibition at the National Gallery in Beijing. One comment states 'you have voiced out the people's voice, thank you—an audience,' and another that 'it's good to make bold artistic attempts and breakthroughs, but don't just take everything from Western art—an audience' (Anon. http://www.shigebao.com).

25 According to Köppel-Yang, the Exhibition of the Stars at the National Gallery in Beijing attracted 200,000 visitors in seven days (Köppel-Yang 2003: 127). Berghuis states that the exhibition included 149 works and attracted around 80,000 visitors (Berghuis 2008: 46). Zhu Zhu asserts that the exhibition attracted between 80,000 and 160,000 visitors with daily attendance of around 5,000 people (Zhu 2007a: 27). A facsimile of an article titled 'An Exhibition which Twice Took Beijing by Storm' taken from an unnamed source and posted on the Stars' official website states that '[a]ccording to the statistics of the ticket office, the number of people queuing up in front of the ticket office [of the Stars exhibition] increased from 2,000 to 4,000, 5,000, 6,000 and even 7,000 on the busiest day […] Including those who held invitation cards or long-term tickets, the daily attendance nearly reached 10,000' (Anon. http://www.shigebao.com). Yan Li's assertion that the exhibition attracted a relatively limited audience may refer to the fact that it was not toured to other parts of China as was the case with exhibitions of the work of semi-official Chinese art groups during the late 1970s and early 1980s. It is also possible that the reported attendance figures are exaggerated.

26 As Köppel-Yang points out, it is important to see 'humanist enthusiasm' within the PRC during the late 1970s and 1980s not simply in terms of calls from 'avant-garde' artists for individual freedom of expression but also as part of a more widespread attempt among

intellectuals to establish a new spiritual order in the PRC in the wake of the Cultural Revolution (Köppel-Yang 2003: 23).

27 According to Berghuis, the Stars drew support from Liu Xun, the Head of the Beijing Municipal Artists Association, who had been denounced as a 'rightist' and jailed for ten years in 1957, and Jiang Feng, who had lost his party membership in the late 1950s but who was restored to the party in 1979 becoming chairman of the Chinese Artists Association (Berghuis 2008: 42).

28 The impact of the Stars' activities on cultural life within the PRC was widely felt. In December 1984, a group of five local artists in the town of Lanzhou in Gansu province staged an exhibition titled 'Exploration, Discovery and Expression' associating their own activities directly with those of the Stars.

29 As Berghuis indicates, some members of the Stars received formal training related to the arts. However, this training was not always focused on the acquisition of skills related to the making of works of visual art. Wang Keping, who produced and exhibited sculptural works as a member of the Stars, was, for example, trained in script writing at the Beijing Film and Television Academy (Berghuis 2008: 40).

30 A lack of technical schooling is also valued as part of China's established cultural traditions. Technical awkwardness is understood to conform to a Daoist desire for spontaneity and truth to nature (*wu wei* 无为) often referred to in an anglophone context as 'non-action.'

31 Zhu Zhu claims that the April 5th group had a significant influence on the Stars' decision to stage their protest march (Zhu 2007a: 25).

32 The Gang of Four was a leftist group of four CCP officials, Jiang Qing (Mao Zedong's last wife and the group's leading figure), Yao Wenyuan, Wang Hongwen and Zhang Chunqiao, who strongly influenced Mao Zedong's decision-making during the latter part of the Cultural Revolution. Following Mao's death in 1976, the group was ousted from its position of power and widely denounced as the principal cause of the social turmoil that had taken place during the Cultural Revolution. In 1981, all four members of the group were placed on trial and received lengthy prison sentences.

33 This notion of shared appreciation among friends is similar to the traditional Chinese (*literati*) concept of *wanshang* (play appreciation); the sharing of subjective aesthetic responses among a select group of cultured individuals (Chang 2005).

34 This is an edited version of a conversation recorded at Qiu Leilei's home in Beijing on 4 February 2010.

35 Qi Baishi (1864–1957) was one of the most influential traditional Chinese painters of the twentieth century. He was elected president of the Association of Chinese artists in 1953.

36 Ren Bonian (1840–1896), also known as Ren Yi, was a member of the Shanghai School of painters who brought together traditional and popular styles of Chinese painting.

37 Xu Beihong (1895–1953) was one of the first Chinese painters during the twentieth century to develop a modern style of painting using Western techniques and stylistic influences.

38 The classic Chinese text *Baijia xing* (Hundred Family Surnames) was first compiled during the early Song dynasty (Song chao 宋朝) (960–1279). It initially included 411 names, but was later revised to include 504 names.

39 *Zhulian jiu zu* (Nine Familial Exterminations) was established during China's imperial period as a punishment for a range of serious offences including treason. Although rarely used, the punishment involved the killing of a convicted criminal's relatives who were divided for the purpose into nine categories.

40 This family history is unverified. Nevertheless, it echoes Qu Leilei's account of his parents' and his own fall from grace with the CCP.

41 The People's Liberation Army (PLA) was established in 1927 as the military wing of the CCP.

42 *Gong-bi* is a meticulous style of traditional Chinese ink and brush painting, first developed during the Han dynasty (Han chao 宋朝;) (206 BCE–220 CE), often associated with the painting of birds and flowers. *Xieyi* is an expressive and freely interpretative style of painting considered to be the complementary opposite of *gong-bi*.

43 This well-known Chinese aphorism originated during the Tang dynasty (Tang chao 唐朝) (618–907). It signifies the uncertain boundary within traditional Chinese culture between painting and the writing of poetry/calligraphy.

44 Lei Feng was reputedly a member of the PLA who, after his accidental death in 1962 at the age of 21, was upheld as model of selflessness and devotion as part of successive 'Learn from Comrade Lei Feng' campaigns initiated by the CCP in 1963. These campaigns were conducted as part of an attempt to restore Mao's reputation after the disasters associated with the Great Leap Forward. Lei Feng's existence as an actual historical figure has been disputed by some scholars. Lei Feng is now a figure of fun among young people within the PRC who regard him as a representative of outdated values. Wang Jie, who is nowadays a less well-known figure than Lei Feng within the PRC, was also a member of the PLA. At the age of 23, Wang is reported to have held his body over an exploding pack of dynamite during a demonstration to other soldiers, sacrificing his own life to save 12 of his comrades. Wang's sacrifice was upheld as an example of moral selflessness to the Chinese people alongside the slogan 'Be not afraid of suffering; be not afraid of death.'

45 This may be an indirect reference to the traditional Chinese proverb '者為王, 敗者為寇' (literally: 'He who wins becomes king while he who loses becomes a bandit').

46 Many of Qu Leilei's later paintings, produced after he left the PRC, are ink and brush depictions of the naked female form.

47 Lin Biao (1907–1971) was a prominent leader of the PLA during its simultaneous struggle with imperial Japanese forces and the KMT before the founding of New China in 1949. Lin died in a plane crash in Mongolia following what appears to have been an attempted coup against Mao. After his death, Lin was condemned by the CCP as a traitor and continues to be blamed by the party for the excesses of the Cultural Revolution.

48 The 'Four Modernizations' were goals set out by Zhou Enlai in 1963 aimed at strengthening the fields of industry, science and technology, agriculture and defence within the PRC. The Four Modernizations remained a focus for national development as part of Deng Xiaoping's reforms after the death of Mao.

49 Qu may be referring here to the Beijing Workers' Cultural Centre (*Beijing gongren wehhua* 北京工人文化).

50 Zhou Enlai (1898–1976) was the first premier of the PRC, serving from 1949 until his death. Although persistently loyal to Mao, Zhou took steps to mitigate the worst excesses of the Cultural Revolution; a stance which earned him widespread popularity within the PRC during the early and mid-1970s. Zhou's death in 1976 led to widespread displays of public grief, including the Tian'anmen incident of that year, as well as increasing public anger against Mao and the Gang of Four.

51 Zhu De (1896–1976) was a founding member of the CCP, and after 1949, commander-in-chief of the PLA. He enjoyed immense public prestige within the PRC in spite of his exile from political power between 1966 and 1973.

52 The Tangshan earthquake, which took place in Hebei province in July 1976, is estimated by official Chinese sources to have killed 250,000 people (although other sources claim that as many as 700,000 died as a result). Traditionally, earthquakes have been seen as precursors of dynastic change within China. The Tangshan earthquake was regarded as a portent of the installation of Hua Guoufeng as leader of the PRC after Mao's death in September 1976.

53 Lu Xun (1886–1931) is a major writer of the twentieth century and is widely acknowledged as the leading exponent of modern Chinese literature.

54 Here Qu refers imperfectly to a well-known aphorism attributed to the classical Chinese philosopher Confucius: '*zhi yu dao, ju yu de, yi yu ren, you yu yi*' 志于道, 据于德, 依于仁, 游于艺. This aphorism can be translated into English as 'Regard "*Dao*" as the aspiration, regard "*De*" as the foundation, respond to "*Ren*" and then master "*Liu Yi*"'. The term 'Liu Yi' refers to the six arts—rites, music, archery, charioteering, calligraphy and mathematics—that were considered to be the basis of refined education during Chinese antiquity. *Dao* (the Way) is arguably the most important concept of the Chinese intellectual tradition and signifies a metaphysical bringing together of all things temporal and spiritual. *Ren* (benevolence) refers to the necessary relations between human beings. *De* has a diffuse significance, but can be understood in simple terms to refer to 'power' or 'virtue.' For extended definitions of *Dao*, *Ren* and *De*, see Zhang (2002). '*Ren*' and '*De*' and '*Liu yi*' are the foundations of Confucian teaching. Achieving '*Ren*' and '*De*,' the Confucian creeds, and mastering '*Liu yi*' enable students to have a thorough and balanced development. The four sentences that make up the aphorism are placed in order of importance. Confucius devoted himself to learning '*Dao*' when he was 15. After he achieved '*Dao*,' he could then go on to achieve '*De*.' '*Ren*' is the complete status of bearing '*De*' in mind. Only with the faithful completion of '*Dao*,' can one have '*De*' in mind. Mastering '*Liu yi*' not only helps to complete one's accomplishments but also advances one's sense of '*De*.'

55 This paraphrase relates to ideas put forward by Mao Zedong as part of his 'Yan'an Talks on Art and Literature.'

56 These related aphorisms paraphrase writings by Mencius 孟子 (372–289 BCE). The first of the actual phrases from Mencius is '*Da zhe jian shan tianxia*' 达则兼善天下, which can be translated as 'when people become established they should spread good values throughout the world.' Qu Leilei's use of the term 'political responsibilities,' is, perhaps, indicative of the habitual commingling of traditional thinking and communist ideology under Mao.

The Northern Art Group (*Beifang yishu qunti* 北方艺术群体)

In July 1984, a small group of university graduates, who had recently returned to Harbin and surrounding cities in northern China to take up employment assigned to them by the Chinese government, initiated an unofficial forum for discussion about culture and the arts known as the Youth Information Communication Centre of Northern Art (*Beifang yishu qingnian xinxi jiaoliu zhongxin* 北方艺术青年信息交流中心). Initially, the discussions of the centre were broad, encompassing literature and poetry as well as the fine arts. Gradually, however, the centre's leading members—who included Shu Qun 舒群, Wang Guangyi 王广义, Liu Yan 刘彦, Ren Jian 任戬, Gao Minglu 高名潞, Li Xianting, Wang Xiaojian 王小箭, Zhou Yan 周彦 and Huang Zhuan黄专—abandoned this broad approach in favour of more focused debate about the practice and significance of painting. To reflect this change of direction, in January 1985, the Youth Information Communication Centre of Northern Art decided to rename itself the Northern Art Group.

The position adopted by the Northern Art Group was similar to that of the Stars insofar as the group chose to work unofficially outside the PRC's state-controlled system of cultural production. In contrast to the Stars, however, the Northern Art Group did not seek simply to promote individual freedom of artistic self-expression. Rather, its leading members attempted to develop a collective view of artistic production rooted strongly in the group's immediate geographical, social and cultural surroundings within northern China. One of the manifestations of this collective approach was the staging of a number of group exhibitions, including the Biennial Exhibition of the Northern Art Group (*Beifang yishu tuanti shuangnian zhan* 北方艺术团体双年展), which was staged at the Jilin Art Academy (*Jilin yishu xueyuan* 吉林艺术学院) in Changchun in February 1987, as well as participation in collective national art events such as the Huangshan symposia. Moreover, unlike the Stars, the Northern Art Group adopted a distinctly hierarchical organizational structure, with Shu Qun as chair of the group responsible for theory and Wang Guangyi as vice-chair responsible for practice, mirroring what was used to direct official artistic production within the PRC at a national governmental level.

The collective vision of artistic production promoted among the Northern Art Group by its leading members proceeded on the basis of three key assertions. The first of these is that the PRC's renewed openness to outside cultural and social influences following on from the adoption of Deng policy of 'Reform and Opening' in 1978 had lead to the beginnings of a move away from the naturalism and irrationality of traditional Chinese society and culture towards Western urbanization, design and rationality. The second key assertion is that the meeting of Western and Eastern culture that had begun to take place as a result of China's renewed openness to outside social and cultural influences would result in the emergence of a new 'Northern Culture'(*Beifang wenhua* 北方文化) replacing those of the East and the West and that the emergence of this new Northern Culture reflected the historical tendency of 'strong' people to move northwards into cold, physically challenging environments (Plate 9).

The third assertion was that the move towards urbanization, rationality and design within the PRC and the supersession of Western and Chinese culture by Northern Culture would be accompanied by a paradigm shift within Chinese culture that would see a radical departure from established modes of artistic production associated with socialist-realism and, in particular, its recent variant, the Rural Realism of the Sichuan School. The key documents setting out these views and aspirations are Shu Qun's manifesto for the Northern Art Group, 'The Spirit of the Northern Art Group' (*Beifang yishu qunti de jingshen* 北方艺术群体的精神), which was published in *Zhongguo meishu bao* (*Fine Arts in China*) in 1985 (Shu 1985),[1] and 'An Explanation of the Northern Art Group' (*Wei beifang yishu qunti chanshi* 为北方艺术群体阐释), which was published in the journal *Meishu sichao* (*The Trend of Art Thought*) in 1987 (Shu 1987).[2] Other important texts relating to the activities of the Northern Art Group include Wang Guangyi's 'We – Participants of the "'85 Art Movement"' (*Women – ''85 Meishu yundong' de canyuzhe* 我们-八五美术运动的参与者), which was published in *Zhongguo meishu bao* in 1986 (Wang 1986b),[3] and 'Which Kind of Painting Is Needed in Our Age?' (*Women zhege shidai xuyao shenmo yang de huihua?* 我们这个时代需要什么样的绘画), which was published in *Jiangsu huakan* (*Jiangsu Pictorial*) in 1986.

In arriving at these ideas, leading members of the Northern Art Group drew on a wide range of writings taken from both the Western and Chinese intellectual traditions. The Western writings that most strongly influenced the thinking of the group included works by Hegel, Nietzsche and E.H. Gombrich. While Hegel's dialectical vision of history as a progressive realization of spirit or *geist* supported the group's belief that the meeting of Eastern and Western culture would lead inevitably to the emergence of a new combinatory Northern Culture, and while Gombrich's appropriation of the concept of 'paradigm shift' from Thomas Kuhn[4] enabled them to think of the emergence of Northern Culture as something that would be marked by a sharp move away from conventional forms of artistic expression, it was Nietzsche's conception of the Übermensch that encouraged the group to see themselves as aristocratic/elitist agents of iconoclastic cultural change.

The Chinese writings that influenced the thinking of the Northern Art Group include those of Confucius and Laozi 老子 (sixth century BCE) as well as texts associated with Buddhist thought. In the case of the writings of Confucius, the group drew principally on traditional northern Chinese Confucian thinking associated with the aesthetic concepts of sublimity and magnificence (*Da* 大).[5] In the group's view, these concepts and their associated feelings could be used as a way of rebuilding Chinese culture and human dignity after the ravages of the Cultural Revolution by upholding the possibility of a metaphysical distancing of Chinese art from the contingencies of everyday life (effectively reversing Mao's belief that

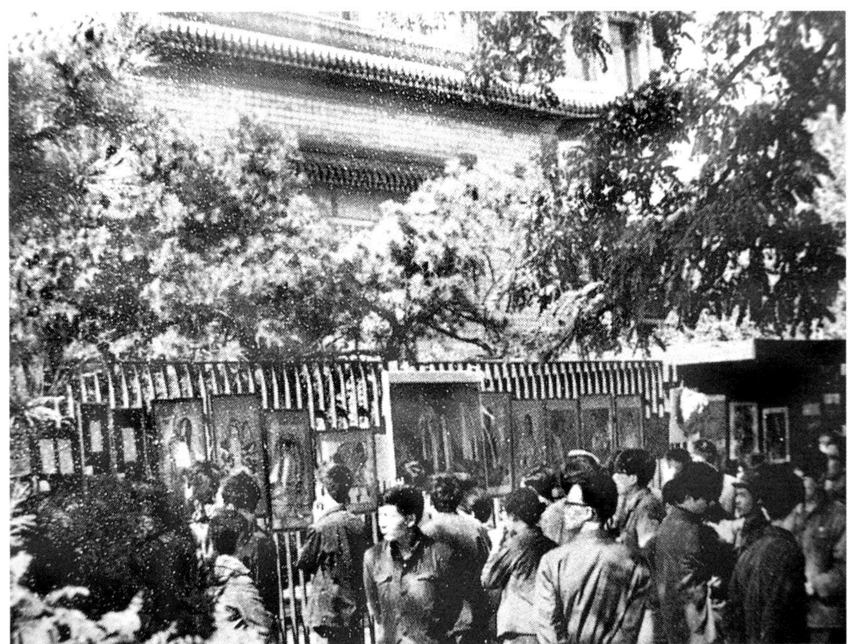

Plate 1: The Stars' first unofficial outdoor exhibition staged next to the National Art Museum in Beijing, 27–28 September 1979. Image courtesy of Yan Li. Reproduced with permission of Yan Li.

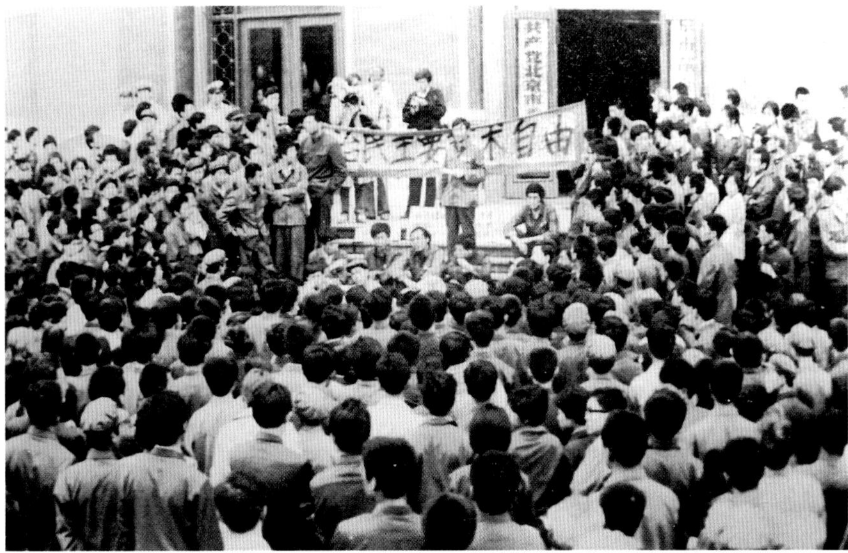

Plate 2: Speeches on the steps of the Municipal Committee of the City of Beijing at the end of the Stars' protest march, 1 October 1979. Image courtesy of Yan Li. Reproduced with permission of Yan li.

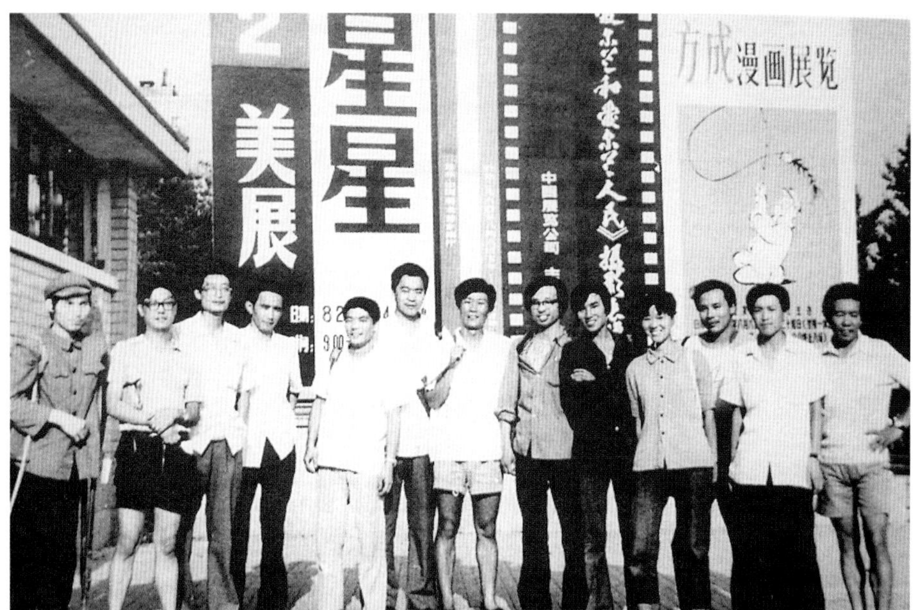

Plate 3: Members of the Stars at the entrance to their second official exhibition at the National Art Museum in Beijing, August 1980. Image courtesy of Yan Li. Reproduced with permission of Yan Li.

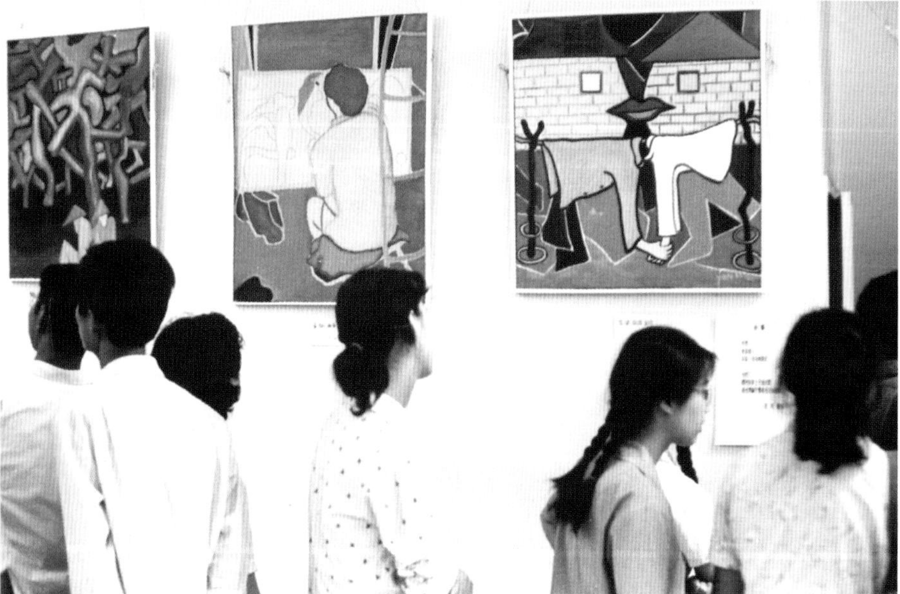

Plate 4: Members of the public viewing works at the Stars' second official exhibition at the National Art Museum of China in Beijing, 1980. Image courtesy of Yan Li. Reproduced with permission of Yan Li.

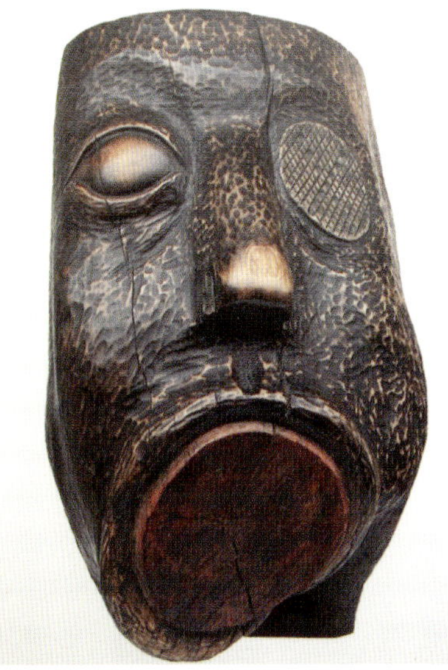

Plate 5: Wang Keping, *Silence* (*Chenmo* 沉默), 1979. Wood carving, height approx. 40cm. Image courtesy of Yan Li. Reproduced with permission of Yan Li.

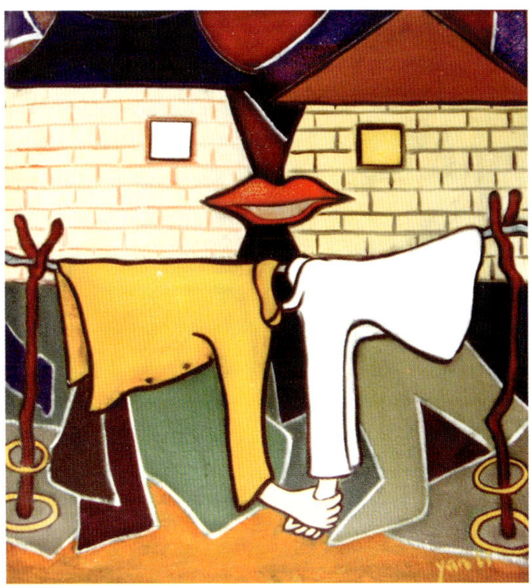

Plate 6: Yan Li, *Home* (*Jia* 家), 1979. Painting, dimensions unknown. Photograph courtesy of Yan Li. Reproduced with permission of Yan Li.

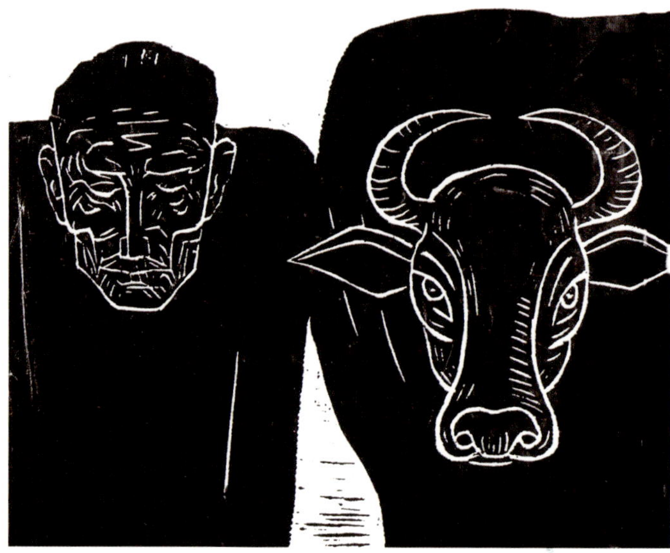

Plate 7: Ma Desheng, *untitled*, 1979. Woodblock print, dimensions unknown. Image courtesy of Yan Li. Reproduced with permission of Yan Li.

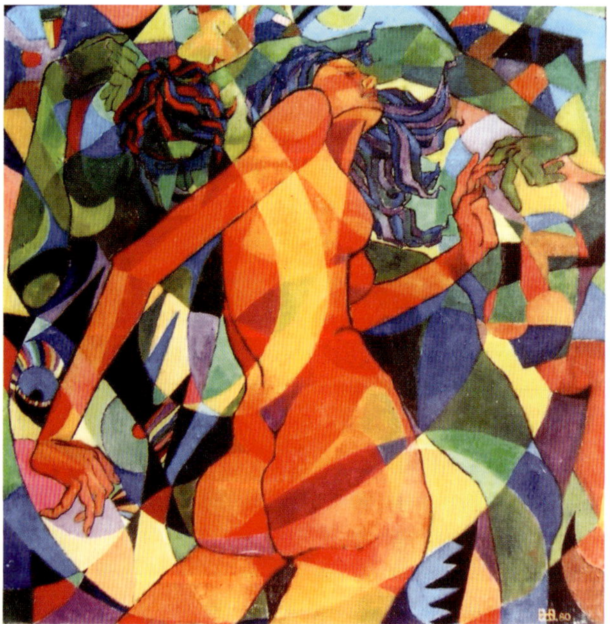

Plate 8: Qu Leilei, *Dance* (*Wu* 舞), 1979. Painting, dimensions unknown. Image courtesy of Yan Li. Reproduced with permission of Yan Li.

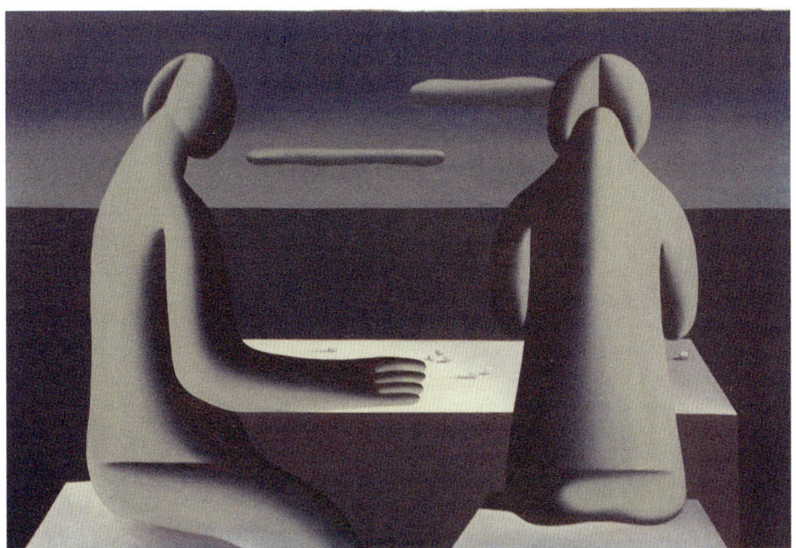

Plate 9: Wang Guangyi, *Frozen North Pole* (*Ninggu de beifang jidi* 凝固的北方极地), 1985. Painting, oil on canvas, 160 × 100cm. Image courtesy of Wang Guangyi. Reproduced with permission of Wang Guangyi.

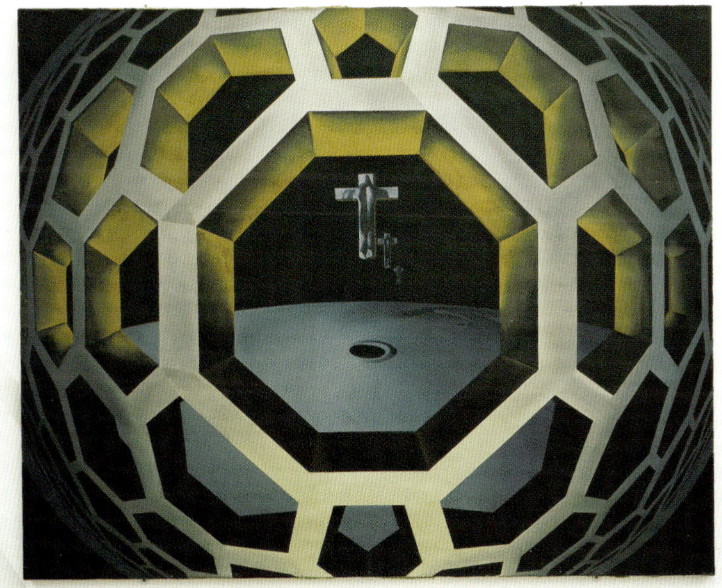

Plate 10: Shu Qun, *Absolute Principle* (*Juedui yuanzi* 绝对原则), 1985–1989. Painting, oil on canvas, 164 × 240cm. Image courtesy of Shu Qun. Reproduced with permission of Shu Qun.

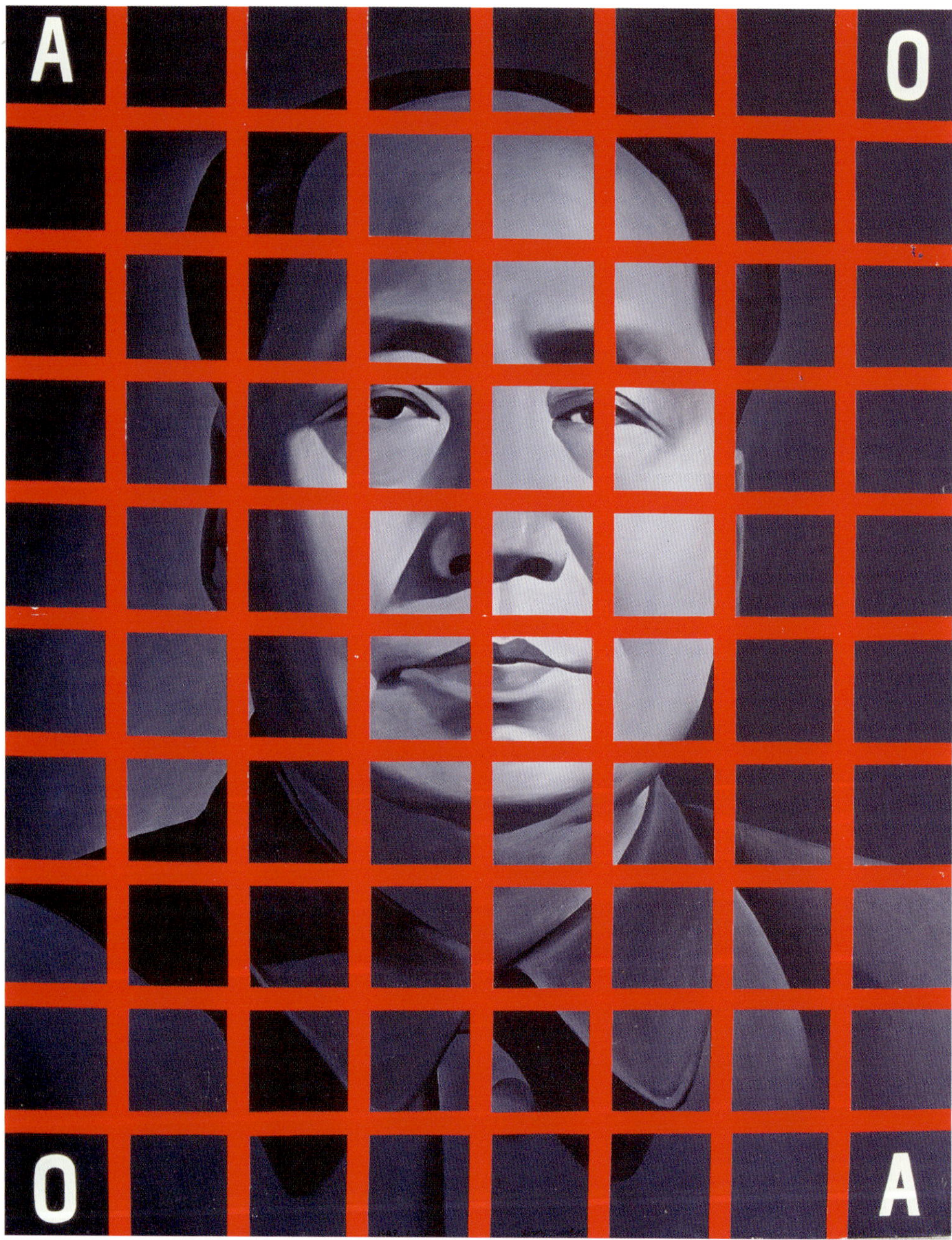

Plate 11: Wang Guangyi, *Red Rationalism* (*Hongse lixing* 红色理性), 1988. Painting, oil on canvas, 150 × 120cm. Image courtesy of Wang Guangyi. Reproduced with permission of Wang Guangyi.

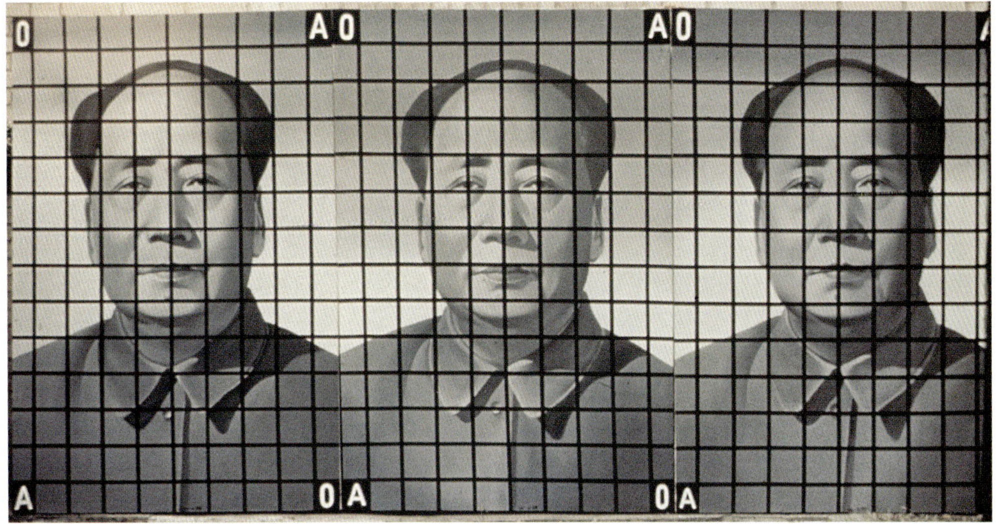

Plate 12: Wang Gaungyi, *Black Rationalism* (*Heise lixing* 黑色理性), 1988. Painting, oil on canvas, 150 × 120cm. Image courtesy of Wang Guangyi. Reproduced with permission of Wang Guangyi.

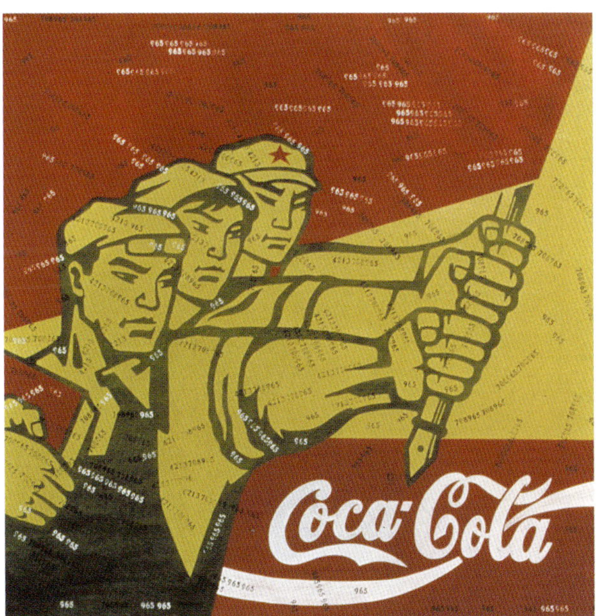

Plate 13: Wang Guangyi, *Great Criticism* (*Da pipan* 大批判系), 1993. Painting 200 × 200cm. Image Courtesy of Wang Guangyi. Reproduced with permission of Wang Guangyi.

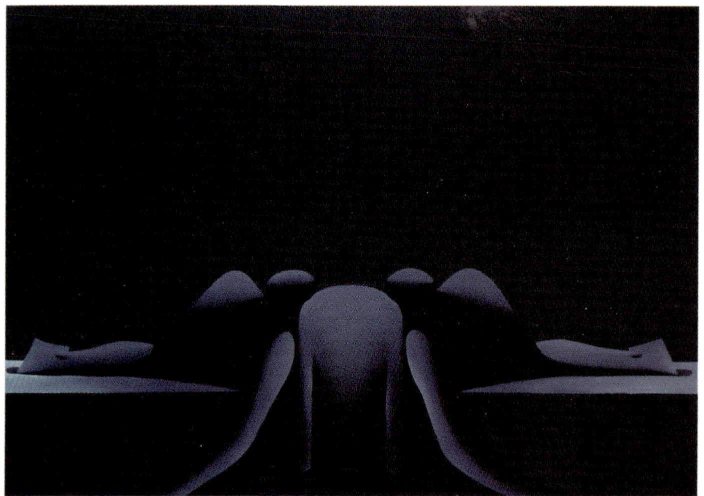

Plate 14: Wang Guangyi, *Post-Classical Series—The Death of Marat* (*Hou gudian xilie Mala zhi si* 后古典系列, 马拉之死), 1986. Painting, oil on canvas, 117 × 169cm. Image courtesy of Wang Guangyi. Reproduced with permission of Wang Guangyi.

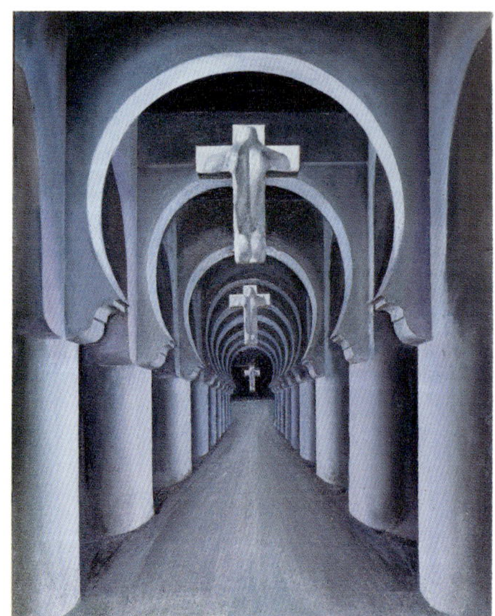

Plate 15: Shu Qun, *Identity Voice—Rigorous Religious Dialogue* (*Xiangzheng de zhixu xilie* 象征的秩序系列), 1985. Painting, oil on canvas, dimensions unknown. Image courtesy of Shu Qun. Reproduced with permission of Shu Qun.

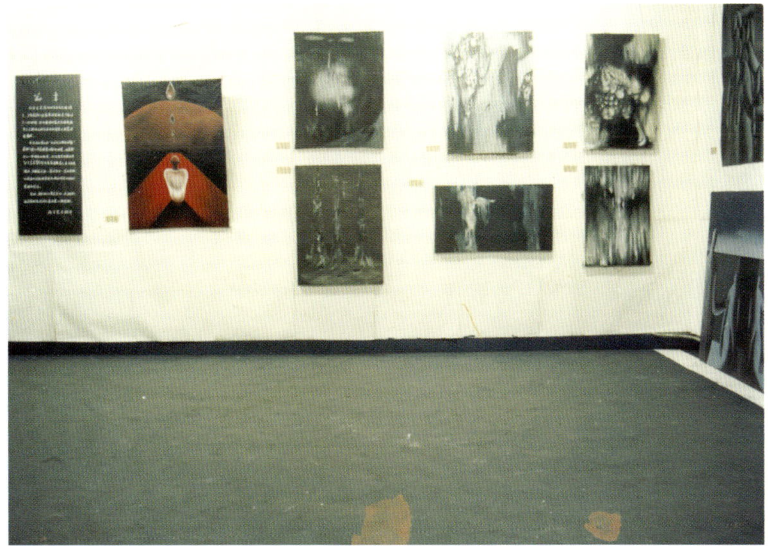

Plate 16: Ka Sang, paintings exhibited at the Northern Art Group Biennale, 1987. Image courtesy of Ka Sang. Reproduced with permission of Ka Sang.

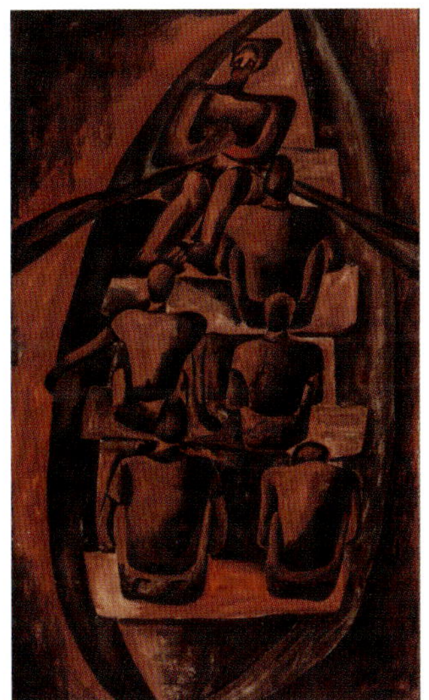

Plate 17: Ka Sang, *Boating on Songhua River* (*Songhua he shang huai chuan* 松花河上划船), 1984 or 1985. Painting, oil on canvas, dimensions unknown. Image courtesy of Ka Sang. Reproduced with permission of Ka Sang.

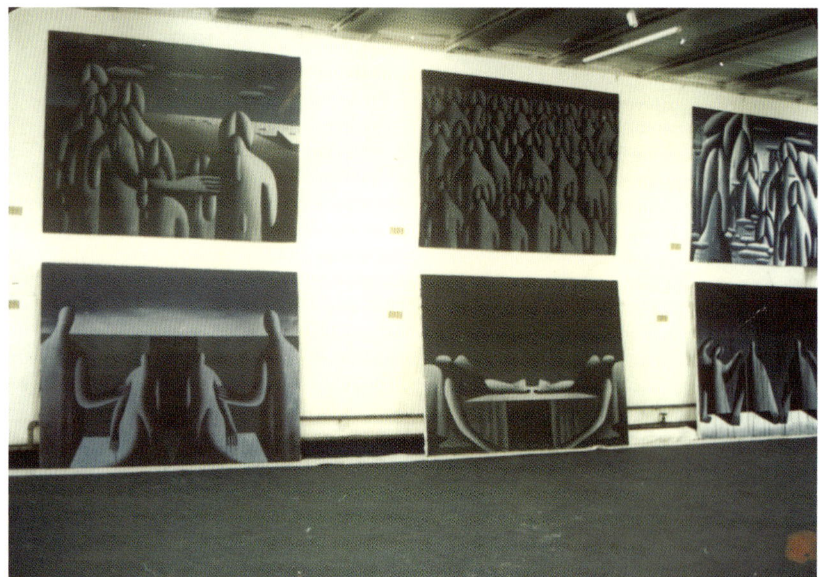

Plate 18: Wang Guangyi, paintings exhibited at the Northern Art Group Biennale, 1987. Image courtesy of Wang Guangyi.

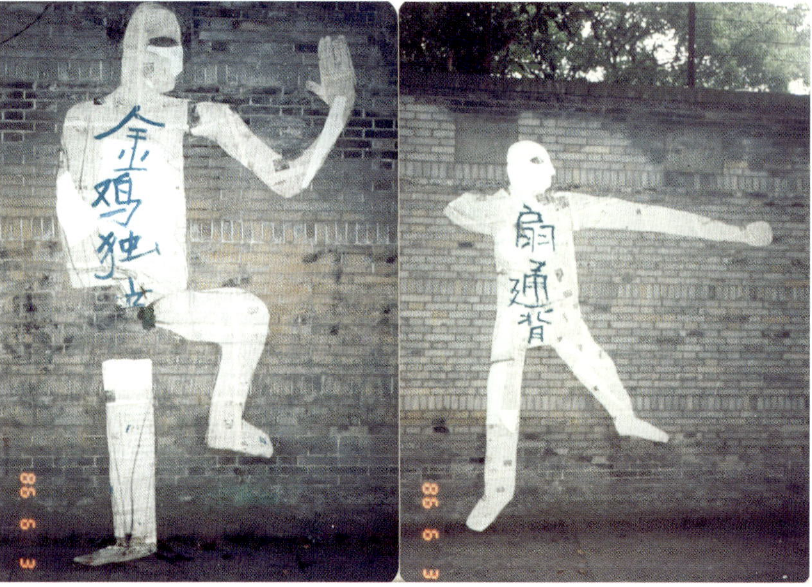

Plate 19: The Pond Association, *No. 1—Yang Style Tai Chi Series* (*Zuopin yi hao—yang shi taiji xilie* 作品一号-杨式太极系列), 1986. Site-specific action. Image courtesy of Song Ling. Reproduced with permission of Song Ling.

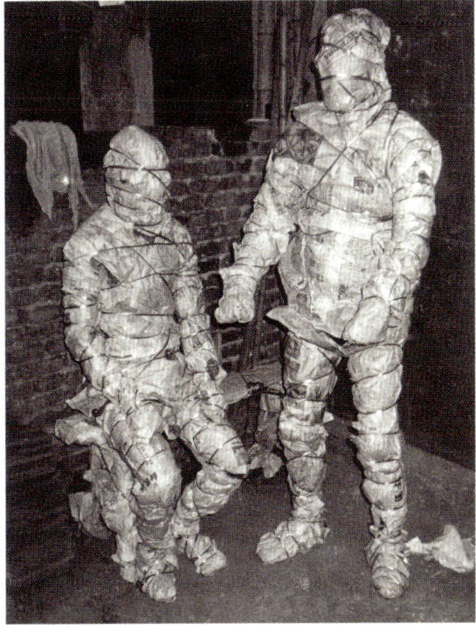

Plate 20: Zhang Peili and Geng Jianyi, *Wrapping Up—King and Queen* (*Baoza-guowang yu huanghou* 包扎—国王与王后), 1986. Performance. Image courtesy of the Asia Art Archive. Reproduced with permission of Zhang Peili.

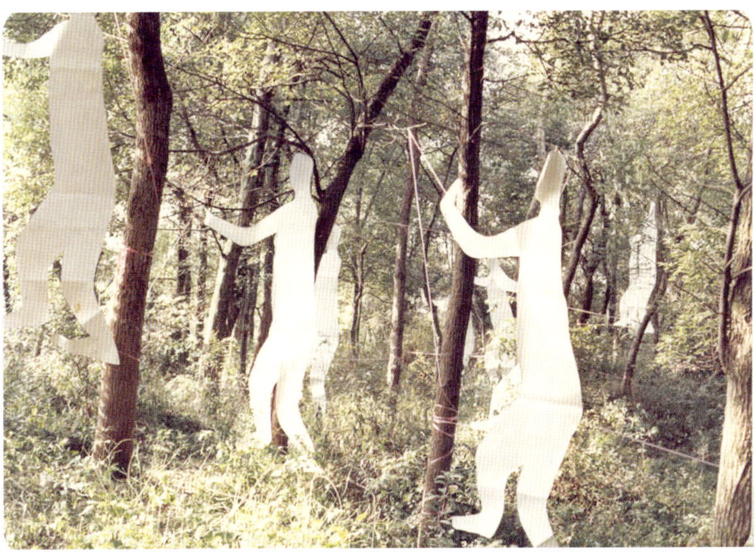

Plate 21: The Pond Association, *No. 2—Strollers in the Green Space* (*Zuopin er hao—Luse hongjian zhong de xingzhe* 作品二号—绿色空间里的行者), 1986. Site-specific action. Image courtesy of Song Ling. Reproduced with permission of Song Ling.

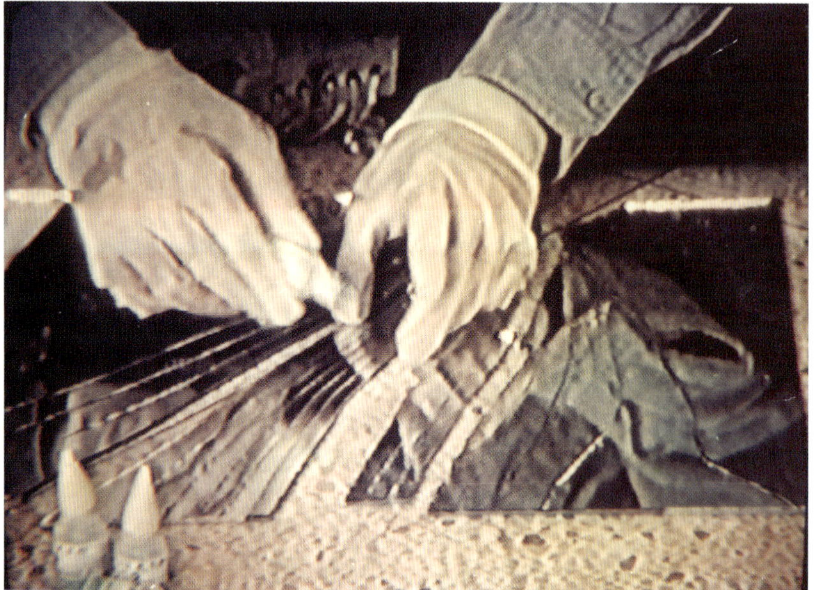

Plate 22: Zhang Peili, *30 × 30*, 1988. Single-channel video. Image courtesy of the Asia Art Archive. Reproduced with permission of Zhang Peili.

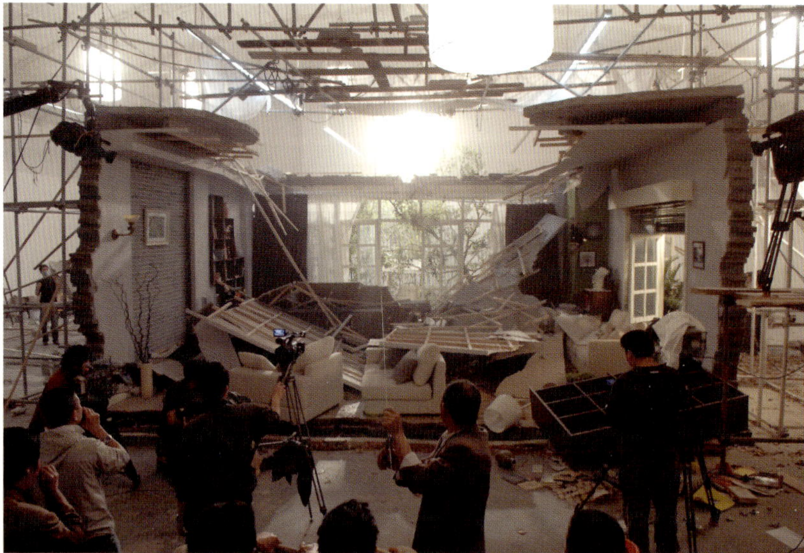

Plate 23: Zhang Peili, *A Gust of Wind* (*Zeng feng* 阵风), 2008. Multichannel video and installation. Image courtesy of Zhang Peili. Reproduced with permission of Zhang Peili.

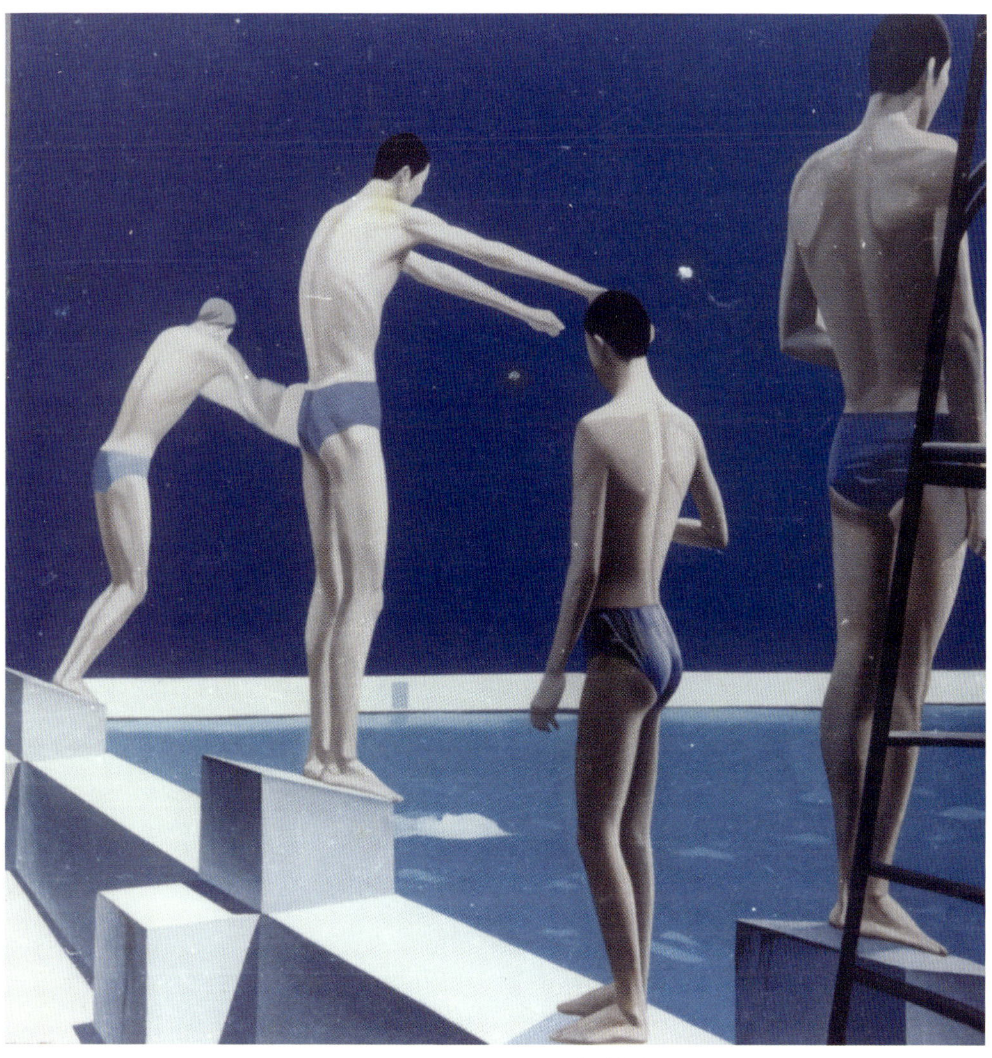

Plate 24: Zhang Peili, *Mid-Summer Swimmers* (*Zhongxia de yongzhe* 仲夏的泳者), 1985. Painting, oil on canvas 120 × 120cm. Image courtesy of the Asia Art Archive. Reproduced with permission of Zhang Peili.

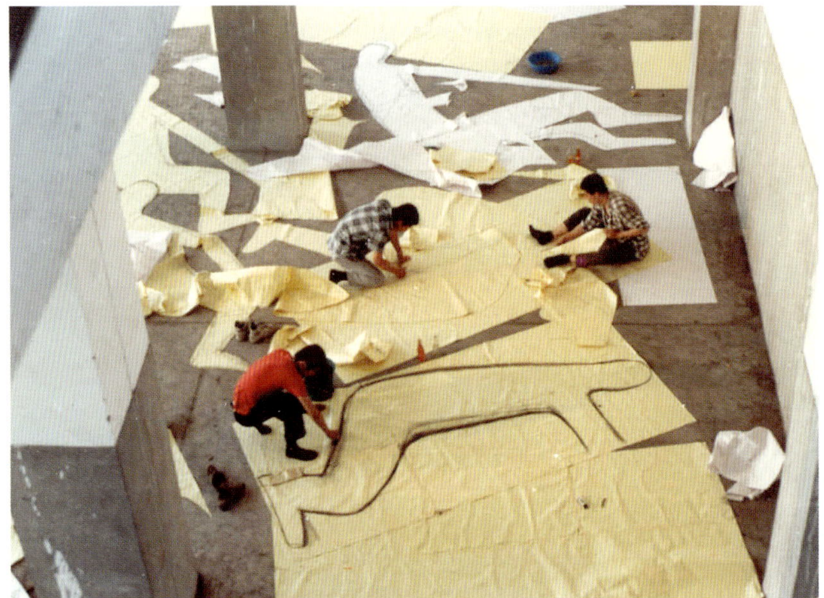

Plate 25: Re-staging of *No.1 Yang Style Tai Chi Series* for Beijing Central Television, 1988. Image courtesy of Song Ling. Reproduced with permission of Song Ling.

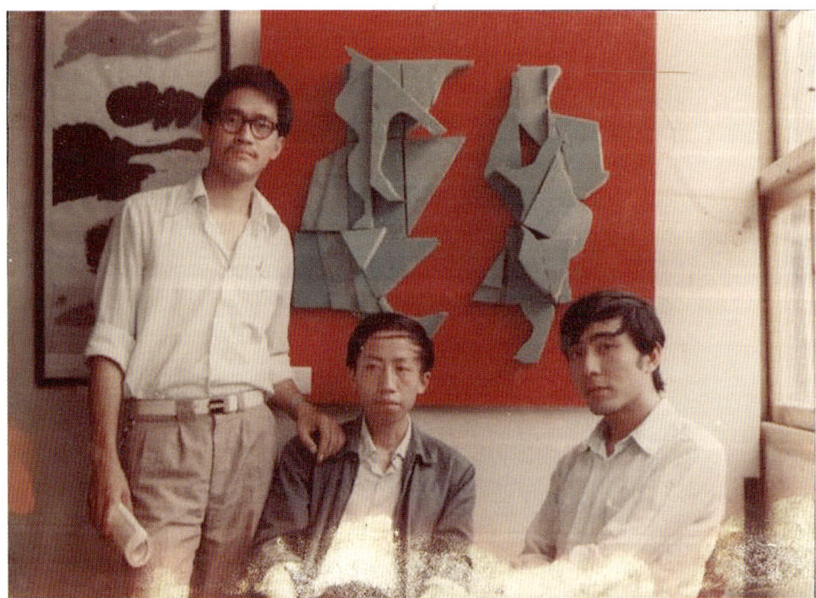

Plate 26: Lin Jiahua, Huang Yongping and Jiao Yaoming, Xiamen, 1983. Image courtesy of Yu Xiaogang. Reproduced with permission of Yu Xiaogang.

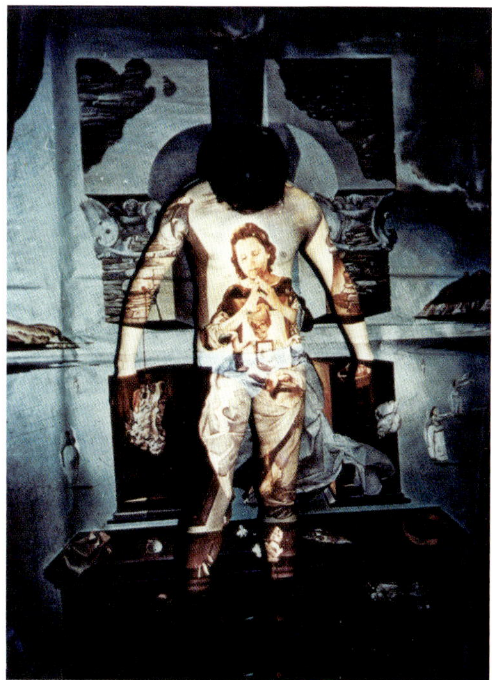

Plate 27: Lin Jiahua, *untitled*, 1986. Performance. Image courtesy of Yu Xiaogang. Reproduced with permission of Yu Xiaogang.

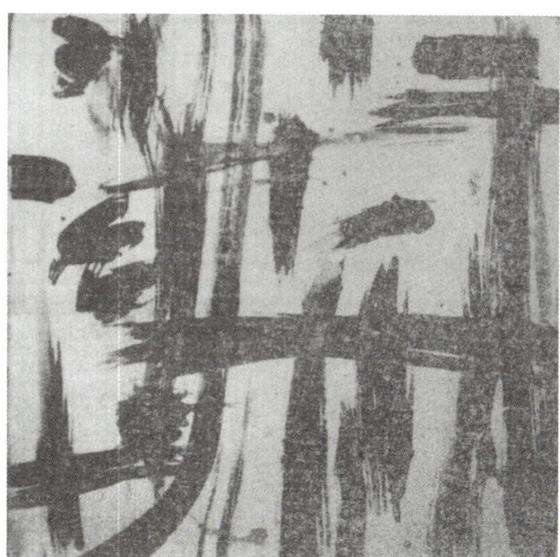

Plate 28: Yu Xiaogang, *untitled*, 1986 (destroyed). Painting, ink on canvas, dimensions unknown. Image courtesy of Yu Xiaogang. Reproduced with permission of Yu Xiaogang.

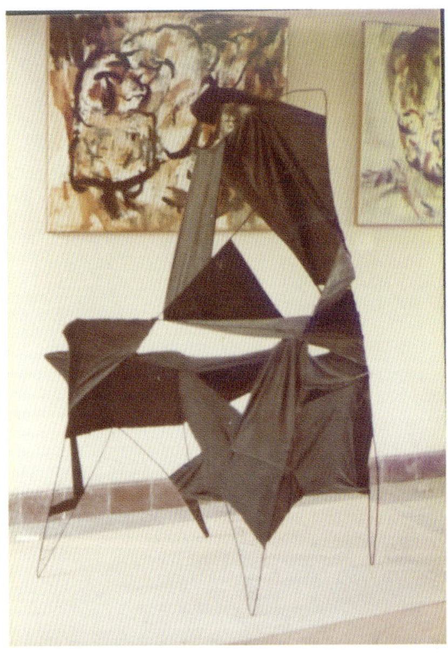

Plate 29: Jiao Yaoming, *untitled*, 1986.
Construct, mixed-media. Image courtesy of
Yu Xiaogang. Reproduced with permission of
Yu Xiaogang.

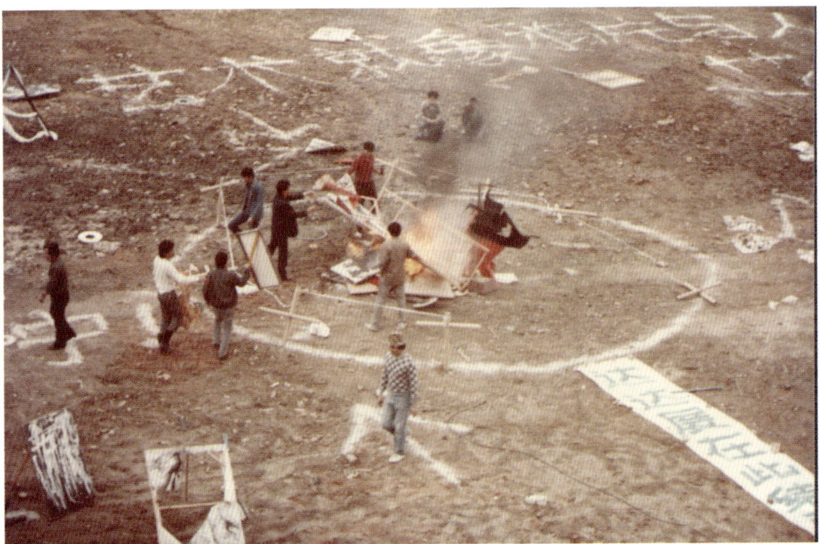

Plate 30: Xiamen Dada, *Burning Event* (*Fenshao shijian* 焚烧事件), 1986. Site-specific action.
Image courtesy of Yu Xiaogang. Reproduced with permission of Yu Xiaogang.

a truly revolutionary art should bring art and life more closely together). The importance of the writings of Laozi to the group lay principally in their assertion of the importance of culture as a focus for individual improvement or self-elevation; a notion referred to in a Mandarin-speaking context as *wenhua* (literally, improvement through writing). This pillar of the Chinese *literati* tradition not only enabled members of the Northern Art Group to shore up the aristocratic/elitist view of cultural agency that they had taken from Nietzsche, it also further supported the reconnection of their work as artists to an extended Chinese cultural tradition in a way that flew very much in the face of the wholesale destruction of traditional Chinese culture that had lain at the centre of the Cultural Revolution. Writings on Buddhist thought had a similar effect by promoting among the group the lofty notion of a non-desiring relationship with the world.

Alongside their thinking on the historical development of culture and artistic production, leading members of the Northern Art Group (principally, Wang Guangyi and Shu Qun) began to develop an approach to painting that contrasted strongly with the aestheticism and emotional warmth of the institutionalized Chinese art of the time. This approach, which came to be known as Rational Painting, is ostensibly similar to that associated with paintings by artists belonging to the European and North American Surrealists in its use of strange dream-like imagery, simplified forms and flat, non-expressive ways of applying paint (having the strongest similarity with the paintings of Shu Qun which draw heavily on the work of Salvador Dalí) (Plate 10).

The similarity of works by members of the Northern Art Group to those of the Surrealists is, however, a largely formalistic one that should not mislead the viewer into direct associations with the aims of the Surrealists and, in particular, their attempt to commingle reality and dreams as part of a revolutionary politics of Eros (Mahon 2005). The Surrealists, like other Western avant-garde movements of the early twentieth century, sought to bring art and life more closely together as a means of initiating a revolutionary reworking of the means-end rationality of the latter along the more playful lines of the former. By contrast, the Northern Art Group aim was to reassert the value of a traditionally lofty northern Chinese aesthetic as a way of rebuilding Chinese culture after the ravages wrought on it by the Cultural Revolution—a move that effectively reverses the aims of the early-twentieth-century Western avant-gardes.

Indeed, explicit within the stated aims of the Northern Art Group is a desire not only to uphold the emergence of a new combinatory Northern Culture but also, as part of that upholding, to bring about a revival of Chinese national-cultural identity. In adopting this position, which is congruent with wider and increasingly strident calls within Chinese society since the early 1980s for a renewal of national-cultural identity alongside social and economic reform, the Northern Art Group can therefore be understood to have promoted a nationalistic agenda strongly at variance with the tendencies of the Western political/revolutionary avant-gardes. As such, the aims of the Northern Art Group are very much open to interpretation as promoting distinctly authoritarian tendencies; a position almost certainly influenced by Chinese (mis-)interpretations of Nietzsche during the early twentieth century that also saw Nietzsche's thought as the basis for a strengthened sense of modern Chinese national-cultural identity (Shen 2009: 363–365).

In spite of the group's strong assertions of collective identity and purpose, it would, however, be a mistake to see the activities of the Northern Art Group as entirely coherent. As Ka Sang, one of the women members of the group, indicates in the conversation with her (included here), the group was actually a heterogeneous one with some members pursuing artistic aims different from those involved in the production of Rational Painting. Moreover, as Ka also makes clear, the structure and actions of the Northern Art Group were informed strongly by the persistence of patriarchal attitudes within the PRC during the 1980s, which served to marginalize the participation of women artists within the group.

Towards the end of the 1980s, there was an increasingly pronounced shift in emphasis in relation to the work of Wang Guangyi away from the Northern Art Group's early alignment with Confucian sublimity towards critical forms of representation similar to those associated with the Western avant-gardes and post-avant-gardes. Exemplary of this shift is Wang's appropriation of iconic images, such as standard portraits of Mao and reproductions of classic Western paintings as part of his *Red Rationalism* (*Hongse lixing* 红色理性) and *Black Rationalism* (*Heise lixing* 黑色理性) series of paintings (Plates 11 and 12).

In these paintings, Wang overlays his chosen iconic images with grids and other diagrammatic symbols—following the example of Gombrich's use of similar devices to illustrate the formal analysis of artworks—in such a way that the images in question are provisionally drained of their aesthetic/auratic impact. As a number of commentators, including Köppel-Yang (2003: 157–158), have argued, the distancing effect of this variation on Rational Painting has distinct similarities to the deconstructive outcomes of grafting and citation in the context of Western avant-garde art and, as such, can be understood to have presaged not only Wang's highly prescient call to 'Liquidate Humanist Enthusiasm' (*Qingli renwen reqing* 清理人文热情) at the Huangshan Symposium on contemporary Chinese art in November 1988[6] but also the Political Pop paintings produced by the artist after the dissolution of the Northern Art Group in 1989.

Although, it should be acknowledged here that, within a Chinese context, Wang's juxtaposition of Maoist revolutionary imagery with that of international capitalism in the *Great Criticism* series (*Da pipan xilie* 大批判系列) is widely perceived to be a subjective-realist interpretation of the hybrid state of contemporary Chinese society after Mao (Plate 13).

Conversations with members of the Northern Art Group

Wang Guangyi (b. 1957)[7]

Paul Gladston: When and where did the Northern Art Group first come together?

Wang Guangyi: The Northern Art Group first came together in July 1984 in the north-eastern Chinese city of Harbin. Harbin is in Heilongjiang Province, part of the area of China formerly known as Manchuria.

PG: When and where did the group's activities come to an end?

WG: There wasn't a specific point in time when the activities of the group came to an end. We didn't say 'right, our group is now finished.' In 1986, I left Harbin to work at the Zhuhai Painting Institute (*Zhuhai huayuan* 珠海画院) in Guangdong in south-western China, near Macau and Hong Kong. But it was really after the China/Avant-Garde exhibition in Beijing in 1989—which was effectively the terminal event for the Chinese avant-garde art of the 1980s—that we no longer got together to discuss things. That's how the Northern Art Group came to an end. The group disintegrated naturally.[8]

PG: Is there still a working relationship between any of the members of the group?

WG: No, after 1989 the group simply disintegrated.

PG: Within the existing literature on contemporary Chinese art of the 1980s there are conflicting accounts of when the Northern Art Group first came together. Some say that the group first came together in January 1985, while others say July 1984.[9] Just now, you said that the group started in July 1984. Can you explain these differing accounts?

WG: The Chinese media started reporting the group in 1986, but we actually founded it in 1984, albeit under another name. Before 1985 the group was called The Youth Information Communication Centre of Northern Art. The Chinese media was not allowed to report the activities of unofficial art groups until 1985.[10] Things became a little bit more flexible after that. That's how the activities of our group came to be reported in the Chinese media. To use a simile, it's just like a couple who have been together secretly for years before the relationship becomes public [laughs].

PG: Under what circumstances did the Northern Art Group come together?

WG: The reason was simple. After graduating from university, a group of us came back to work in Harbin and got together quite often, chatting and talking about art. Gradually, we made it a regular meeting, just like a salon. Previously, I had been a student in the Oil Painting Department at the Zhejiang Academy of Fine Arts (*Zhejiang meishu xueyuan* 浙江美术学院) in Hangzhou.[11] I graduated from there in 1984 and then became a teacher at the Harbin Institute of Architectural Design (*Harbin jianzhu yu sheji xueyuan* 哈尔滨建筑与设计学院). I was born and brought up in Harbin.

PG: Who was involved in or associated with the group and what role did they play?

WG: Many people were involved in the group, including Shu Qun, Liu Yan, Ren Jian, Gao Minglu, Li Xianting, Wang Xiaojian, Zhou Yan and Huang Zhuan.[12] Zhang Peili, of the Pond Association in Hangzhou, also corresponded with Shu Qun and me by letter.

PG: Were there any women members or associates of the group? What role did they play? Did they have an equal standing with the men associated with the group?

WG: Yes, Wang Yaling, Wang Haiyan and Ka Sang. They joined the group initially because it was interesting to them. But the group became more serious later on and they stopped coming to our discussions.

PG: What you have just said suggests that Wang Yaling, Wang Haiyan and Ka Sang played only a marginal role in the group.

WG: Yes. It might have something to do with traditional Chinese culture. Traditionally, Chinese society has been very patriarchal.

PG: In recent years, women have contributed strongly to the development of contemporary Chinese art. What is your opinion of that contribution?

WG: I think it's a good thing.

PG: How did you and Shu Qun come to correspond with Zhang Peili, who was based in Hangzhou?

WG: Peili and I were students together at the Zhejiang Academy of Fine Arts. As students, we shared our views on art. We continued that exchange by letter when I returned to Harbin.

PG: Apart from art, what else did the members of the Northern Art Group talk about? For example, did you discuss wider cultural, social or political issues?

WG: The topics were varied: art, philosophy, poetry and social issues. However, our discussions were mainly related to art.

PG: Could you say more about the discussions you had; in particular, discussions about the relationship between art and philosophy?

WG: We talked a lot about philosophical thought, especially that of Nietzsche. Though there was no direct relationship between Nietzsche's thought and our art-making, we liked the spirit of Nietzsche, particularly his theory of the Übermensch. Our discussions were actually quite contradictory because we liked both Nietzsche and Hegel even though their philosophical approaches were very different—Hegel's approach to philosophy was rational and dialectical while Nietzsche's wasn't.

PG: One of the similarities between Hegel and Nietzsche is that they both hold out the possibility of some sort of historical transcendence; in the case of Hegel the progressive dialectical realization of spirit or *geist*, and in the case of Nietzsche a critical departure from established morality, religion and rationalist forms of philosophical thought. Was it Hegel and Nietzsche's shared belief in the possibility of historical transcendence that you were interested in, particularly in the context of mainland China during the mid-1980s, which had embarked falteringly on a period of momentous change?

WG: Yes, I think so. Principally, there was a desire among the members of the Northern Art Group to break with existing cultural values, both those of China and the West. We believed that Western and Chinese culture had collapsed and that they would be superseded by the birth of a northern civilization. We also believed that there is a historical tendency for civilized culture to move north—both in Northern Europe and Northern Asia—and that this illustrates the tendency of strong people to move to areas of conflict.

PG: As a result of your readings of Nietzsche did you, as individuals, identify yourselves directly with the Nietzschean concept of the Übermensch?

WG: Yes, we had that idea at the time.

PG: How did you get access to the writings of Nietzsche?

WG: I read a translation of Nietzsche made during the early 1980s by a friend of mine, Zhou Guoping.

PG: During the early 1980s, there was a turn towards more formalist/aestheticist attitudes within the Chinese art world. I'm thinking here of not only the highly aestheticized Rural Realism of the Sichuan School but also the sustained debate about formalism (*xingshi zhuyi* 形式主义) and the beauty of form (*xingshi mei* 形式美) initiated by Wu Guanzhong 吴冠中 that took place within the PRC between 1979 and 1986.[13] Did the Northern Art Group's desire to break with existing cultural conventions involve a direct challenge to these formalist/aestheticist attitudes?

WG: Yes. During the early 1980s, there was too much emphasis on formalism within institutionalized Chinese art, which we considered to be a weakness, as something not so important. More important to us was the content of art, a kind of content with 'superpower.' We thought art should be injected with powerful stuff. This position may well have been influenced by our readings of Nietzsche.

PG: Can you give a specific example of the kind of content you are referring to?

WG: It's difficult to give a specific example of the content that I'm talking about. It's more like an atmosphere than a set of specific concepts, something we called 'absolute *geist*' in light of our readings of Hegel. At the time we used words like 'sublime' (*chonggao* 崇高), 'order' (*zhixu* 秩序) and 'tranquility' (*ningjing* 宁静) to describe our artworks.

PG: Why was the sublime so important to you?

WG: The content I mentioned is a kind of feeling. When we said art should be sublime, it was an abstract, vague notion. The Northern Art Group placed a great deal of emphasis on the sublime because we thought it was a good way to recover the dignity of human nature and culture and, in doing so, to rebuild Chinese civilization. We thought too much emphasis on formalism in art was a backward and dispiriting step. Formalism and beauty were something bad as far as we were concerned. We made a connection between the sublime and the cold, apparently limitless landscapes of northern China. In a series of paintings, which I produced during the mid-1980s, titled *Frozen North Pole* (*Ninggu de beifang jidi* 凝固的北方极地), I depicted abstracted figures in cold, limitless landscapes as a graphic interpretation of the sublime (Plate 9).

PG: During the mid-1980s, were you aware of the relationship that had been discussed in the West between postmodernism and the sublime?

WG: Yes, we had heard of postmodernism.[14] However, we thought the sublimity that we were trying to achieve was in conflict with postmodernism. We recognized the concept of postmodernism, but our desire was to construct a sublime or lofty culture that was actually contrary to the blurring of the boundary between high and low art associated with postmodernism.

PG: At the time, were you aware of Jean-François Lyotard's notion of the postmodern sublime?

WG: No, not really.

PG: One of the most influential ideas associated with postmodernism in the West is that of the postmodern sublime. Lyotard argues that postmodernist artworks habitually fail to present objects that adequately match the concepts to which they give rise. Lyotard aligns this failure with the eighteenth-century philosopher Immanuel Kant's conception of the sublime: first, feelings of pain experienced in the face of objects of such power or vastness that they defy the human imagination; and second, feelings of pleasure experienced through the capacity of human reason to supersede the imagination by intuiting the illimitability of the phenomena in question. As Lyotard would have it, postmodernist art therefore affirms the mismatch between freedom and attempts—such as those found in the writings of Hegel and Marx—to represent historical events in their totality. In Lyotard's view, it therefore follows that freedom is dependent upon the persistent application of human judgement and not upon established principles (Lyotard 1984 [1979]: 71–82).

WG: The concept of the sublime represents something else in a Chinese cultural context: something big or vast that is also a powerful source of moral authority.[15] It's somewhat different from the Western concept of the sublime.

PG: So, your conception of the sublime differs from the one that I'm using.

WG: Yes. Different cultures have differing interpretations of certain concepts. For instance, when Western scholars interpret Chan Buddhism, it's different from the way that it's understood in its original context as part of Chinese culture. Culture creates new meanings and significances through misinterpretation.

PG: Yes, I would agree with that. Western avant-garde art has been influenced by vernacular Chinese thought and practice. But as a result of the transference of that thought and practice from one cultural context to another, it has been subjected to a process of cultural translation/mediation involving inescapable refractions of meaning. By the same token, contemporary Chinese art can itself be understood to be a hybrid of Western and Chinese cultural influences; one that is also a focus for the translation/mediation of vernacular Chinese cultural thinking and practice previously translated/mediated by the West. This is why it's short-sighted to talk about contemporary Chinese art simply from either a Western or a Chinese cultural perspective. Indeed, it's not really clear in this respect where the dividing line between Western and Chinese culture actually lies.

WG: Yes, and from an artistic point of view, that's more interesting. Though contemporary Chinese art has been greatly influenced by Western and Chinese culture, it has become a new form.

PG: In the West we associate the sublime with a romantic desire to transcend or transgress established limits. Did you see your art as romantic in that sense?

WG: There's a contradiction here. We were anti-romanticist, as well as anti-formalist. We thought romanticism and formalism made art into entertainment—that is to say, into a kind of kitsch.[16] By contrast, we were trying to make an art of sublime thoughts; one which was not purely formalist, but which presented graphic interpretations of those lofty thoughts.

PG: The North American art critic Clement Greenberg has also objected to art as entertainment—to art as kitsch (Greenberg 1939: 34–49; 1965: 193–201). Did you draw upon his writings in reaching these conclusions?

WG: No, not really. It was an instinctive leap of the imagination.

PG: Some of the paintings produced by you as an individual during the late 1980s involve the appropriation of existing images—in some cases of Mao Zedong and in others of classic Western artworks—that have then been overlaid with grids and/or symbols of one sort or another in a manner highly reminiscent of the analytical diagrams one sometimes finds in art-historical texts. In doing this, what was your intention?

WG: It was my own idea, which I called 'rational analysis.' (*Lixing fenxi* 理性分析)

PG: What exactly do you mean here by rational analysis?

WG: Here rational analysis is also a vague concept. It's a hint, a kind of attitude. It's not the same as it's usually understood in the West: a form of critical reasoning opposed to feeling and intuition. When facing classical culture or images of Mao, I played the role of objective analyst. Titles of some of my paintings had the prefix *Red Rationalism* (*Hongse lixing*), while others had the prefix *Black Rationalism* (*Heise lixing*) (Plates 11 and 12). I tried to keep an objective attitude towards historical cultural facts. One point I'd like to make here is that I was influenced a lot by the work of the art historian Ernst Gombrich. In his books, Gombrich often applied grids and symbols to reproduce paintings in order to signify some aspects of their design or formal composition. To me, that had the effect of objectifying the works of art in question; of placing them at a distance and of reducing their aesthetic impact. I now realize that I misunderstood or misinterpreted Gombrich's ideas. Even so, his thoughts were very important to me at the time. I was particularly interested in Gombrich's use of the concept of 'paradigm shift'; that is to say, a historical shift from one order of pictorial representation to another.

PG: It's perhaps important to add that rational analysis, as you describe it here, can be understood to involve a critical response to the perceived irrationalism of the instrumental reasoning associated with Maoist ideology. With this in mind, at least one commentator has interpreted your version of rational analysis from a contemporary Western theoretical perspective as a self-consciously applied form of deconstruction; that is to say, as an analytical intervention that recontextualizes and critically re-motivates a given text (Köppel-Yang 2003: 157). Were you aware of the theory and practice of deconstruction during the late 1980s?

WG: I wasn't conscious of the theory and practice of deconstruction during the late 1980s. I got to know deconstruction in the 1990s, during which time I began to apply the concept unconsciously to my work—for instance, the *Great Criticism* (*Da pipan* 大批判系) series of paintings,which involved the juxtaposition of images derived from the Cultural Revolution with international brand names, such as Marlboro and Cartier (Plate 13). Before the 1990s, I didn't know about deconstruction. Sometimes you do things without realizing. I thought I was applying Gombrich's concept of paradigm shift, but I was using deconstruction instead. It's as though I tried to make a cup, but made a tea table instead [laughs].

PG: So, the way in which you have interpreted your own work has altered over time?

WG: Yes, that's right.

PG: Were the aims of the Northern Art Group written down or recorded? Were they published? If so, where?

WG: Yes, there was a statement relating to the work of the Northern Art Group by Shu Qun, 'The Spirit of the Northern Art Group' (*Beifang yishu qunti de jingshen*), which was published in *Fine Arts in China* (*Zhongguo meishu bao*)[17] in November 1985.[18] I also wrote a statement relating to the work of the Northern Art Group, 'Which Kind of Painting Is Needed in Our Age?' (*Women zhege shidai xuyao shenmo yang de huihua?*). This statement was published in *Jiangsu Pictorial* (*Jiangsu huakan*)[19] in 1986—but it's not really a declaration of intent.[20]

PG: Could you say something about the exhibitions and events that the Northern Art Group took part in during the 1980s?

WG: There were two principal events: one was the Biennial Exhibition of the Northern Art Group (*Beifang yishu tuanti shuangnian zhan* 北方艺术团体双年展), which was staged at the Jilin Art Academy (*Jilin yishu xueyuan* 吉林艺术学院) in Changchun in February 1987.[21] The other was a forum on northern Chinese culture. I can't remember the exact details of the forum now. It was mainly about sublimity. As I said before, we related the concept of the sublime to the living environment in northern China, where the landscape is wide and solemn. We made a symbolic association between the northern Chinese landscape and concepts such as sublimity, solemnity and religiosity. That's why our group emphasized natural scenes, whereas in the south, art groups such as the Pond Association and Xiamen Dada placed more emphasis on the inner world. Chan Buddhism, for example, was very important to Xiamen Dada.

PG: Could we pursue that line of argument further? What other differences would you see between the work of the Northern Art Group and that of the Pond Association and Xiamen Dada? Let's talk about the Pond Association first.

WG: There were many differences between these groups, mainly caused by differences in regional culture

PG: Such as?

WG: It's difficult to say. We saw the work of the Northern Art Group as characterized by *i-ching*.[22] We thought the concept of the sublime might be affected by this. Traditional Chinese aesthetics places emphasis on the integration of man and nature. However, what we were trying to do was to break away from nature and lay stress on the highness and greatness of man in a way that moves against traditional Oriental philosophy. So we were anti-tradition, which was very different from the Pond Association, who wanted to bring art and life more closely together, and Xiamen Dada, who aligned themselves with Chan Buddhism. The reason we were anti-tradition may have had something to do with the influence of the Western avant-gardes.

PG: During the 1980s, Chinese critics used the term Rational Painting (*Lixing huihua* 理性绘画)[23] to categorize paintings produced by the Northern Art Group and artists associated with the Pond Association. Western commentators have also continued to use this term (e.g. Köppel-Yang 2003: 25, 61). Do you entirely agree with this description, given the differences in approach you have just described between the Northern Art Group and the Pond Association?

WG: I think it's simplistic to describe both of our groups as 'rationalist' in their approach. This simplistic approach to the categorization of contemporary Chinese art may be helpful when doing research and in writing down readily understandable historical narratives. Personally, I don't like to look at things from such a simplistic point of view. It's fascinating to see the complex cultural cross-currents in contemporary Chinese art. Though, I don't really mind how scholars do their research or how they categorize contemporary Chinese art.

PG: Does the work produced by the Northern Art Group have any relationship to traditional forms of Chinese art and aesthetics, apart from associations within the concept of *i-ching*?

WG: We mainly made oil paintings. If there's any influence from traditional Chinese art, I think it's an unconscious aesthetic thought; for instance, the solemn aesthetic feelings revealed in my early work which are similar to those associated with some traditional forms of Chinese landscape painting.

PG: Did members of the Northern Art Group collaborate in the production of shared artworks?

WG: We mainly made two-dimensional artworks…paintings. We made our own works, though we shared similar thoughts.

PG: Did the group have an agreed political position or stance?

WG: No, we didn't have a clear political position or stance. We were yearning for freedom; which is also paradoxical, because we had leanings at the time towards the centralization of power. We followed the traditional Chinese notion that when one dynastic power is overthrown another dynastic power will replace it. Now I think we should build a more democratic system in China. Both the Chinese political system and Chinese culture are turning towards a more democratic way of doing things. I think it's important to have this transitional period. I think transition is better than a sudden revolutionary breaking with the past because the latter would cause a lot of trouble.

PG: Did humour, satire, anti-intellectualism, anti-social behaviour, work avoidance, law-breaking, violence or deliberate non-cooperation with authority play a significant role in the activities of the group?

WG: No, mentally we were quiet or peaceful and this kind of mentality was enough to express our cultural attitude.

PG: How was the Northern Art Group organized?

WG: We had leaders: Shu Qun was the chairman, in charge of theories; and I was the vice-chairman, in charge of practice.

PG: Does the hierarchical structuring of the group have any thing to do with the way in which labour, production and political initiatives were managed in the PRC during the revolutionary period after 1949, through work units, large-scale political, campaigns or movements or government committee structures, for example.

WG: Yes, I think so. It was a small model of centralized government power.[24] In the case of the Northern Art Group, however, this power wasn't totally centralized. Even though we had a chairman and vice-chairman, the roles were parallel. Theory provides guidance to practice, but still it's difficult to say who leads whom. It's a bit like a game.

PG: Did the organizational structure of the group change?

WG: No it didn't change. The group was an organization, but quite loose. If someone wanted to join, they could join; if they wanted to leave, they could leave.

PG: What kept the group together other than shared artistic goals?

WG: We were all classmates, and friendship brought us together.

PG: Were there any disputes or conflicts within the group? If so, what was the nature of these disputes or conflicts? Also, when, where and between whom did these disputes and conflicts take place and how long did they last?

WG: Yes, we had our disputes, but the debates or arguments were a kind of intellectual game. Shu Qun and Liu Yan debated quite a lot. I was the mediator. The disputes didn't last that long.

PG: As a member of the group, what were your personal aims? In what ways were these aims supported by the group? In what ways, if any, did they differ from or come into conflict with those of the group?

WG: Our main goal was to represent individual values.

PG: What was the relationship between the group and the authorities in China, both at a national and at a local or regional level?

WG: It had nothing to do with the government.

PG: In what ways did wider social, economic or cultural events—both within and outside China—influence the activities or the group?

WG: The work of the group had nothing to do with events outside China. It was influenced more directly by the political and cultural situation within China at the time. Yes, there was a relationship to the wider historical context, but it wasn't that important. Our inner world at the time was the most important thing—it was more a matter of ideology than facts.

PG: What is the legacy of the group for subsequent generations of contemporary Chinese artists?

WG: Probably the spiritual values and cultural values of the group, which are very important in art. They should surpass the art's potential standing as a source of entertainment.

PG: What kind of values? And why are they important?

WG: Our group wanted to do something to help bring about the renaissance of our nation's culture after the destructive events of the Cultural Revolution. We saw it as a kind of social responsibility. I think a country's cultural myth is realized by its artists.[25]

PG: What do you think of the recent exhibition of the work of the 1985 New Wave at the Ullens Foundation in Beijing? (Fei 2007)

WG: I think the exhibition represented the historical facts. As for the disagreements or arguments surrounding the exhibition, they're not important.

PG: I interpreted that exhibition as an attempt to establish a national-cultural myth—that of the 1985 New Wave as a 'heroic' cultural movement—and, in doing so, to affirm the continuity of a specifically Chinese national-cultural identity.

WG: Sure. It's just like we say Shakespeare is part of the British cultural myth.

PG: The Museum of Modern Art in New York does something similar in relation to American modernist art….

WG: Right.

PG: Personally, I would have preferred to see an exhibition that actively sought to uphold differing interpretations of the 1985 New Wave, to present the 1985 New Wave as a contestable phenomenon. As someone involved at the time, do you think that the 1985 New Wave is open to differing interpretative points of view? Or is it important that we start to define the significance of the 1985 New Wave in absolute historical terms?

WG: Yes, it's important to do academic research and to define the historical facts. I believe some scholars have started. As a member of one of the Chinese art groups of the 1980s, I have been waiting for this kind of serious scholarly discussion.

Shu Qun (b. 1958)[26]

Paul Gladston: I would like to begin by asking you to say something about your views on the context within which contemporary Chinese art first emerged during the late 1970s and early 1980s and, in particular, the renewed openness of Chinese artists to Western cultural influences.

Shu Qun: Up until the beginning of the Warring States (*Zhan guo* 战国) period in ancient China,[27] religious culture in the East and the West were quite similar. Both were based on stories about mythological civilizations. However, after the beginning of the Warring States period—which was contemporaneous with ancient Greek civilization in the West— Chinese culture and that of the West began to diverge. Chinese culture developed along a naturalistic line—which resulted in the concept of *i-ching*—while that of the West became increasingly abstract and rationalist. After 1985, Chinese culture and Western culture came back together and inevitably collided, which can be thought of as China's entry into globalization. There was no choice for Chinese people. If Chinese people could choose, they would probably still prefer to follow a naturalistic way of life, which means living close to nature—somewhere near the mountains and water. Historically, the conceptual order of Western culture has been very different from that of China; for example, the Western concept of the hero, which emphasizes human mastery over nature. Western culture has emphasized rationality and design, while Chinese culture has emphasized naturalism. Greek rationality is a kind of architectural rationality. Plato's ideal society, as presented in *The Republic*, is based on the theory of designing. The management of Western society is also based on this kind of theory. Chinese and Western attitudes towards society have differed strongly in this regard. In China, there was a kind of village-based family management system, which involved a patriarchal ordering of society. This is in marked contrast to Western societies, which adopted organizational forms of social management. After 1985, Chinese culture was forced to follow the West's unnatural, rationally designed way of doing things.

PG: So, in your view, after 1985 there was the beginning of a shift within the PRC away from a traditional naturalistic culture to one strongly informed by Western rationality, design and conceptual abstraction?

SQ: Yes. This shift was also accompanied by stylistic changes in Chinese art. Before 1985, most artworks within the PRC were like Luo Zhongli's painting *Father*; that is to say, sentimental forms of realism. After 1985, artistic style began to turn in another direction— towards rationalism and abstraction. There was a paradigm shift. My own work at the time intuitively marked this shift. Some philosophers have argued that there are two elements in Western culture: one is the inheritance of rationality from ancient Greece, and the other is the inheritance of the Hebrew spirit.[28] If you look at rationally designed paintings I produced during the 1980s that represent the Christian Crucifixion (a symbol for the Hebrew Jesus), paintings such as *Absolute Principle* (*Juedui yuanzi* 绝对原则) (1989), it is possible to see the influence of the two elements of Western culture: the Greek and the Hebrew (Plate 10). I interpreted this significance ten years after making those paintings. Artists often work unconsciously [laughs]. I'd like to add another point, which may be more vivid than the last. Western culture since Ancient Greece has been an urban culture. By contrast, Eastern culture has traditionally been a rural culture—objective and resistant. Even now, Chinese people are still eager to live as part of a rural culture. For instance, we have theme parks, such as Penglai Fairyland and Xanadu in Shandong Province, that continue to display the characteristics of rural culture. The coming together and collision of Western and Chinese culture after 1985, which I alluded to earlier, has resulted in the transformation of Chinese culture from a rural culture to an urban culture. As a consequence of the collision between Western and Chinese culture, China has had no choice but to follow the urban cultural system first established by Ancient Greece—globalization means urbanization. Of course, that's just my personal understanding. If cultural transformation involves changes in attitudes and points of view, then it will inevitably be accompanied by linguistic transformations involving semiotic changes in the appearance of symbolic characteristics. For instance, the conventional symbolic characteristic of rural China is a girl with pigtails. This symbolism still persists today. However, nowadays, as part of urban culture, Chinese girls have a variety of hairstyles that change constantly. This contrast can be thought of as a metaphor for changes of discourse as part of the transformation of Chinese culture. In the context of urban culture, the functions of language have changed and diversified markedly. Life is no longer natural. Many differing points of view have been added. Life in China is now like a game, or an opera.

PG: During the 1980s, members of the Northern Art Group developed a style of painting that Chinese critics referred to at the time as Rational Painting. How should we interpret the use of the term 'rational' in this context?

SQ: During the Cultural Revolution most paintings in China were warm. They evoked feelings of happiness and togetherness. Though paintings by the Sichuan School, such as Luo Zhongli's *Father*, that emerged after the Cultural Revolution were not as warm as those during the Cultural Revolution, they were still humanistic and sympathetic. Rational Painting involved the making of cold, self-contained images. Rationality can be interpreted in this context as a kind of cold, resistant state represented by a rigid and mechanical ordering of form that is neither organic nor vivid. Here, rationality emphasizes coldness and even a bit of antipathy. A lot of themes in Chinese painting just prior to the emergence of Rational Painting were about returning home. Rational Painting refuses this: in Rational Painting there's no longer any home to go back to, there's only wasteland. The Bengali novelist and poet Rabindranath Tagore once wrote that there is no longer a home to which we might return and that in order to follow our mysterious calling we are compelled to travel in search of values elsewhere.[29] Members of the Northern Art Group no longer accepted China's traditional rural values. We no longer appreciated the conventional image of the 'poor old soul', which had become a mainstay of Chinese painting after the Cultural Revolution. We intuitively felt the impending arrival of urban civilization in China. A Belgian designer once said that artists are the only purveyors of truth. I agree with what he said. That's why artists are different from ordinary people. While the majority of people are still asleep, we have awakened.

PG: Paintings produced during the 1980s by the Hangzhou-based artists Zhang Peili and Geng Jianyi—who became members of the Pond Association—have also been referred to by Chinese critics as examples of Rational Painting. Do you agree with this use of the term?

SQ: I think Zhang Peili and Geng Jianyi also had a premonition about the arrival of urban civilization in China. But unlike the Northern Art Group they did this by representing the phenomena of everyday urban life. Take here, for example, Zhang Peili's painting *Mid-Summer Swimmers* (*Youyong zhe* 游泳池) of 1985 and his series of paintings *Please Enjoy the Jazz* (*Qing nin xinshang jueshiyue* 请您欣赏爵士乐) of 1985–1986, which are all about the coolly detached representation of people or objects in urban settings. This was considered avant-garde at the time and couldn't be understood by the majority of people. The coldness of these paintings reflects the artist's impressions of urban life.[30] One can see that there's a big difference between Zhang Peili's work and naturalistic paintings such as Luo Zhongli's *Father*. As for my own work, the coldness comes from an engagement with principles rather than with phenomena. Zhang Peili's and Geng Jianyi's paintings were about the phenomena of everyday urban life while my works were more abstract, expressing a kind of conceptual point of view.

PG: So, you would consider your own version of Rational Painting as more conceptual than that of Zhang Peili and Geng Jianyi; that is to say, more abstract…more detached from everyday phenomenological experience?

SQ: If we look at Zhang's early paintings, most of them depicted figures in urban settings. Though some works were not about people, they were still related to urban life. They broke away from the conventional characteristics of the countryside. They were different from works such as *Father* of 1979 by Luo Zhongli and *Spring Wind Has Been Awakened* (*Chunfeng yijing shuxing* 春风已经苏醒) of 1982 by He Duoling, which dominated the Chinese art world during the late 1970s and early 1980s. By contrast, paintings produced by the Northern Art Group approached painting from a conceptual point of view. So, we can say that while rational paintings produced by Zhang Peili and Geng Jianyi depicted phenomena, those produced by the Northern Art Group were related to concepts.

PG: Could you say more about the relationship between Rational Painting and the emergence of an increasingly urbanized society within the PRC during the 1980s?

SQ: Actually, this relationship involved both an aesthetic and a cognitive transformation. What I mean by cognition here is our interpretation of things—a critical system. During the period of agricultural civilization and rural culture in China, beauty was the dominant aesthetic. However, after 1985, coolness came to the fore. The goal of Rational Painting was to turn beauty into coolness. Coolness says no to beauty. Agricultural civilization was warm and direct, but had a very low capacity for self-reflection. We tried to refuse this kind of state. I think the style of my work changed drastically from beauty to coolness. Zhang Peili's and Geng Jianyi's work probably changed like that too. As you know, if one looks at paintings by Geng Jianyi, such as the series *Haircut—Another Bald in the Summer of 1985* (*Nian xiaji de you yige guangtou* 年夏季的又一个光头) of 1985, the images are of modern life. Most of my works were not about warm personal experiences. I was inspired by textbooks. This is different from Wang Guangyi, who was inspired by nature, kinsfolk and his relationship to his surroundings. My works were more influenced by the work of Michelangelo and textbooks. That's why my works are cold and dry. In contrast to the drastic stylistic changes which took place in relation to my own work, Wang Guangyi's style changed gradually. Early rational paintings produced by him, such as *Frozen North Pole*, still had a sympathetic air—this was because of sympathetic feelings he had towards his wife. However, in his later works such as *The Death of Marat* (*Hou gudian xilie Mala zhi si* 后古典系列, 马拉之死), which transforms a painting by the French neoclassicist David as a way of establishing a detached cultural perspective, there's no sympathetic feeling (Plate 14). That's the measure of semiotics. I would also like to add a detail. I first began to make unsentimental rational paintings in 1984. Wang Guangyi produced *The Death of Marat* in 1986. After 1986, Wang's styles changed dramatically. Before that, the changes were gradual. As for myself, my styles have always changed drastically. At this point I would also like to mention the relationship between metaphysics and the coolness or coldness of the work of the Northern Art Group. Paintings produced by the Northern Art Group sought to raise coolness and coldness to the level of metaphysics. Metaphysics is a kind of absolute principle, not an ordinary phenomenon or a short-term phenomenon. The metaphysical coldness of rational paintings produced by the Northern Art Group was meant to signify the birth of a new northern civilization in China. After that, the image of *Father* and the naturalistic state to which it refers would disappear and never come back again. Coolness and coldness would become the main principle.

PG: Arguably, the Cultural Revolution led to a catastrophic loss of critical distance between art and life by effectively negating the existence of a relatively autonomous cultural sphere within the PRC. Was the coolness and detachment of the Northern Arts Group's work an attempt to rebuild a sense of critical distance in response to not only the uncritical sentimentality of official Chinese art but also the destructive events of the Cultural Revolution?

SQ: Yes, before 1985, Chinese people were living together in a sympathetic state; a state in which people knew each other and lived together contentedly. This sympathetic state was not self-critical. Only coldness and rationality can provide space for examining, measuring and checking. That kind of observation is just like using a microscope or a telescope. After 1985, we started to emphasize the value of that kind of observation.

PG: One thing that intrigues me here is that at roughly the same time as you were developing these ideas in China, Western theorists had already begun to lose faith in the capacity of the Western avant-gardes to engage in a direct critical transformation of the lifeworld (Bürger 1984 [1974]). From a certain Western postmodernist theoretical standpoint, it can be argued that the Western avant-gardes had sublimated artistic production within the lifeworld, thereby bringing about a problematic negation of art as an autonomous—or relatively autonomous—and therefore critically objectivist sphere of human activity. Were you aware of this theoretical position? Were you aware of differences in outlook between your own attempt to establish a coolly detached, critical art after the Cultural Revolution and a Western postmodernist sense of despair at the Western avant-garde's perceived inability to sustain any sort of critical distance from the lifeworld?

SQ: We were influenced by Dadaism and surrealism. Dadaism is very critical. We were also aware of modernism and postmodernism. Modernism is aesthetic and not spiky. However, Dada is very spiky and difficult to manage. We were closer to Dada and surrealism.

PG: Politicized avant-garde artists in the West, including those associated with Dada, have often been suspicious of conventional aesthetics—especially the notion of beauty (Meecham and Sheldon 2005: 27). They have tended to see aesthetics as something that distances art from life…as something that brings about an ideological sense of false consciousness in relation to actual socio-economic conditions. Hence, attempts by artists associated with the Dada movement to arrive at various forms of anti-art. By negating aesthetic feeling—so the thinking goes—the historical Western avant-gardes would then be able to engage more directly and more critically with modern life. It seems to me that the priorities of 'avant-garde' artists in China during the 1980s were somewhat different from those of Western avant-garde artists during the early twentieth century. Yes, you were critical of the sentimental false consciousness of official Chinese art. However, instead of questioning or abandoning the aesthetic, you attempted to replace the sentimentality of official Chinese art with a new—though still distinctly aestheticized—sense of critical detachment. In some ways this is closer to the strategic return to beauty that has recently taken place as part of international postmodernism than the aggressive critical negativity of the Western historical and neo avant-gardes.

SQ: Yes, you could put it that way. Classical aesthetics can be described as something that is complete, harmonious and distinctive. We did not depart from that framework.

PG: I think that it's also important to recognize that you and I have differing cultural viewpoints on the significance of aesthetic feeling. I understand that you see the sentimental realism of the Sichuan School as beautiful insofar as it can be understood to evoke warm feelings associated with a traditional Chinese belief in the closeness of human beings to nature. For me, however, it isn't at all beautiful. To me it's just kitsch. If we view the aesthetic as something that has the capacity to radically engage the viewer at the level of feeling—that is to say, bring about a radical change in the consciousness of the viewer as a result of its affective impact—then I would have to say that the sentimental realism of the Sichuan school simply leaves me cold.

SQ: So, you would see Luo Zhongli's painting *Father* as anti-aesthetic? That could be because of differences in our cultural backgrounds, which give rise to differing interpretations. When Chinese people look at this work, they feel that they can immerse themselves in feelings of beauty. What do you think of this work?

PG: It's not so much that it's anti-aesthetic from my particular cultural point of view. For me, it's so conventional and so boring that it doesn't engage me affectively at all. It's very much like the kind of painting one sees in conservative commercial galleries in the United Kingdom; a kind of painting that appeals to the sentimentality of an unsophisticated bourgeois audience who have little or no knowledge of, or interest in, critical forms of contemporary art. I have no direct connection to its cultural themes. I understand that you look at it in a different way—that you continue to see it as aesthetic because of its relationship to rural life in China and traditional Chinese notions of the beauty to be found in a close relationship between human beings and nature. I accept that there are differing cultural points of view here.

SQ: Yes, the cultural contexts are different. Within the Chinese artistic field, it's common sense to see *Father* as beautiful; it's an embrace.

PG: Within the existing literature on contemporary Chinese art of the 1980s, the perceived rationalism of the Northern Art Group is often contrasted with the perceived non-rationalism of Xiamen Dada, who can be understood to have adopted a deconstructive approach towards artistic production similar to that of Western Dada (Köppel-Yang 2003: 25). Do you think these characterizations have a relationship to historical differences in regional cultural identity within China? For example, differences between the historical prevalence of Confucian pragmatism in northern China and of the metaphysical irrationalism of Daoism and Chan Buddhism in southern China. During the mid- to late1980s, Huang Yongping, one of the leading members of Xiamen Dada, made the case for an affinity between the deconstructive irrationalism of Dada and Chan Buddhism (Huang 1986: 1; 1989: 30–32, 72).

SQ: I think the work of Xiamen Dada is also rationalist, but in a deeper way. Western irrationality is actually a kind of rationality. It's quite different from the traditional Chinese emphasis on an empathetic or sentimental aesthetic associated with *i-ching*. Chinese culture emphasizes the integration of human beings with nature, which is sentimental and not at all rational in the Western sense. Western irrationality is not sentimental. I think Xiamen Dada made a contribution to the transformation of artistic languages within China by going beyond established forms of painting and sculpture, and the Northern Art Group made more of a contribution to the transformation of cognition. About your question on the influence of regional culture and philosophy on contemporary Chinese art groups, I think the Northern Art Group was principally influenced by Confucianism and Xiamen Dada was greatly influenced by Chan Buddhism. Northern Chinese culture places emphasis on responsibility and heroism.

PG: It seems to me that the regional identity of the Pond Association sits somewhat uncertainly between the two positions you have just described. On the one hand, their work as a group emerges in relation to the rational paintings produced individually by Zhang Peili and Geng Jianyi; hence, their perceived identity as rationalists alongside the Northern Art Group. While, on the other, the group's signature making of immersive, site-specific artworks as well as some of their published statements suggest an affinity with the irrationalism of Daoism and Chan Buddhism.

SQ: Hangzhou was the capital of China during the Song dynasty. It was a place where northern Chinese culture and southern Chinese culture mingled. That's why the paintings of some of the members of the Pond Association are similar to those of the Northern Art Group. At the same time, work by the Pond Association shares some things with Xiamen Dada, especially the group's nihilism and sense of the ridiculous.

PG: One thing I find interesting here is the idea that contemporary art in China is not simply contemporary 'Chinese' art—that is to say, an art defined by its congruence with a single national-cultural identity—but, instead, one whose production and reception is inextricably enmeshed with localized differences in social relations as well as cultural conventions and meanings. That is not to say that contemporary Chinese art can be subdivided simply according to differing regional identities. Rather, it is to assert that contemporary Chinese art is something that has developed and continues to develop as a multiplicity in relation to specific, though historically shifting, circumstances of both time and place—for example, regional differences in climate and geographical setting, or genealogies of cultural inheritance. Indeed, I would go further by arguing that when we look back at the development of contemporary art in China over the last three decades we can see a multiplicity of inheritances, with artists constantly varying the ways in which they interweave differing cultural attitudes, practices and techniques in relation to differing circumstances of time, place and cultural memory.

SQ: Yes, that's right. Artistic creation operates at a micro level. That's why very small differences that ordinary people wouldn't notice can be reflected by artists and their works. Vernacular culture and environment definitely influences the work of artists. The differences between regions can also be at a micro level. However, the differences between contemporary art and traditional art are macro; very obvious. To use a metaphor, these big differences are just like the differences between urban culture and rural culture. The differences between manifestations of contemporary Chinese art in different regions of China are related to differences between the cities in those regions. All of them are part of urban culture, not rural culture.

PG: Let's try to work that through in more detail. When I interviewed Wang Guangyi, one of the things he talked about was a relationship, as he saw it, between the coolness of the work of the Northern Art Group and the Confucian conception of the sublime; something so big, vast or magnificent that it acts as a powerful source of moral authority. Do you think it is possible to identify a resonance between the cool detachment of the work of the Northern Arts Group and the Confucian conception of the sublime as a localized way of conceptualizing aesthetic feeling?

SQ: The 'sublime' and 'magnificence' are synonymous in Chinese culture. Northern Chinese culture emphasizes magnificence, which is a characteristic of Confucian thinking, while southern Chinese culture, which tends to be nihilistic and playful, has Daoist characteristics. The north takes lightness as heaviness, whereas the south considers heaviness as lightness. This difference has something to do with the landscapes of the northern and southern China. The traditional aesthetic of the south and of the southern landscape is beauty while that of the north and the northern landscape is the sublime. As for contemporary artworks, satire and playfulness are often used in both contexts.

PG: When I began to study Chinese art, I made the mistake of assuming that the feelings of immersion—loss of defined subject-object relations—which are often ascribed to traditional forms of Chinese *shan-shui* ink and brush painting and also seem to resonate with the site-specific works of the Pond Association, are coextensive with Chinese aesthetics as a whole. But, I can now see that this sense of immersion is a predominantly southern Chinese conception of aesthetic feeling. The south-eastern Chinese city of Hangzhou is, after all, the place where traditional Chinese *shan-shui* painting was first developed during the Song dynasty (Li 1999: 208–231).

SQ: Yes, it has something to do with the environment. I was born in Changchun in the north-eastern province of Jilin. The northern part of China is very cold and severe—the temperature can fall below −20 or −30 centigrade. The beauty of the northern landscape can only be appreciated from a distance rather than from a position of being immersed.

PG: The notion of distant appreciation resonates strongly with a series of paintings you produced during the 1980s that depict images of endless architectural recession titled *Identity Voice—Rigorous Religious Dialogue* (*Xiangzheng de zhixu xilie* 象征的秩序系列) (Plate 15).

SQ: Yes, it's a vivid visual metaphor. We used images representing the distance between human beings and between human beings and nature to symbolize the distance between cultural cognition and life.

PG: We've spoken here at length about the work of the Northern Art Group and localized ways of conceptualizing aesthetic feeling in northern China; could you say more about the relationship between these localized conceptions and the Western cultural influences, which also informed the work of the Northern Art Group?

SQ: Our works were mainly influenced by the West in terms of their formal construction. For example, *The Death of Marat* by Wang Guangyi is a modification of a Western neoclassical painting. Some of my own works of the 1980s are similar to Wang Guangyi's in this regard.

Though our works are 'Western' from the point of view of their formal construction and their appropriation of a kind of surrealistic sensibility, there's also a serenity that can't be found in relation to a lot of Western works. Western surrealistic works are restless and anxious, whereas our works have a serene feeling which is influenced by Chan Buddhism.

PG: So there are feelings not only of coolness and distance in relation to the work of the Northern Art Group but also of stillness and tranquility; a combination, perhaps, of Confucian attitudes towards aesthetic feeling with the more meditative attitudes of Daoism and Chan Buddhism. Would you see the intellectual position adopted by Northern Art Group—like the Chinese intellectual tradition as a whole—as an interweaving of differing cultural thoughts and practices? (Wang 2009: 3).

SQ: I think most government officials in China are influenced by Confucianism, and most intellectuals and *literati* are influenced by Daoism. Painters and artists are part of the intellectual and *literati* class, so they are influenced too. The spirit of the *literati* is romantic and transcendent. The essence of Chinese painting is *literati* painting. The Rational Painting of contemporary Chinese art can be considered as a new form of *literati* painting or scholar painting. It was often referred to as such in 1985—as being similar to *literati* painting in antiquity. The background to *literati* painting in antiquity was village civilization, whereas the background to scholar painting nowadays is urban civilization.

PG: In the West, contemporary Chinese art has been interpreted in relation to theories associated with, amongst other things, postmodernism, post-colonialism and feminism. Were you aware of these theories during your time in the Northern Art Group? Was your artistic practice influenced by contemporary Western theoretical discourse in any way?

SQ: We were aware of postmodernist and post-colonialist theory during the 1980s; more so postmodernism in the beginning. Our works may have had something to do with postmodernism or post-colonialism. However, what inspired us to create these works was the environment we were in at the time. They were made instinctively and spontaneously rather than by first paying attention to theory. We made our artworks and then with a gradual understanding of some Western theories we realized that there was some kind of relationship between our artworks and Western theories. There was a kind of *mo qi* 默契 (tacit understanding), as Chinese would call it. So, we were not influenced directly by Western theories. It's understandable though that our works have been interpreted through the application of Western theories. Interpretations should be various. There's a saying in China, 'The benevolent see benevolence and the wise see wisdom.' Different people have different points of view. Because of this, people are inspired in diverse ways.

PG: The theorization of contemporary Chinese art is highly problematic. While it would be wrong to dismiss Western theoretical interpretations of contemporary Chinese art entirely out of hand because of the undeniable historical relationship between that art and Western modernist and postmodernist art, it would also be wrong to assume that contemporary Chinese art can only be interpreted meaningfully from a Western theoretical point of view, given the differences in social organization and cultural outlook which pertain to the immediate circumstances of its production and reception within the PRC.

SQ: Yes, I agree. More Western scholars or critics should do field work here in China. Many Western critics simply apply Western theories to works of contemporary Chinese art rather than analysing the particularities of Chinese society and culture.

PG: Was the work of the Northern Arts Group influenced by particular writings, theories or texts—Chinese and/or non-Chinese?

SQ: Yes. For example, *Being and Time* (1927) by Martin Heidegger, *Being and Nothingness: An Essay on Phenomenological Ontology* (1943) by Jean-Paul Sartre, *The Interpretation of Dreams* (1899) by Sigmund Freud and *The Origin and Goal of History* (1953) by Karl Jaspers. One of the most influential books we read was *Thus Spake Zarathustra* (1883–1885) by Nietzsche. Since there were no new printed copies, I read a copied 1930s' version of Nietzsche's works in 1984, which had been translated by Gao Han. As a result, my world perspectives were changed. If we, the Northern Art Group, hadn't read Nietzsche's works, we wouldn't have adopted the idea of the Übermensch. Before we read these philosophical writings, we were influenced by other works of Western literature; for instance, *Jean Christophe* (1904–1912) by Romain Rolland, *Les Confessions* (1782) by Jean-Jacques Rousseau, *Call of the Wild* (1903) by Jack London, *The Old Man and the Sea* (1951) by Ernest Hemingway, *My Life* (1927) by Isadora Duncan. Among these, *Les Confessions* was considered to be a bit rebellious because of its criticism and questioning of civilization.

PG: Many of the books you mention can be understood to embody a Romantic search for transcendence—a striving to exceed conventional limitations.

SQ: The novels I referred to earlier helped stimulate our sensitive feelings. As for the philosophical books we read later on—for instance, Nietzsche's books—they helped us reach another peak; one that we were aiming to reach and that helped us to judge things more clearly. We felt that we were standing on the top of a hill and that our surroundings were small.

PG: Where there any Chinese writings that strongly influenced the members of the Northern Art Group?

SQ: Besides Western books, we also read many Chinese books. For example, books by Laozi and Zhuangzi.

PG: Did the work of the Northern Art Group involve a self-conscious bringing together of ideas from the Chinese literary tradition with others from the Western tradition?

SQ: That's right. Nietzsche emphasizes the power of the Übermensch, while Daoist thought places emphasis on the cultivation of one's body and soul and the enhancement of one's stature.

PG: Given what you have said throughout our conversation, you would appear to hold the view that artists occupy an elevated or elitist position in relation to the rest of society. Is that the case?

SQ: Yes, this notion of an elitist culture has a relationship to Daoism. Actually, Chinese intellectuals and *literati* artists have always been greatly influenced by the romantic side of Daoism. As for government officials and common people, they are more influenced by Confucianism. After all, the tradition of Daoism is a kind of *literati* tradition, or, as I would call it, a 'micro-linguistic tradition.' Traditional Chinese culture is inclined towards humanities.

PG: By elitism, you mean the elitism of the Chinese *literati* tradition?

SQ: What I meant by elitism is having a heart/mind (*xin* 心)[31] that is sensitive enough to feel. However, we might become too reclusive if we only absorb Daoist thought. Daoism seeks to cultivate the heart/mind by paying attention to one's own individual moral uplift, whereas Nietzsche inspires us to radiate our beams outwardly. So the value of Nietzsche is in encouraging us to turn a humanistic ethos into one of the Übermensch.

PG: In other words, during your time with the Northern Art Group you saw Nietzsche's philosophy and Confucianism as providing some sort of foil to the relative introspection and passivity of traditional Chinese *literati* culture?

SQ: Confucianism encourages responsibility and Daoism cultivates our humanistic ethos. Nietzsche encourages us to enlighten the world like the sun.

PG: What influence do you think the work of the Northern Art Group has had on the work of subsequent generations of Chinese contemporary artists?

SQ: The cool ethos of the work of the Northern Art Group brought about a change of artistic styles which may well have had a strong influence on subsequent generations of contemporary Chinese artists. We were the first generation to adopt cold and cool artistic styles.

PG: I'm thinking here, in particular, of the video and film installation artist Yang Fudong 杨福东, whose work, it seems to me, exhibits a cool stylistic and aesthetic detachment similar to that of the work of the Northern Art Group. When I recorded a conversation with him recently, like you, he also spoke about the influence of Chinese aesthetics and of Nietzsche on his work.

SQ: That's right. Yang Fudong's approach is very cool. As some critics suggested at the time, the Rational Painting movement 'froze' the sky. We turned the red, bright colours of the Cultural Revolution into black, white and grey. This quick freezing process in 1985 was very important because it radically changed people's point of view. The artists of Yang's generation were brought up in relation to a cold background, which was quite different from that of my generation. Yes, his works are very cool.

Ka Sang (b. 1961)[32]

Paul Gladston: You were a member of the Northern Art Group during the mid-1980s. How did you come to be involved with the group?

Ka Sang: I became involved with the Northern Art Group because of Shu Qun. I got to know him when I was in my second year at university in Changchun. The name of my university is Jilin Architecture and Engineering College (*Jilin jianzhu gongcheng xueyuan* 吉林建筑工程学院). At the time, in 1983, Shu Qun had just graduated from the Traditional Painting Department of the Luxun Academy of Fine Arts (*Luxun meishu xueyuan* 鲁迅美术学院) in Shenyang[33] and had started working at the Changchun Cultural Centre for Workers. Although I was studying architecture at the university, I liked painting very much. I had been very interested in painting when I was a child, but I had never learned how to paint formally in class. The only time was probably in fine art lessons during my first year at the university, where I was taught how to draw and sketch.

PG: When did you first become involved with the group and when did you leave?

KS: I graduated from university in 1984. For one or two years before and after 1984, I participated in and witnessed the preparation, founding and initial exhibition activities of the Northern Art Group. I didn't participate fully in the activities of the group after I left Changchun for Beijing in 1986. After 1986, I joined in the activities of the group occasionally when I went back to the north of China for holidays. Around 1987, or even later—I can't remember clearly—I took part in the Huangshan Conference, which was the last time I participated in activities organized by Northern Art Group. I joined the group mainly because of Shu Qun, who was a key member and one of the organizers of the group, and someone with whom I had a close personal relationship. I wasn't really that active or consistent in attending the group's activities. The reason I finally withdrew from the group is not because of a change in my interests, but because I couldn't find space for self-development. It was a male environment.

PG: Could you say more about what you did during your time with the Northern Art Group, and what you did after you left the group?

KS: Some members of the Northern Art Group had not studied fine arts. They had a background in poetry and literature instead. There were poets in the group, such as Meng Fanguo and Ba Wei. In the beginning, we talked a lot about literature. 'Misty Poetry' was quite influential at that time. We expressed our feelings initially through literature. We exchanged ideas. We learned from each other and we were inspired by each other. At that time, it was different from nowadays. People couldn't get information through the Internet. Talking to people was the main way to get information. During the 1980s, the atmosphere wasn't as open as it is nowadays and the ways we had to express ourselves were not as diverse as today. So it was common for people to come together in groups and to choose poetry, drawing or painting to express themselves because they are direct forms of expression; whereas today, a lot of people can express their feelings or opinions through the Internet. Gradually, we began to talk more about fine art. Personally, I liked literature very much and it's nice to talk to poets and writers. After 1986, I travelled back to Harbin from Beijing to attend several seminars organized by the group. Most of the time, I accompanied Shu Qun when joining in with the activities of the group. After 1987, I was assigned to work in an architectural design institute to design residential houses, food processing factories and the like. From then on, I was mainly involved in architectural design rather than in the making of art.[34]

PG: What did the Northern Art Group discuss during its meetings?

KS: The discussions probably inspired Shu Qun and Wang Guangyi more than me. They didn't influence me that much. I just wanted to be myself and to paint something I liked.

PG: Did the group have a particular aim, or was it simply a forum in which its members could talk and share their ideas?

KS: In the beginning it was shared interests in literature, philosophy and poetry that brought the group together. But gradually there was a practical goal, which was about painting. Shu Qun liked theories. He raised the concept of 'Cold Culture', (*Handai wenhua* 寒带文化, literally: 'frigid zone culture') which was about northern Chinese culture. Because of the geographical and climatic characteristics of that region, he thought that the people there were comparatively cold. This was probably the reason why the Northern Art Group's paintings were more rational than other groups.

PG: How did this idea of 'Cold Culture' influence the group as a whole? What was the group seeking to achieve by adopting this idea?

KS: The group was trying to form a unified style among its members. The group also wanted to make an impact through the exhibition of its work.

PG: So, there was an attempt to unify the group around a shared artistic vision; one rooted in the particular geographical locality of north-eastern China. Shu Qun and Wang Guangyi's paintings at that time clearly conform to the notion of a cold, rationalist aesthetic. The handling of the paint is relatively flat—it avoids the use of conspicuous brushstrokes—and their palette is very limited in its use of colour, which is usually cool and monochromatic. They also depict vast, apparently limitless spaces, similar in feel to the landscapes of north-eastern China. Much of your own work at that time doesn't seem to conform to this shared aesthetic. Your paintings are rather more expressionistic in style; they make use of obvious brushstrokes and of strongly contrasting tones and colours—they are discernibly hotter in temperature than those of Shu Qun and Wang Guangyi. They also involve intimate representations of everyday events rather than depictions of big abstracted spaces. Did you see your work as distinct from that of others within the group?

KS: I painted one or two pieces of work which catered to the demands of the Northern Art Group's first biennial exhibition, which was held in 1987 (Plate 16). But most of my paintings at the time were related to daily life. A good example would be the painting of people boating on a river (Plate 17). The painting was made in 1984 or 1985 after I came back from one of our group activities; we went boating together on Songhua River.

PG: Was your aim simply to depict this event or did you have another purpose in mind?

KS: I didn't think too much. The figures in the painting represent some of the members of the Northern Art Group at the time; that's all. I was trying to recall the scene of the group event.

PG: What interests me here, are the apparent stylistic influences on your work. First of all, your approach, the style of the image and the way that you have handled the paint, is very reminiscent of German expressionist painting of the early twentieth century. Was that something you were aware of at the time when you made the painting?

KS: I wasn't conscious of it. When I saw some paintings that touched me, I might have unconsciously learned their styles. I seldom read books related to fine arts before I met Shu Qun. I read more after I met him because he had a collection of books, such as *World of Fine Arts* (*Shijie meishu* 世界美术)[35] and *Jiangsu Pictorial* (*Jiangsu huakan*). I was so excited after I read them, and I think I was influenced by them.

PG: Could we now look at one of the photographs you have of the Northern Art Group's 1987 exhibition? It shows one of Wang Guangyi's paintings (Plate 18). I'd like to discuss your painting of the boating trip in relation to this painting by Wang Guangyi. Are you conscious that the way you have depicted the figures in your painting is similar to the way in which the figures are depicted in Wang Guangyi's painting. Were you influenced by Wang Guangyi's stylistic approach, or might he have been influenced by yours? Is influence within the group something you were aware of, or talked about at the time?

KS: We painted similar paintings at a similar time. For example, Wang Guangyi and I both made paintings titled *Shadow* during 1985. Wang Guangyi painted his version first…before I got to know him. We didn't discuss the paintings beforehand…before we painted them. But afterwards we saw each other's paintings. We talked about the similarities and thought we might have drawn similar figures by coincidence. Both of us exhibited our paintings titled *Shadow* during the biennial exhibition of the Northern Art Group in 1987.

PG: Do you still have any of the paintings you made for the Northern Art Group exhibition in 1987?

KS: No. My works were lost after the exhibition. I don't have the original works, only some photographs. When the Ullens Centre for Contemporary Art staged the 1985 New Wave show in Beijing in 2007, they used some of my photographs instead of the actual works.

PG: One of the interesting things about the 1985 New Wave exhibition at the Ullens foundation is that the work of only two women artists was included in that show. There were rather more women artists involved in the 1985 New Wave and in the work of contemporary art groups at that time. What did you feel about the exhibition's effective marginalization of women artists? Did the 1985 New Wave exhibition fairly represent contemporary Chinese art at that time, given that the vast majority of the works included in the show were made by men?

KS: It's difficult to say whether it's fair or not, but it might not be comprehensive.

PG: If you were organizing an exhibition of the work of the 1985 New Wave, how would you go about it?

KS: I would probably try to cover all sides; for example, present all of the works made by the members of the Northern Art Group at that time, regardless of whether those members had gained wider recognition or not.

PG: What would be achieved by including the work of these other members? What difference would it make?

KS: It would be a better representation of the historical facts…but, of course, these things are always selective.

PG: I wrote a critical review of the 1985 New Wave show, which was published in the journal *Yishu* (Gladston 2008a: 98–104). In that review I argued that the exhibition's organizers had constructed a myth about the contemporary Chinese art of the 1980s by focusing on the 'heroic' efforts of a predominantly male group of artists—a myth not dissimilar to that associated with American Abstract Expressionism. I also argued that, in doing so, the exhibition's organizers were helping to confirm the reputation of a select group of artists and the value of their work on the international art market at the expense of a richer, more critically searching analysis of historical events.

KS: In China during the 1980s, the principal purpose of making art was to bring about cultural change, because there was no art market. In fact, it was illegal to sell art commercially at that time. Just after the adoption of the opening-up and reform policy in 1978, the atmosphere was still quite spiritual, and it became more and more materialistic and more practical afterwards. Personally, I think painting expresses the inner world better when there is an emphasis on spirituality. If we just pander to the international art market, making art becomes a way to make a living and to make profits; it obscures our true feelings.

PG: During the last 30 years, far more men have established careers as contemporary artists in China than women. The careers of talented women artists have often been short-lived. Why do you think this is the case? Why has it been easier for men to establish artistic careers in China than women?

KS: This happens not only in the field of art. It's the same in other fields. It seems that it's easier for men to be successful in all fields. The reason for that is that men are good at expressing themselves—in promoting themselves—while women are, by comparison, too shy to do that. Men are also more competitive.

PG: Is there still work to do in opening up a bigger space for women artists in China? Do you think it's important to establish a Chinese society in which there is genuine equality of self-expression between men and women?

KS: Yes, I think we need that. Generally speaking, I don't think women are as aggressive as men in fighting for things. They tend to wait quietly. This is the same in the natural world.

Notes

1 For an English translation of Shu's 'The Spirit of the Northern Art Group,' see Fei (2007: 31).
2 For an English translation of 'An Explanation of the Northern Art Group,' see Shu (2010: 79–82).
3 For an English translation of 'We – Participants of the '"85 Art Movement'" see Wang 2010: 78–79.

4   Gombrich's use of the term 'paradigm shift' in relation to the visual arts is derived from Thomas Kuhn's original use of the term in his book *The Structure of Scientific Revolution* (1962) to describe abrupt, non-evolutionary changes in Western scientific thinking (Gombrich 1979: 184–188).

5   In traditional Chinese culture, there is no term whose meaning corresponds exactly to the Western concept of the sublime. The Confucian notion of '*da*' (big or vast) is, however, broadly equivalent. In the *Analects*, Confucius uses the term *da* to praise the emperor Yao (Confucius, *The Analects*, VIII 1979, 19). According to the present-day Chinese philosopher, Liu Yuanyuan, da is used by Confucius in this context to signify the limitlessness of Yao's power which, he asserts, can be understood to instill feelings of horror and fear in the viewer. In contrast to a Western Kantian conception of the sublime, these feelings of horror and fear are not overcome through the intervention of reason, but instead persist in making the viewer hold the object of vision in awe and veneration (Liu 2006: 69–70).

6   For an English language translation of Wang Guangyi's paper 'On Liquidating Humanist Enthusiasm,' see Köppel-Yang (2003: 203).

7   This is an edited version of a conversation recorded in a coffee bar in Beijing on 11 January 2008.

8   Following the Tian'anmen incident of 4 June 1989, there was a sustained crackdown on unofficial organizations throughout Chinese society. As a result, for a while it was no longer possible for 'avant-garde' artists to exhibit their work publicly or to come together openly in groups.

9   According to the Asia Society website, the Northern Art Group first came together in March 1985 (Anon. http://www.asiasociety.org). A catalogue accompanying the 1985 New Wave: the Birth of Chinese Contemporary Art exhibition, which was staged at the Ullens Centre for Contemporary Art in Beijing in 2007, states that the Northern Art Group was first established in Harbin in January 1985 (Fei 2007: 30). Smith also states that the Northern Art Group first came together in 1985 (Smith 2006: 20). Köppel-Yang identifies the founding of the Northern Art Group as having taken place in July 1984 (Köppel-Yang, 2003: 60).

10   The Anti-Spiritual Pollution Campaign, initiated in October 1983, came to an end in February of 1984. As a result, there was an increasing liberalization of attitudes towards unofficial forms of cultural production within the PRC.

11   The Zhejiang Academy of Fine arts, which is now known as the China Academy of Fine Arts, was established in 1928 and is regarded as one of the PRC's leading art institutions.

12   A catalogue accompanying the 1985 New Wave: the Birth of Chinese Contemporary Art exhibition at the Ullens Centre for Contemporary Art in Beijing lists the main members of the Northern Art Group as Shu Qun, Wang Guangyi, Ren Jian and Liu Yan (Fei 2007: 30). Ren Jian was born in Harbin in 1955 and graduated from Luxun Academy of Fine Arts, Shenyang in 1983. Liu Yan was born in Harbin in 1960 and graduated from the Department of Physics at Jilin University, Changchun, in 1982.

13   In June 1960, the artist Wu Guanzhong wrote an article titled 'On the Beauty of Form in Painting' (*Huihua de xingshi mei* 绘画的形式美). The content of this article diverged

strongly from the established conventions of Maoist socialist-realism by asserting that the principle value of painting lay in its formal beauty rather than its capacity to represent reality, that form should consequently not be subordinated to content and that content should be made to coincide with form. Understandably, this article remained unpublished during Mao's lifetime. In 1978, a new edition of Mao's *Letters on Poetry* was published, which included writings on the positive role which *xingxiang siwei* 形象思维(image-thinking) might play in the process of artistic creation. The publication of these ideas opened up the possibility of a renewed debate on the relationship between form and content in official Chinese art. This debate was initiated by the publication of Wu Gaunzhong's article 'On the Beauty of Form in Painting,' which appeared in the magazine *Art* (*Meishu zazhi*) in May 1979. The publication of Wu's article led to the publication of a string of other articles between 1979 and 1986, including follow-up articles by Wu in 1980 and 1981 as well as official rebuttals by Jiang Feng and Feng Xiangyi (Wu 1979: 33–35; 1980: 37–39; 1981: 52–54).

14   Debates on the subject of postmodernism were initiated within the PRC by the publication of an essay by Shao Dazhen 邵大箴 in the journal *Waiguo meixue* 外国美学 (Foreign Aesthetics) in February 1985. In this essay, which was later republished in *Zhongguo meishu bao* (*Fine Arts in China*) in November 1986, Shao argued that the use of the term postmodernism to describe artistic trends in the West since the 1960s was an extreme view reflecting a 'unilateral development of modernism.'

15   This statement by Shu Qun argues that 'the cultures of the West and the East have collapsed and that a new branch of culture has emerged instead: the birth of the Northern Civilisation.' The statement also argues that 'the world's cultural history and the West's cultural center have tended to move north – both in Northern Europe and Northern Asia' and 'that the inherent tendency of moving north illustrates the inherent tendency of strong peoplemoving to areas of conflict' embodying 'a healthy spirit of humanism.' See Shu (1985: 1). For an English translation, see Fei (2007: 31).

16   Within the PRC, there had been an established connection between indigenous romantic sentiment and official socialist-realist art since the late 1950s. In 1957, Mao Zedong issued a slogan: 'revolutionary romanticism combined with revolutionary realism' (*Geming xianshizhuyi yu geming langmanzhuyi xiang jiehe* 革命现实主义与革命浪漫主义相结合) This slogan supported an official directive that while art in China should continue to follow socialist-realist principles imported from the Soviet Union, there should also be an insistence on the romanticism of traditional Chinese culture. The combination of romanticism and realism persisted into the 1980s, informing the sentimental aestheticism of the Sichuan School.

17   *Zhongguo meishu bao* (*Fine Arts in China*), which was launched at the Cultural Palace of Nationalities in Beijing on 3 June 1985, was published by the Visual Arts Research Institute (*Zhongguo yishu yanjiuyuan meishu yanjiusuo* 中国艺术研究院美术研究所) of the Chinese Arts Research Academy. The publication was closed on the instruction of the Chinese authorities in 1989.

18   This statement by Shu Qun argues that 'the cultures of the West and the East have collapsed and that a new branch of culture has emerged instead: the birth of the Northern Civilisation.' The statement also argues that 'the world's cultural history and the West's cultural center have

tended to move north – both in Northern Europe and Northern Asia' and 'that the inherent tendency of moving north illustrates the inherent tendency of strong people moving to areas of conflict' embodying 'a healthy spirit of humanism.' See Shu (1985: 1). For an English translation, see Fei (2007: 31).

19 *Jiangsu huakan* (*Jiangsu Pictorial*) has been published each month since its initiation in 1974.

20 This statement by Wang Guangyi advocates 'the magnificence of humanism and the harmony of nature' as well as calling for a return to a 'sublime and healthy spirit' in art (Wang 1986a: 33). For an English translation, see Fei (2007: 26).

21 According to a contemporaneous report by Gao Minglu, the artists taking part in the exhibition were Shu Qun, Ni Qi, Liu Yan, Ka Sang, Wang Yalin and Wang Guangyi (Gao 1987).

22 This supports the notion that the aim of the group was to elevate Chinese society through the engendering of feelings of sublimity.

23 The term 'Rational Painting' was first used by the curator and art critic Gao Minglu in relation to the work of the Northern Art Group during a discussion accompanying the Northern Art Group Biennial Exhibition at the Jilin Art Academy in Changchun in February 1987. Participants in the discussion included Gao Minglu, Zhui Qingsheng and Zhou Yan as well as members of the Northern Art Group. During the discussion, Gao reportedly sought to justify his use of the term Rational Painting in relation to the work of the Northern Art Group by contending that 'to express philosophical propositions or beliefs through formality of feeling is a kind of metaphysical statement' (Gao 1987: 98).

24 This bifurcated organizational structure is similar to that used by the CCP to administer artistic production at times during the Maoist period.

25 As Koppel-Yang indicates, the belief that Chinese civilization could be rebuilt through the promotion of a sublime-elevated spirit coincides with the humanist enthusiasm that dominated China's cultural climate during the 1980s (Köppel-Yang 2003: 25).

26 This is an edited version of a conversation recorded at the artist's studio in Chengdu on 7 March 2008. A Mandarin Chinese version of this conversation was previously published in Shu Qun (2009: 484–495).

27 Ancient China's Eastern Zhou dynasty (*Dongzhou* 东周) (770 BCE–256 BCE) is conventionally divided into two periods: The Spring and Autumn Period (*Chun qiu*) (722 BCE–476 BCE), and The Warring States Period (475 BCE–221 BCE). The Warring States Period precedes the Qin dynasty (Qín 秦) (221 BCE–206 BCE), China's first imperial dynasty.

28 The classical scholar Oswyn Murray also identifies the dual influence of Ancient Greek and Hebrew civilization on modern Western society and culture (Murray 1986: 186–203).

29 Here Shu is almost certainly referring to Rabindranath Tagore's novel *The Home and the World* (1916), which addresses the author's struggle to reconcile the influence of Western culture and localized resistance to that culture in his homeland of Bengal. Tagore was a major influence on modern Chinese cultural thinking during the early twentieth century.

30 According to Köppel-Yang, the paintings by Zhang Peili and Geng Jianyi to which Shu Qun refers here can be understood to 'symbolize the alienation of the individual in the urban centres impregnated by Deng Xiaoping's modernization program' (Köppel-Yang 2003: 61).

31 The Chinese word *xin*, which is usually translated into English as 'heart', is conventionally understood within a Chinese cultural context to signify an uncertain relationship between heart and mind (or soul) and therefore an indeterminate coming together of feeling and cognition.

32 This is an edited version of a conversation recorded at Ka Sang's home in Beijing on 7 November 2008.

33 Shu Qun graduated from the Luxun Academy of Fine Arts in 1982.

34 Within the PRC, the assigning of individuals *to danwei* (work units) continued into the 1990s.

35 *Shijie meishu* (*World Art*), which was published by the Central Academy of Fine Arts in Beijing, was established in 1979.

The Pond Association (*Chi she* 池社)

The Pond Association was formed in the south-eastern Chinese city of Hangzhou,[1] sometime between March and May 1986, by five artists who had recently graduated from the Zhejiang Academy of Fine Arts—Zhang Peili 张培力, Geng Jianyi 耿建翌, Song Ling 宋陵, Wang Qiang 王强 and Bao Jianfei 包剑斐—and a self-taught writer and artist Cao Xuelei 曹学雷. Previously, the graduate members of the group had belonged to the Zhejiang Youth Creation Group (*Zhejiang qingnian chuangzuo she* 浙江青年创作社), a short-lived collective that came together under the leadership of Zhang Peili to organize an exhibition of contemporary Chinese art titled '1985 New Space' (*Bawu xin kongjian* 85 新空间), which had opened in Hangzhou in December 1985. The 1985 New Space exhibition, which included some of the first installation works to be produced and exhibited within the PRC, was a major influence on the development of contemporary Chinese art during the latter part of the 1980s, providing impetus and encouragement to the wider development of the 1985 New Wave.

Following the 1985 New Space exhibition, Zhang Peili, Geng Jianyi, Song Ling, Wang Qiang and Bao Jianfei decided to build on the work of the Zhejiang Youth Creation Group by founding a new smaller group that they hoped would support them in the making and exhibiting of art outside the PRC's official party system. This new group, which was eventually named The Pond Association, was, for the most part, little more than a talking shop or social club, whose members continued to produce artworks independently of one another. Nevertheless, much of the Pond Association's reputation rests on three experimental artworks that were produced collectively by the group between June and November 1986: first, a site-specific work, titled *No. 1—Yang Style Tai Chi Series* (*Zuopin yi hao—Yang shi taiji xilie* 作品一号-杨式太极系列), involving large-scale paper cut-outs of figures representing traditional *tai chi* poses that were pasted along a wall opposite the Zhejiang Academy of Fine Arts on Nanshan Road in Hangzhou on 3 June 1986 (Plate 19); second, a performance, often referred to as *Wrapping Up—King and Queen* (*Baoza-guowang yu huanghou* 包扎—国王与王后), in which Zhang Peili and Geng Jianyi posed as living sculptures tightly wrapped from head to foot in newspaper at a private event, staged at or near an artist's studio in Luoyang, Henan Province, on 2 November 1986 (Plate 20); and third, another site-specific work known as *No. 2—Strollers in the Green Space* (*Zuopin er hao—Lüse kongjian zhong de xingzhe* 作品二号-绿色空间里的行者), made up of large paper cut-outs of running figures that were suspended from trees in a green space known as *Wan song lin* 望松林 near Hangzhou's West Lake on 4 November 1986 (Plate 21).

As a declaration distributed privately by the Pond Association in 1986 and the conversations with members of the group published here indicate, the collective vision that lead to the production of these site-specific works and the performance by Geng and Zhang was based on three interrelated beliefs: first, that artists should produce artworks in response to internal needs rather than a desire to fulfil existing social and/or ideological requirements; second, that the process of making an artwork is more important than its existence as a concrete outcome/artifact in the service of social and/or ideological requirements; and third, that artists should seek to make artworks that bring art and life together by immersing the artist in everyday social situations.

Furthermore, during the mid-1980s, Geng and Zhang began to develop a profound scepticism with regard to the capacity of language to communicate authoritative meanings which would go on to inform much of their work as artists after the dissolution of the Pond Association in 1989. Traces of this scepticism can be discerned in relation to *No. 1—Yang Style Tai Chi Series*, which is very much open to interpretation as a playfully deft satire of the use of *dazibao*; a view borne out by the conversations with Song Ling and Wang Qiang presented here in which both draw attention to strong formal similarities between *Chi she*'s collectively produced work and the use of *dazibao* (big character posters) as a public means of communication during the Cultural Revolution. Against the background of these beliefs, works produced collectively by members of the Pond Association can therefore be understood to have a strong affinity with those produced historically by the Western avant-gardes insofar as both not only involve a resistance to artistic convention as well as an intention that art should engage as directly as possible with everyday life but also what might be interpreted as a critically deconstructive attitude towards the production of meaning.

Unlike much of the work of the Western political avant-gardes, however, it is by no means clear to what extent that produced collectively by the Pond Association could be described as overtly political/revolutionary in intent. As the conversations with members of the group published here attest, while members the Pond Association were sensitive to prevailing social and political issues within the PRC and beyond, they did not choose to adopt an explicitly political stance in relation to the public staging of their collectively produced works. Nor, despite contemporaneous claims by the Dutch critic Hans van Dijk, who was living in Hangzhou at the time (Berghuis 2008: 50), did the group seek to engage in direct/violent confrontation with governmental authorities and established institutions. This political reticence and avoidance of any direct/violent confrontation with authority may, of course, reflect continuing concerns within the group over the consequences of dissent within the politically suppressive context of the PRC during the 1980s. However, it can also be interpreted as an oblique form of resistance to the still immanent and pervasively controlling presence of Maoist ideology during the decade following the adoption of Deng's reforms.

Doubts of this sort are less justifiable in relation to work produced individually by some members of the Pond Association after 1986. Since the mid-1980s, Geng and Zhang have drawn consistently on the example of the site-specific and performance experiments of the Pond Association to produce works that, while still understandably ambiguous in their significance, nevertheless have a discernibly critical relationship with society and politics. Consider here, for example, Zhang's video work *30x30* (1988), which shows the artist in the process of intermittently smashing and repairing a mirror (Plate 22), as well as his more recent video installation *A Gust of Wind* (*Zeng feng* 阵风) (2008), which involves the simulated destruction of a well-appointed domestic interior by a violent storm (Plate 23). Both of these can be interpreted as signifying the persistent threat of disorder in relation to ideologically grounded assertions of stability and continuity (Gladston 2011c).

Although the work produced collectively by the Pond Association amounted to only two site-specific works and one performance work, it is important to note that members of the group established a critical profile within the PRC initially because of paintings produced individually by Geng and Zhang during the mid-1980s, such as Zhang's *Mid-Summer Swimmers (Zhongxia de yongzhe* 仲夏的泳者), 1985 (Plate 24), which were seen by critics as part of the artistic tendency known as Rational Painting, as well as their contribution to the staging of the 1985 New Space exhibition, which included a ground-breaking Beuys-like installation by Wang Qiang, included in the 1985 New Space exhibition titled 'The Start of the Second Movement of the 5th Symphony' (*Di wu jiaoxiangyue di'er yuezhang kaitou de rouban* 第五交响乐第二乐章开头的柔版) (Plate 24). The key text in this regard is an essay by the critic Shi Jiu, titled 'On New Space and the Pond Association' (*Gunyu xin kongjian he 'Chi she'* 关于新空间和池社), which was published in *Meishu sichao* 美术思潮 (*The Trend of Art Thought*) in 1987 (Shi 1987).[2]

To some extent the inclusion of paintings by Geng and Zhang alongside those of the Northern Art Group within the category of Rational Painting is a justifiable one given that they both share in the use of simplified forms and non-expressive approaches to the application of paint. However, the underlying intention of rational paintings produced by Geng and Zhang and those produced by the Northern Art Group are very different. While the Northern Art Group sought, for the most part, to evoke a sublime art detached from everyday phenomena, Zhang and Geng's work, though formally abstracted, depicts closely observed scenes from everyday urban life that nevertheless evoke a critical sense of alienation. Despite claims to the contrary by the originator Gao Minglu, the term Rational Painting should not therefore be seen as a coherent stylistic category but as one encompassing formal similarities and contrasting intentions. Moreover, care should be taken in describing the Northern Art Group and the Pond Association as both being rational in intent given that the latter's belief that art and life should be brought more closely together has a distinct affinity with the deconstructive intentions of the Western avant-gardes, which was very much absent as part of the early development of the Northern Art Group.

The Pond Association's particular sense of rationality is, perhaps, better interpreted as a state of cool, non-desiring objectivity arrived at, somewhat paradoxically—as the group's declaration indicates—through (what would be seen in Western terms as) a decidedly non-rationalist or immersive blurring of subject-object boundaries. The Pond Association's approach to the making of artworks can thus be understood to have a strong conceptual affinity with three aspects of traditional, non-rationalist Chinese cultural thought and practice: first, the Buddhist notion that enlightenment (*satori*) can be achieved through non-desiring meditative states; second, traditional Chinese *shan-shui* painting where the absence of any strict perspective geometry or unequivocal visual depth cues encourages a spatially, temporally and aesthetically indeterminate relationship between the viewer and the viewed associated with the aesthetic concept of *i-ching* (Jullien 2004: 35–39); and third, the concept of 'tracklessness'—as expounded in chapter 27 of the *Daodejing* 道德经—where 'reality' is viewed as an abstraction shuttling somewhere between subjectivity and objectivity (the limitless and the limited) and 'knowledge' as something that arises out of an active and constantly unfolding relationship between subjects and objects (Mainusch 2006: 141–42)— all of which is commensurate with *Chi she*'s reported desire to create a style redolent of China's historical Southern School of Chan Buddhism (Köppel-Yang 2003: 61).

As such, the Pond Association's stated approach to the collective making of site-specific artworks can also be thought of as having an affinity with the sublime/immersive—cool/ depthless spaces characteristic of Western postmodernism (Jameson 1992: 38–45). However, as I have pointed out elsewhere, there are significant grounds for caution in arriving at the view that there is an absolute correspondence between these historically and spatially differing cultural positions (Gladston 2008b: 63–69).

Conversations with members of the Pond Association

Zhang Peili (b. 1957)[3]
Paul Gladston: When and where did the Pond Association (*Chi she*) first come together as a group?

Zhang Peili: It was here in Hangzhou in May 1986, or perhaps a little bit earlier—maybe even around March or April. The Pond Association was not a group with a clear or explicit structure; in fact, it was very loose. We didn't have a fixed place of work or an office of our own. We held our meetings in various places.

PG: When did the activities of the group come to an end?

ZP: Actually, we never discussed it. We almost began to think about bringing the group to an end when we first got together [laughs]. But, basically the group's activities came to an end in 1989, after the China/Avant-Garde exhibition in Beijing. Around that time, one member of the group, Song Ling, went abroad to Australia and another, Bao Jianfei, moved to Shenzhen. Another member of the group, Cao Xuelei, was assigned a job as a dispatcher at the North Railway Station in Hangzhou. We simply lost touch with him after that. Some gave up their careers as artists, while others stopped making art for a time before starting again shortly afterwards. Consequently, the Pond Association has not held any meetings since 1989.

PG: Is the name, the Pond Association, the only one we should use in this context? At least one source refers to the group as '1985 New Space' (*Bawu xin kongjian* 85新空间) (Tong 2005: 21).

ZP: Yes, it's the only one. 1985 New Space was the name of the exhibition that led to the formation of the Pond Association. After I graduated from the Oil Painting Department of the Zhejiang Academy of Fine Arts in 1984—which was the same year as the staging of the Sixth National Art Exhibition (*Diliu jie quanguo meizhan* 第六届全国美展) in Beijing—I was assigned to a teaching job in a polytechnic school known as the Hangzhou Crafts School (*Hangzhou gongyi meishu xuexiao* 杭州工艺学校).[4] Later, I was seconded to the Zhejiang Association of Fine Arts where I was asked to organize an exhibition of young artists. I had classmates and friends who had recently graduated from the Zhejiang Academy. They included graduates of the academy, such as Geng Jianyi and Song Ling, who had graduated in 1985, as well as Zhai Li and Bao Jianfei, who had graduated earlier. We got together and called ourselves the Zhejiang Youth Creation Group (*Zhejiang qingnian chuangzuo she* 浙江青年创作社). This group began to discuss issues related to Scar Art and the work of the Sichuan School, both of which were prominent in China at the time, as well as similar paintings by the American artist Andrew Wyeth. We wanted to do something new—something different from the official art exhibited at the Sixth National Art Exhibition—both in terms of form and content. We also discussed unofficial exhibitions by groups such as the Stars and the Same Generation Painting Association (*Tong shidai huihua xiehui* 同世代绘画学会).[5] At the end of 1985, the Zhejiang Youth Creation Group staged a group exhibition called 1985 New Space in an exhibition hall on Nanshan road in Hangzhou.[6] At that time, quite a few people were involved, about 20 or 30.[7] We found that the artists involved in that larger group had many different ideas and interests as well as attitudes towards the making of art. Actually, the Zhejiang Youth Creation Group wasn't really a coherent organization; we came together temporarily for one exhibition and we didn't all share the same ideas. After the 1985 New Space exhibition, a number of the artists who had participated in the exhibition discovered that they did have certain things in common. So they got together to plan other events and activities. That's how the Pond Association first came together. After the 1985 New Space exhibition, some of the artists who took part in the exhibition went on to form the Pond Association.

PG: What were the aims of the Pond Association?

ZP: We had a discussion about what to do after the 1985 New Space exhibition. At that time we began to have doubts and raised questions about domestic attitudes towards the making of art within China. We began to think of Scar Art and the work of the Sichuan School as artificial or mannered. We thought that we should find alternative ways of expressing ourselves in relation to our own particular environment and background in Hangzhou, which was different from Sichuan. We wanted to emphasize the 'here and now', rather than pursue a particular style or sentiment.

PG: Were the aims of the Pond Association written down? Were they published?

ZP: Yes. We wrote a declaration, but it was poetic and obscure rather than constructive in tone. We drafted and discussed the declaration, made some modifications and then printed it out using an early form of oil-based printer. We had to type the declaration out by hand and print it using the oil-based printer because there were no computers at that time. This is our declaration:

The Declaration of the Pond Association

Art is a 'pond',
We rely on carbohydrates to live.
It's not because we would like to be like this,
But we have to rely on carbohydrates…

We are eager to purify our mind properly,
Our thoughts are flowing and vague.

Have you ever experienced a rational impulse?
The moment of immersion makes people intoxicated.
The moment of resurgence is a kind of 'enlightenment'.

The result is not so important,
However, the seeds are sprouting.[8]

The declaration wasn't published at the time…it wasn't reported in a newspaper or magazine. It was perhaps in June 1986 that some reports about the activities of the Pond Association first began to emerge. They were related to a collective work named *No. 1—Yang Style Tai Chi Series* that we had just completed. We made big paper cut-outs of figures in different *tai chi* poses and pasted onto a wall opposite the Zhejiang Academy of Art in Hangzhou. *Art* magazine reported the work, and so it was communicated nationwide to our friends in the Chinese artworld and to the Chinese media (Zhu 1986).

PG: Could you say more about the intended significance of the declaration?

ZP: The declaration emphasized the concept of immersion—like someone dunking themselves in water during the summer. In our view, being immersed in the process of making a work of art was far more important than the finished result. Actually, we emphasized two points. One was that the process of making a work of art is more important than the outcome. We thought that if we dispensed with the idea of an outcome, then our art would become more meaningful. The other was that we thought art should be non-utilitarian. Actually, historically speaking, utility has always had a lot to do with art. Even when art isn't commercial, it's utilitarian in other ways. Historically, art was a product that served the interests of religious ritual and political ideology. We felt that this utilitarian aspect was harmful; that it drew attention away from the process of artistic creation and what that might bring to people. When new art (*xin meishu* 新美术) started in China after 1979, it faced the same question. While the new art in China differed from the old in a variety of ways, it still involved the pursuit of utility as part of a conventional approach towards art-making. By emphasizing the concept of immersion we wanted to blur the boundary between art and society as well as that between the professional and the amateur. Immersion should not, however, be thought of here as self-intoxication. It's not simply a matter of subjectivity…or a lack of objectivity. We believed that art should have a connection with society. We wanted it to be a pure thing; a pure process and pure experience similar to an act of religious meditation. Another point is that we saw immersion in the process of artistic creation as something similar to the destruction of art; in other words, by merging art into society and social life, art could become part of life rather than existing in a closed state as before. Although it may not always be obvious when looking at our work, we felt that art should have a relevance to daily life within society. We thought that this function was of great importance. That's why the Pond Association staged artworks in public spaces. One passage from the Pond Association's declaration may best represent our ideas:

We rely on carbohydrates to live.
It's not because we would like to be like this,
But we have to rely on carbohydrates.

The general meaning of this passage is that we should do things not out of want but out of necessity. In other words, art should respond to internal demands or needs. If one does things out of want…out of desire, one focuses on utility and its external causes. One might behave like this because it's useful or profitable to do so. If one does things out of necessity, because one has internal needs, the outcome is different. The process of immersion in art we referred to in our declaration relates to bodily needs. Supposing one feels cold—that results in a need… one has a need for clothes in order to keep warm, otherwise, one may freeze to death. Supposing someone wears clothes to look good—that's a want. So, it's different. From our point of view, art could be judged in relation to whether it was made in response to internal needs or external influences. As for immersion, we wanted to suggest that everyone's experience of art is different. We also wanted to suggest that everyone needs the psychological relaxation provided by art— like the experience of bathing in warm water—because human beings are exhausted by want.

In recent years, the tendency towards utility has become increasingly prominent in relation to contemporary Chinese art. But I think that at least some artists continue to face these questions in a serious way and to set their own interests aside.[9]

PG: Why did you call the group the Pond Association?

ZP: I've forgotten exactly how we got this name, perhaps it came about accidentally. Before we thought of the name and wrote the declaration, we held numerous parties where we chatted and drank tea. Then, suddenly, we thought of the name. I can't remember the first person who said it. Anyway, we all liked the name. The Chinese word *chi* means a 'pond' or 'pool.' But in the context of the name, the Pond Association, it's not so concrete. It refers to the concept of immersion. *She*, which means 'association,' signifies communication. Anyone can dip freely into the pond—to some extent at least.

PG: Does the use of the word 'pond' and the concept of immersion have a relationship to the Pond Association's immediate geographical surroundings—to Hangzhou and the famous West Lake?

ZP: Maybe it's because of the location, as you suggest. As you know, southern China is full of water; rivers, canals and lakes. That's not the case in northern China. We all lived in Hangzhou, so water meant a lot to us. I was born here.

PG: What were the group's artistic and intellectual influences? Are there particular artworks, writings, actions or theories that directly influenced the group's development?

ZP: At the time, there was no particular starting point or formative intellectual influence on the group's activities. Looking back, I now realize that the Pond Association was more like an attitude than a coherent group or organization. To be frank, as a group, we just wanted to have the opportunity to discuss certain issues together—to raise questions and doubts and to figure out problems. The Pond Association did not want to influence others. That was not our intention. Sometimes we had fun together; playing *Go* 围棋 (Chinese chess), enjoying tea and even watching movies together. Sometimes we made artworks together or talked about art, sometimes we didn't.

PG: How many people were involved in or associated with the group and what role did they play?

ZP: No more than ten people—maybe six key members. Most group members were artists who had graduated from the Zhejiang Academy of Fine Arts, including myself, Song Ling, Wang Qiang, Geng Jianyi and Bao Jianfei. As I mentioned before, there was also a member called Cao Xuelei.[10] He didn't attend the Zhejiang Academy of Fine Arts. He worked on the railways. He was mainly interested in philosophy and literature and often went to the Party School Library near the railway station. He read a lot of books. He was also interested in music and attempted to write some experimental novels. Cao Xuelei was a self-taught artist who made drawings as a way of relaxing during the hot summer weather; you have to understand that there was no air conditioning in China at that time. He was a very important influence on both 1985 New Space and the Pond Association.

PG: Did the membership of the group change?

ZP: No. Everything proceeded naturally. We didn't press anyone to join or to leave the group. It all depended on them. Actually, we didn't think of the Pond Association as a formal organization. If we heard that someone had made a good artwork, we might invite that person to join in with our discussions. We never formally asked anyone if they would like to join the group or whether they would like to be asked to join. Such things never happened.

PG: Could you say more about the relationships between the various members of the group?

ZP: Basically, apart from Cao Xuelei, we were all classmates at the Zhejiang Academy of Art in Hangzhou. We were all of a similar age, born in the late 1950s or early 1960s; some maybe five or six years older than the others. Consequently, we seldom made plans in a serious way—most of the time we just chatted and enjoyed drinking tea together.

PG: Where there any women members or associates of the group? Did they have an equal standing with the male members of the group? Also, what role did they play within the group?

ZP: Yes, we had one female member, Bao Jianfei. She was an artist who had graduated from the Zhejiang Academy of Art at the same time as the rest of us. Mostly, she made paintings. We were all equals, even among the men [laughs]. There was no leader or director of the group. Everyone was a leader.

PG: You mentioned earlier that Bao Jianfei moved to Shenzhen towards the end of the 1980s. What did she go on to do after she left the Pond Association?

ZP: I am not entirely sure. I know she doesn't make art anymore. I believe that recently her work has been related to commerce and real estate as well as selling furniture. I think she owns a shop and finds old Chinese furniture to sell in Australia.

PG: During their time with the Pond Association, did any of the members of the group have individual exhibitions?

ZP: No, not as far as I know.

PG: Could you say more about the events and exhibitions that the Pond Association was involved in as a group?

ZP: Actually, the Pond Association did not hold any public exhibitions of its work as a group. The group was only together for a relatively short period of time and most of its members were concerned more with their own work as artists rather than that produced by the group. There were two or three collective works, but there were no actual group exhibitions or publications. The group was mainly a forum for discussion. Many artists had their work publicized in magazines during the 1980s and there were many exhibitions in different places across China. However, as a group, the Pond Association didn't hold an exhibition of its own. To some extent, the artists involved in the group shared a similar approach to the making of art. They often held parties together. Consequently, they may well have been influenced by one another. But, basically, we completed our works independently. For the most part, we worked as individuals rather than through group collaboration.

PG: Nevertheless, the group is perhaps best known for two site-specific works and a performance work that were produced collaboratively.

ZP: Yes. A few of us collaborated in the production of artworks shown in public spaces. I think it influenced our approach to the making of art for a long time. As for me, I believe that many of the artworks that I produced in 1987 and 1988, such as *30x30*,[11] have a lot to do with the work of the Pond Association.

PG: Could you say more about the artworks that were made collectively by members of the Pond Association?

ZP: When we had an idea for an artwork we were all interested in, we would then make time to do it together. The most obvious example is *No. 1—Yang Style Tai Chi Series*. It was staged in a street opposite to the Zhejiang Academy of Fine Arts. On the one hand, it was a suitable position with a very quiet atmosphere…along one side of the street there was a beautiful brick wall that was very well suited to having something stuck onto it. On the other hand, it was a discrete place away from the rigid atmosphere of the Zhejiang Academy. We glued newspaper into sheets two metres wide and three metres high. One of our friends worked in a middle school that had a big gymnasium. We used the gymnasium to make drawings of body shapes on the prepared paper sheets. We made cut-outs of human figures in different *tai chi* 太极 poses.[12] We then slunk out under the cover of darkness to stick the cut-outs onto the wall at night. Because the wall was three metres tall, we could stick the figures from the top to the bottom of the wall. The funny thing was that a guy who lived nearby selling old newspapers eventually ripped off the bottom part of the paper figures. The paper came off layer by layer, cascading down the wall. But he was only able to tear off the bottom of the figures. The upper parts of the figures remained intact for over a year because he wasn't tall enough to reach them [laughs]. What a pity that we don't have a record of the remains of the paper figures; that would be very interesting. No one was concerned with the aftermath of what had happened except us. We often passed the place and found that it was disappearing gradually into its surroundings.

PG: When exactly was the work *No. 1—Yang Style Tai Chi Series* made?

ZP: In June 1986.[13]

PG: Why did you make this site-specific artwork? What was its intended purpose?

ZP: We tried to merge an artwork into the public environment…to make an artwork in public surroundings that would have a direct relationship to public life. We wanted to reflect an attitude that emphasized the relationship between art and non-art; in other words, a deviation from art or an experience that couldn't be defined simply as art. It was also intended as a signal to the Zhejiang Academy of Fine Arts, or, at least, one that would attract the attention of the students. That piece was totally open. We chose to make *No. 1—Yang Style Tai Chi Series* because every morning a group of people met to practice *tai chi* on the street opposite the academy. By sticking the cut-outs on the wall, we were looking to create an incident. The people who practiced *tai chi* on the street where the work was staged realized that something uncertain had happened. Some may have thought that it had something to do with them, while others may have thought that it didn't. It all depends on people's individual attitudes.

PG: Who executed the work?

ZP: Me, Song Ling, Geng Jianyi and…Wang Qiang…I think.

PG: Could you say more about how others responded to the work?

ZP: There were many differing responses. We went back to the location of the work many times. Some wondered why there was such a big image on the wall. Some insisted that it had something to do with the man who taught the *tai chi* group. Some thought that we made the work for the sake of fun. Later on, I heard that students studying at the academy thought that artists had made the work and that it was undoubtedly a form of artistic expression.

PG: Did you get into any difficulty with the authorities as a result of making the work.

ZP: No, not in relation to that work. But, maybe the declaration of the Pond Association was a little bit weird and they, the authorities, seemed not to understand it. I know that the

Hangzhou branch of the National Security Bureau (*Guojia anquan ju* 国家安全局) investigated the declaration and contacted art academies and art colleges to ask what the Pond Association was. Someone told me that they had investigated us and that we should be careful. I said that we had done nothing wrong or anything that was against the government.

PG: Does the work of the Pond Association have any relationship to traditional Chinese modes of art-making?

ZP: No. I feel that the works produced collectively by the Pond Association didn't look like artworks, or might not be considered simply as artworks. At least, they didn't give others a strong indication that they had something with art. You can call it art if you want. But, we didn't consider it wholly as art when we did it.

PG: Did the group have an agreed political position or ideological stance?

ZP: It's a little bit complicated. As for political position, in my opinion, an artist can't make art in an isolated way. He or she lives in society and must therefore be affected by society or the whole environment in which he or she works, including the government. As I indicated before, the Pond Association did not respond directly to such things, nor was there any intention to do so. I have to say, that it was actually different in Hangzhou from Beijing during the 1980s. At that time, in Hangzhou, our involvement in art-making activities didn't attract much trouble. I am afraid to say, that was not the key issue.

PG: Did humour, satire, anti-intellectualism, anti-social behaviour, work avoidance, law-breaking, violence or deliberate non-cooperation play a significant role in the activities of the group?

ZP: As I just said, we had no intention of adopting an anti-administration or anti-government stance. In the cultural and political life of Beijing, there were aggressive anti-government attitudes. We didn't think that the Pond Association should act in that way. Of course, we were concerned about political problems, but we did not intend to solve those problems directly through our involvement in art-making activities. We simply wanted to propose problems in relation to the use of language in art. Actually, we behaved a little obscurely. We opposed a kind of philosophical tendency or symbolism that focused itself on rationality. In our opinion, art-making should not be thought of in such detached terms. We thought that art should be more socially engaged. At the same time, we opposed the use of art as a means of expressing subjective emotion. So, to that extent, we had a rather eclectic stance.

PG: Could you say more about the Pond Association's decision not to adopt an aggressive anti-government stance?

ZP: First, most members of the Pond Association did not wish to adopt a radical, revolutionary stance or to place too great an emphasis on philosophy in art. This was a kind of sociological function in our view. We were more concerned with the development of art from the point of view of language. Our interest lay in language itself. We considered language as a fundamental aspect of artistic production and believed that one may only begin to think about other things such as culture, history, politics and society by starting from this point. In this way, we avoided a violent revolutionary attitude towards politics and society. That said, we never fully excluded political factors from our work. Actually, as an artist, by using language as a basis, one may be affected by many external factors. The purpose of an artwork can be complicated. Politics is only one part of that purpose…of an overall conception that should be more extensive in its scope. I think that politics doesn't manifest itself simply as a political or anti-political attitude, but more in terms of the conflict between the system and the individual. From a broad perspective, nobody can avoid such an issue.

PG: None of the collective works executed by the Pond Association make any obvious reference to Chinese cultural identity.[14] Why is that?

ZP: We were always against ethnic identity. But, at that time, during the 1980s, it was not entirely clear what stance we should take on this issue. The world did not have as much knowledge of Chinese modern art as it does today. Nevertheless, we were opposed to the use of simple ethnic symbols in Chinese art regardless of whether they were traditional or modern, or political or non-political, including well-know symbols of Chinese culture such as calligraphy and Chinese characters. We doubted the purpose of such behaviour. Everything should develop spontaneously from our point of view. Some Chinese artists at the time chose to use symbols referring to political figures like Mao Zedong. However, we thought it was the most superficial and obvious thing to do and an attitude that we were against. We did not embrace this form of symbolism because it was meaningless from the point of view of language.

PG: Did the Pond Association make contact with other art groups in China?

ZP: We didn't really think of ourselves as an art group. It was more like a party or an informal meeting. Later on, many people began to think of us as a group or an organization. But, I think that we should just let that idea go. In actuality, we did not have a clear structure or direction. Even though we wrote a declaration, we wrote it because, at the time, someone thought that we should make a record of our ideas…that was all. We usually drank tea, read poems or made paintings together. We didn't appoint someone as a leader. We got together when we had the opportunity to do so and then disbanded. We had personal relationships with members of other groups based on friendship. I was a classmate of Wang Guangyi at the Zhejiang Academy of Fine Arts. I corresponded with him and Shu Qun by letter during the 1980s. I also attended a symposium in Zhuhai (*Zhuhai huiyi* 珠海会议) in 1986 organized by the Zhuhai Painting Institute and *Fine Arts in China*, which brought artists together from all over China to discuss their contribution to the 1985 New Wave movement.[15] But for the most part there was hardly any communication between groups during the 1980s. Many artists came to Hangzhou from all over the country and, basically, we knew each other very well. Once they came to Hangzhou, we would get together and chat. But there were no structured relationships between groups.

PG: What kept the Pond Association together other than shared artistic interests?

ZP: We usually had tea at home. We didn't like to play *mah-jong*. We preferred to play *Go*. Some liked to play cards. Sometimes we watched movies together. It was not easy to get access to movies in the 1980s.

PG: What kind of movies did you watch?

ZP: At that time, there were only a few movies of poor quality that had been copied onto videotape many times. We didn't watch experimental movies, because we hardly saw movies of that sort in China until the beginning of the 1990s. We almost always watched commercial movies. There were a variety of these movies available in the 1980s. Actually, they were not easy to find or see. Some were European movies. They were a little different from domestic Chinese movies—we were not very interested in Chinese movies. At that time we watched a movie—perhaps set in America or Europe—called *The Day of the Jackal*. It was about someone trying to assassinate President de Gaulle…or whatever. We saw it many times. That one was copied on videotape from one friend to another.

PG: So, you watched these movies together as a group?

ZP: Not always; sometimes yes and sometimes no, because we couldn't always wait until we all got together. At that time there were no private telephones, and contacting people was very inconvenient. In fact, I can't remember how we contacted each other at that time. Anyway, it was casual. We liked to watch movies together and then usually exchanged books.

PG: Did the watching of movies copied many times onto videotape influence your eventual use of video as your principal medium of artistic expression?[16]

ZP: Not consciously at the time. I travelled to New York for the first time in 1992. I hardly saw any art videos while I was there, but I did see movies by the likes of Ingmar Bergman, Sergio Leone, Wim Wenders, Bernardo Bertolucci, Volker Schlöndorff and Michelangelo Antonioni. I think they definitely influenced my later work and artistic language after I started working with multimedia.

PG: What sort of books did the members of the Pond Association exchange with one another?

ZP: We were fond of drama and existential literature. There were two books we all liked, one called *Walk to Zhi puyi*[17] and another *Towards a Poor Theatre* (1968), which had been written by an experimental dramatist from Poland, Jerzy Grotowski.[18] There were Chinese versions of these books, and Cao Xuelei bought copies. Almost everyone read them. *Walk to Zhi puyi* had a great influence on the group. Many of us, including Geng Jianyi and me, got inspiration and ideas from that book, including the concept of immersion and relationships with society. We also had some other reading in common, including works of South American literature; black humour…*Catch 22*; and existential philosophy…Sartre, for example.

PG: Were there any disputes or conflicts within the group?

ZP: Sometimes there were disputes, but generally we got along very well. Of course, relationships may have been a little closer or more distant from time to time, but no real conflict at all. There may have been some disputes about art, life and other things. But they only lasted a short time…usually during the tea break [laughs].

PG: Did your personal ambitions as an artist differ from or come into conflict with the collective aims of the Pond Association?

ZP: I think my own aims fitted in well with the general aims of the group, even though there were some small differences. It all depended on individual style or on a personal understanding of media and language. I did not have any serious conflict with the aims of the Pond Association. The Pond Association didn't require its members to follow a particular path or way of working. We were together out of tacit understanding or intuition. We knew each other and never restricted one another. Sometimes we may have gone to someone's studio or house to see his or her work and then gave some comments. But they were personal opinions. We never asked others to follow our personal ways of working and we never imposed some sort of requirement. I think that there was more freedom in the Pond Association than in some other groups at the time.

PG: You mentioned earlier that there were some contemporaneous publications relating to the activities of the Pond Association published in a Chinese art magazine.

ZP: Yes. I remember there were some comments on the work of the Pond Association published at the time, including some in the magazines *Art* (*Meishu zazhi*) and *Art Trends* (*Meishu sichao*) that impressed me deeply. They were about *No. 1—Yang Style Tai Chi Series* and they approved of the blending of art into society that was expressed by that work. It was an important trend and many other artists didn't notice or realize it. Actually, it started with an open letter from a professor, Zhu Qingsheng, at the art college in Peking University, who later went to Germany. At that time, I mailed him some materials relating to the *No. 1—Yang Style Tai Chi Series* and he wrote back to me. He then published our exchange of letters openly in *Art* (Zhu 1986). The open letter was called 'Return Art to the People,' (*Ba yishu huang gei renmin* 把艺术还给人民) which seemed like a political statement but actually didn't reflect the attitude of the government. This aroused some comments on our works…they were all about our paintings. Some comments said that our paintings represented a rationalist trend. Some even said those works involved some sort of grey humour (*huise youmo* 灰色幽默) or whatever; I can't remember them clearly (Shi 1987: 16–20).[19]

PG: What was the relationship between the Pond Association and the authorities in China, both at a national and at a local level?

ZP: There was no direct relationship with the government—no direct relationship or conflict. We made our works without attracting much attention, so few people in the culture department or police had heard of us. Actually, our works were not of great influence on society, or, at least, not a negative influence. I don't think that the authorities ever fully traced or investigated us. Actually, at that time, we were seldom concerned with the government. We focused on the so-called new art, on experimental art or art for its own sake. That had nothing to do with the government.

PG: In what ways did wider social, economic or cultural events—both within and outside China—influence the activities or the group?

ZP: There were definitely some outside influences. It was a period full of ideas. The economy was just opening up, so it was not very well advanced. The mass media and entertainment industry were not yet booming. However, ideology and the arts flourished, including writing, movies, painting and music. Almost all artists at that time paid attention to the development of foreign art as well as to philosophy, literature and cinema—from a cultural perspective rather than as a matter of linguistic expression. Numerous books by Western philosophers were published in China during the 1980s. These books influenced many Chinese artists. At the time, there were three prominent art magazines in China; namely, *Art, Jiangsu Illustrated* and *Art Trends* (*Meishu sichao*), and one art newspaper, *Fine Arts in China. Art Trends* and *Fine Arts in China* were not published after 1989. Around 1984, reproductions of foreign paintings became more widely available to us through these magazines and newspapers. There were also some less well-known magazines that were of great importance during 1980s. Among these was the magazine *Art Worm* (*Yishu chong* 艺术虫), which was published by the Zhejiang Academy of Fine Arts in Hangzhou—actually, it was the journal of the Zhejiang Academy of Fine Arts. Many artists got information from this magazine. During the 1980s, it was difficult to get information about art made outside China. *Art Worm* translated the latest information about overseas art into Chinese and printed it alongside photographs of the artworks in question. It influenced many artists at the time. The name of the magazine has been changed. It's now called *New Art* (*Xin meishu* 新美术). It no longer specializes in introducing information about foreign art, but in publishing papers written by foreign academics. In doing so, it has helped to change the direction of academic study in China.

PG: What is the legacy of the Pond Association for contemporary Chinese art since 1989?

ZP: There are definitely some inheritances. We were born in the 1950s or 1960s and lived through a series of great social changes, such as the Cultural Revolution, opening-up and reform and other political movements. I think these changes left an indelible mark on our memories and have had an undeniable influence on subsequent attitudes towards art and life within China. But it doesn't mean that all artists within China think or make art in the same way. There are many variations. Nevertheless, I would insist that some of the points raised by the Pond Association are still relevant today, including the emphasis which the group placed on the relationship between art and society and our collective attempts to make art part of daily life. I think that contemporary artists in China are now at more of a distance from the society. Many artists are now a little introspective or their starting point is the construction of a generic Chinese culture. As an artist, I still believe in getting rid of the gap between art and daily life. From this point of view, I believe we achieved something of continuing importance. Having said all of that, young artists who were born during the late 1980s have their own life experience and background. During the last quarter of a century, China has undergone yet more social changes. Young people living through these years have been exposed to lots of information. Young artists have gradually come to understand the question of art and have established their own world view in a variety of ways, and many of their works are pretty good.

PG: Published views on the significance of the work of the Pond Association vary. Karen Smith and Thomas Berghuis have argued that public artworks produced by the group, such as *No. 1—Yang Style Tai Chi Series*, should be considered as something of a failure because they did not succeed in engaging a positive public reaction. Berghuis also claims, with reference to a contemporaneous report by the Dutch art critic Hans van Dijk—who was reportedly living in Hangzhou at the time—that, as a result of this failure, the Pond Association began to turn inwardly towards a more specialized artistic audience, producing increasingly 'provocative' performance works, such as *Wrapping Up—King and Queen* (Smith 2005: 383; Berghuis 2008: 49–51).[20] What is your opinion of these readings? Should we consider public artworks produced by the Pond Association as failed attempts to engage with Chinese society?

ZP: I don't really care. Right from the beginning we didn't care how the group would develop or how it would come to an end. It wasn't important to us how and when the group might come to an end…and I think, looking back, it actually lasted for quite a long time. I also think that the experience has been useful to a wider audience, or at least it was a significant experience for its members. Take Geng Jianyi and me for instance, we have not stopped making art. I think that the Pond Association means a lot to us. For the others, I'm not entirely sure of its influence. But I think it was pretty good on the whole. Since it was a worthwhile experience for its members, it makes no difference whether it lasted for one week, a month, a year or whatever. It's the same as human life. If one's life is full of value, it makes no difference whether one lives to be 30, 60 or 80 years old. We didn't think about how long the group would last, what it would achieve or what to save from our work together. As for the historical standing of the group, both at home and abroad, the research on the group so far has not been detailed. Such research is valuable and I think this way of interviewing is a good method. Nowadays, people seldom do such work.

Wang Qiang (b. 1957)[21]
Paul Gladston: When and under what circumstances did the Pond Association first come together?

Wang Qiang: The background to the founding of the Pond Association was China's Sixth National Art Exhibition, which was held in Beijing in 1984. This exhibition was similar to previous national art exhibitions in that it required certain kinds of artistic content—content that matched government propaganda. In fact, the exhibition strongly reaffirmed the political themes and the propagandist styles of the Cultural Revolution. We wanted to do something more individualistic. Compared to the situation nowadays, the whole country was comparatively closed at that time. Nevertheless, we were very curious about foreign philosophy and ways of thinking. As artists, we looked at things or judged things from an artist's point of view. We didn't try to use foreign thinking directly. We made things according to our own thoughts and feelings.

PG: What exactly is the significance of the name 'The Pond Association'?

WQ: The word 'pond' suggests a condition of being totally immersed…immersed in art or in an atmosphere—for instance, an academic atmosphere or, perhaps, something else—that inspires one's enthusiasm. It's just like the relationship between a fish and water as mentioned by Laozi. When people bathe in a big pond together, they're a group sharing the same surroundings; there's no individuality. We used this metaphor to describe our condition as a group. That's why we called ourselves the Pond Association. When I was a fourth-year student at the Zhejiang Academy of Fine Arts, the desire to be a master was very strong. However, this desire became less important after graduation. Art has always been part of my life. The state of being immersed has never changed. During my time in the Pond Association, the water in the pond was tempestuous, while the water now is calmer. There was a very strong desire to be immersed during the period of time when the Pond Association was active. The desire is no longer that strong, but I'm still immersed in the water of art.

PG: As a group, were you also interested in Chinese philosophy and ways of thinking? According to at least one source, the Pond Association was strongly influenced by Chan Buddhist thought and practice (Köppel-Yang 2003: 61).

WQ: No. The background to the formation of the Pond Association had nothing to do with Chinese religion or philosophy. Following the Sixth National Art Exhibition, some recent graduates from the Zhejiang Academy of Fine Arts, including Zhang Peili, Geng Jianyi, Song Ling and myself, got together to organize the exhibition 1985 New Space, which was held in Hangzhou in December 1986. The content of the artwork shown in that exhibition was relevant to ourselves—to the city we lived in and the situation we were in at the time. The exhibition 1985 New Space was staged just after I had graduated from the Zhejiang Academy of Art in 1985. There seems to have been an inevitable trend towards such exhibitions in China during 1985 and the latter part of the 1980s. At the time, many exhibitions of this sort were held in places such as Sichuan, Beijing and Hunan. We neither thought too much about the outcomes of the exhibition, nor did we expect anything to happen as a result. Our starting point was really simple: we wanted to express our own perspectives on reality and the things around us. There were two meanings associated with the title '1985 New Space': first, it indicated the year the exhibition was mounted; and second, it indicated the opening-up of new space in our everyday lives. Most of the time, we followed our instincts and inner thoughts. When I look back at the artworks we exhibited in the 1985 New Space exhibition, things are clearer than at the time we made them. Things were very vague at the time. The notion of doing something that we were interested in became even stronger after the 1985 New Space exhibition. The Pond Association was formed to provide a place for artists to get together and to keep a clear state of mind—a state of mind distinct from that associated with official Chinese art. After the 1985 New Space exhibition, we went to Beijing to see a retrospective exhibition of the work of the American artist Robert Rauschenberg at the National Gallery in Beijing.[22]

PG: How do you think we should interpret the work of the Pond Association? Are there particular ideas, conceptual frameworks or perspectives that allow us to see the work of the group more clearly?

WQ: No doubt, there was something meaningful or valuable about the Pond Association's activities. At the very least, the group promoted the development of contemporary art in China. When we talk about historical criticism, we should ask the question: 'what is the essence of historical events.' We should assess the impact of those events on subsequent developments. Before the Sixth National Art Exhibition, art in China was strongly controlled. The authorities provided guidance to artists, telling them what they should do. However, we believed that art should be an artist's personal view of the world shown or expressed through a particular medium. I think this is the function of art. It's very important that artists are not controlled by a particular organization. After the Sixth National Art Exhibition and the emergence of the 1985 New Wave, more emphasis was placed on artistic self-expression. If we look at Western art history, regardless of whether the art is modern or traditional, it's quite individual. While in China, for a long period of time, art was controlled by a system that told us what to do. It was after 1985 that more emphasis was placed on artistic self-expression. Breaking restrictions may be the significance of the 1985 New Wave. Nowadays, a lot of artistic activities or exhibitions are quite similar to those which took place during the 1980s. I think the Pond Association provided a meaningful foundation for the way artists work today. Currently, artists and art groups are very individual. They may join an exhibition and do something according to a theme, but still their works are quite individual.

PG: Was the Pond Association a politicized group in any sense?

WQ: Not really. Hangzhou is quite a way from Beijing. The local government wasn't so strict with exhibitions. My own work did cause some misunderstandings, but I didn't really care. I made a piece for the 1985 New Space exhibition representing the headless conductor of an orchestra. It was called *The Start of the 2nd Movement of the 5th Symphony in Adagio*.[23] Some people commented that the work showed that I had ambitions to be a leader. But, in fact, I never thought like that. Hangzhou was a gentle city, which didn't get involved with politics. Hangzhou is like that. It's not so easy to get angry about things.

PG: During the 1980s, the work of the Pond Association was described by Chinese art critics as 'rationalist' in its stylistic approach. Do you agree with this categorization? I accept that Zhang Peili and Geng Jianyi were responsible for the making of formally abstracted paintings prior to the forming of the Pond Association, which could conceivably be described as rationalist. However, the collective work of the group involves the making of site-specific and performance works, which, to me at least, have an affinity with non-rationalist—that is to say, deconstructive—artworks produced by the Western avant-gardes.

WQ: During the 1980s, critics argued that artists belonging to the Pond Association were rationalist in their approach, while art groups in Hunan and Sichuan tended to be more emotive. Art groups in the northern part of China were also seen as rationalist. However, when critics tried to classify these groups during the 1980s, they made superficial judgements. They didn't fully understand the significance of our work. They judged things simply from the point of view of linguistic form…the formal appearance of the artworks. The paintings produced by artists in Hunan and Sichuan may have appeared to be less rational than those produced by artists in Hangzhou and in the northern part of China. But that was just an easy way for critics to classify differences between artworks according to a dialectical point of view. I think artists are quite individualistic sometimes. However, critics like to categorize artists. Recently, critics have started to be more objective.

PG: The Pond Association also wrote a declaration which reads more like a poem than a rationalist statement of intent.

WQ: Before the Sixth National Art Exhibition, art in China was too restricted. We pursued change. We were quite young and we were passionate. We wrote our declaration hoping to break the restrictions on art in China.

PG: In pursuing change, to what extent were you influenced by the work of the Western artistic avant-gardes? When I recorded a conversation with Zhang Peili about the work of the Pond Association, he said that the group was aiming to break down the boundary between art and life. This is similar to the aims of the Western historical and neo avant-gardes.

WQ: It was very natural that we paid attention to the city in which we lived and the people living in the city. It was also natural that we brought life and art together. We didn't pay much attention to Western avant-garde art because it was not easy to get access to those kinds of resources. What we did might be similar to Western avant-garde art. However, I don't think it was influenced that strongly by the work of the Western avant-gardes. We looked at some books on Western philosophy, but not at Western art. We were able to read foreign magazines in the resource room at the University. However, these resources were still quite limited.

PG: Could you give some specific examples of the Western books that you and other members of the Pond Association were reading during the 1980s?

WQ: *Being and Nothingness* by Jean-Paul Sartre; also, books by Nietzsche.

PG: Philosophical writings by Sartre and Nietzsche were highly influential on the work of contemporary Chinese artists during the 1980s. In what ways did these writings influence the work of the Pond Association?

WQ: I'm not sure whether the books I read during the 1980s had a direct influence on my work as an artist at the time. I think they may have had some effect, for example, the adoption of different value systems. Actually, the Pond Association didn't stay together for that long as a group. It wasn't very long before we returned to our individual ways of working and to doing our own things. We graduated in 1985 and founded the Pond Association in 1986. We stayed quite close for a time and did things together. For example, we borrowed a basketball court to do photographic shows. The group drifted apart not long after that. I started reading the books I mentioned after the Pond Association. We didn't really talk about art that much; it was just like friends sharing daily feelings. We talked a lot about things that we had noticed in society. Sometimes, we also tried to answer the question: 'what is art?' Through talking and sharing ideas within the group, our discussions became more meaningful and fruitful. The discussion enlightened my thoughts sometimes. We also played Go and drew together.

PG: Were there ever any disagreements within the group?

WQ: Yes, once, I think. We had a disagreement because I thought we should be more individualistic. We should work as a group but we shouldn't deny that we were still independent individuals. Zhang Peili and I were very close friends. We shared our thoughts and debated a lot with each other. As an artist, I was a bit individualistic. We didn't really try to work as a group in a premeditated way. We just shared an interest in art. This provided us with the opportunity to work together as a group. However, the group didn't last long.

PG: Was the Pond Association's decision to make site-specific artworks, such as *No. 1 — Yang Style Tai Chi Series*, directly influenced by the example of public artworks produced during the Cultural Revolution—for example, big character posters (*dazibao*) or large-scale public murals? Moreover, as a group, did you make a connection between the art of the Cultural Revolution and that of the Western avant-gardes, both of which can be understood to involve a conscious attempt to break down the boundary between art and everyday life?

WQ: The Western avant-garde's attempt to bring art and life more closely together was a self-conscious one, while the bringing of art and life together as part of the Cultural Revolution took place unconsciously, as part of China's national reformation. This is different from the West. The Cultural Revolution was primarily a political movement. We might think life and art were merged during the Cultural Revolution from our current point of view, but the starting point of the Cultural Revolution was not to demonstrate that art was life, or that life was art. As an artist, we might think there's an artistic side to the Cultural Revolution, but ordinary people wouldn't see it like that. Though Western avant-garde art may appear to be similar in its aims to that of the Cultural Revolution, their backgrounds are different. As for the work of the Pond Association, that was produced somewhere between consciousness and unconsciousness. My mates and I all experienced the Cultural Revolution, so the art produced during the Cultural Revolution had some influence on us. Actually, we didn't think that much at that time. The Pond Association might have been unconsciously influenced by the Cultural Revolution because the end of the Cultural Revolution and the founding of the Pond Association were very close.

PG: Nevertheless, would you agree that the public art of the Cultural Revolution and the site-specific works of the Pond Association are similar, insofar as both can be understood to involve attempts to bring art and life more closely together?

WQ: Yes, the goal was similar. The building of cultural value has continuity. My generation experienced the Cultural Revolution, seeing or experiencing something that Western artists haven't experienced, which made us want to continue to bring art and life more closely together. During the Cultural Revolution, the official policy on art was to immerse oneself into life and to represent life. However, what was life and what wasn't life? What was culture, what wasn't culture? These questions were controlled by the government. From this angle, the Pond Association can be understood to have broken away from the Cultural Revolution by resisting official government policy on art. On the other hand, all of the Pond Association's members had direct experience of the Cultural Revolution. The work of the Pond Association continued the state of being involved or immersed in life that came with the Cultural Revolution. Seen from this point of view, the work of the Pond Association was a continuation of the Cultural Revolution. As an artist, I think putting up posters or handing out leaflets during the Cultural Revolution was quite artistic, just like performance art. A lot of conventional art forms were destroyed or suspended during the Cultural Revolution and replaced by these more public ways of working. As an artist, I don't want to comment too much on the Cultural Revolution. I often say to my students: 'politicians are there to solve problems.' As artists, we are very sensitive to our surroundings. We may raise a lot of questions, but not comment practically on what should be done, or what shouldn't be done. It seems to me that, by comparison, Western artists are quite idealistic. In China, a lot of things are handed down by the Party. There's just no way to refuse. People are expected to have a sense of being part of a collective. It seems tomorrow has nothing to do with each individual.

PG: What effect did the Cultural Revolution have on your personal circumstances and those of your family?

WQ: It had an effect on my family, but not on me personally.

PG: You are now a teacher at the China Academy of Fine Arts in Hangzhou. Do you ever discuss the work of the Pond Association with your students?

WQ: I have mentioned the Pond Association to postgraduates rather than undergraduates. Undergraduate lessons are more restricted.

PG: How does the experience of students currently studying at the China Academy of Fine Arts compare with your experience as a student at its forerunner, the Zhejiang Academy of Fine Arts?

WQ: I think the atmosphere is much better than before; there's more freedom. Both teachers and students have a certain degree of freedom. I think the development of Chinese art is just like a chain of connected elements. The development of Chinese art is a continuous process.

During the Cultural Revolution and the period just after the Cultural Revolution, people started to re-examine and rethink Chinese art. But most Chinese artists were lacking in thoughts at the time. I personally feel that it was the worst period of time for the development of Chinese art. We did what we were asked to do and learned what we were asked to learn. That's not enough. When we went to university, we started to pay special attention to philosophy and other very natural and essential aspects of what it means to be a human being. We realized art is something that should be natural. At that time my feelings were quite pure and I had quite vague ideas about what art might be. However, because of that purity of feeling, my work was really natural and really artistic. I think artists come to be driven by gaining financial profits or benefits at some stage. But for me and my workmates, we didn't think too much about gaining anything special. We just followed our instincts. We were also quite humble. We realized that we couldn't change reality too much. We couldn't go to government officials and argue with them. We knew that the arts would open up as well as the economy sooner or later. Normally, the development of culture follows economic development. Culture is open to the outside world without being aware of it. I personally did what I thought I should do and tried my best to do it well. I followed my heart. We didn't have any long-term plans or strategies. Having a university education can make the production of art very unnatural sometimes. When you study art at university, you have to pass examinations, and teachers tell you what is right and what is wrong. It destroys the natural and down-to-earth feeling of art. Art cannot be judged as being either right or wrong.

Song Ling (b. 1961)[24]

Paul Gladston: During the 1980s you worked closely with Zhang Peili, Geng Jianyi, Bao Jianfei and Wang Qiang first as a member of the group that organized the 1985 New Space exhibition in Hangzhou and later on as a member of the Pond Association. I think I'm right in saying that you were also invited to take part in the China/Avant-Garde exhibition in Beijing in 1989, but you were unable to do so.

Song Ling: That's right. By then I had already left China to live in Australia. I had a solo show in China during the Pond Association period,[25] and I should have shown my paintings in the China/Avant-Garde show in Beijing. But, at that time I was really struggling with my life, so I didn't have enough energy to send my work back to Beijing. The organizers contacted me, but my life in Melbourne was made difficult because of the interference of lots of personal things. So I missed that exhibition.

PG: Why did you go to live in Australia?

SL: Before I left for Australia, I had a good job. When I graduated from college, I went directly to work at the Zhejiang Academy of Fine Arts. I was a full-time artist, supported by the government. Zhang Peili worked in a school, and Geng Jianyi did something similar. I had a job that was supported by the government, so I didn't need to worry about money.

It was at this time I began working with Zhang Peili, helping to mount the 1985 New Space exhibition and starting the group, the Pond Association. Later, I had a chance to go overseas. During the 1980s, lots of people in China would have liked to have gone abroad. A lot of artists went to America or to other foreign countries. So I got the chance. And I didn't realize I would stay. I went there to study English. I wanted to see the West. When I got there, I had problems with studying. At that time, I knew no English at all. I had problems with life. I had to work washing dishes and also studying. But after six months, Tian'anmen Square started. So I stayed, sort of struggling with life.

PG: How long was it before you resumed your work as an artist?

SL: After a year, I got back to doing some artwork. But I didn't come back to China to do it. I got a studio in Australia. I had a solo show there in 1991. I also found a big gallery in Melbourne that wanted to represent me.

PG: As part of your involvement with the Pond Association, did you participate in the making of the site-specific pieces involving paper cut-outs? One of them, *No. 1—Yang Style Tai Chi Series*, had figures in *tai chi* poses pasted along a wall on a street near the art academy in Hangzhou on 3 June 1986, and another, *No. 2—Strollers in the Green Space*, involved similar figures suspended from trees on 4 November 1986.

SL: Yes, I was directly involved in both. The one on the wall is the one I remember the most from my time in the Pond Association. Actually I haven't talked about the Pond Association for a long time, for almost 20 years.

PG: Can you remember another piece, *Wrapping Up—King and Queen*, that involved two people wrapped from head to foot in newspaper which was staged on 2 November 1986?

SL: Yes, I remember that one, too.

PG: Were you actually there, or do you just remember it as having taken place?

SL: I don't really have any specific memories of that particular piece. I have photographs which I took, at the time, of the one hanging in the bushes and the one on the wall.

PG: At the time, what were you and the other members of the Pond Association trying to achieve with this work?

SL: At that time, we were trying to make environment art. Because the 1985 New Space exhibition mainly involved paintings and sculpture, we thought we would make installations, which had not really made their entry into China yet. So we did a sort of environment art.

We used characters from *tai chi*. I can't remember why we chose that. I think it was probably a kind of Chinese cultural thing. *Tai chi* is part of traditional Chinese culture. We also thought that it was a nice shape.

PG: So, it had an aesthetic dimension?

SL: Yes. We made characters with different motions and poses. We were also trying to explore our emotional feelings for art—love, yes, a kind of love for art. At that time it wasn't like now. There was nothing commercial, nothing involved money, just a kind of love…very pure. Now, it's very different. There's a lot of money involved in art. In those days, we spent our own money buying materials—pure love and a kind of inspiration. During the 1980s, Chinese people were more innocent. It was kind of a new thing, environment art. And we were also thinking that art is usually seen in colleges and among a small group of people—among artists like us. We studied art in college. We made environment art so that we could give something back to ordinary people. We wanted a kind of art that involved having a conversation with people.

PG: To what extent was this attempt to bring art and everyday life together influenced by Western avant-garde art, and to what extent might it have been influenced by your collective experience of the Cultural Revolution?

SL: Yes, that's right. During the Cultural Revolution, we had paper sticking on the wall. In the Pond Association we did it as a form of art.

PG: What about the influence of Western avant-garde art?

SL: Both were influential. At that time, we wanted to make some environment art. We didn't have the right conditions to do actual installations. Environment art was simple. It was something we could do—painting on paper and sticking it on walls. It may have led to doing something with installation. I think Zhang Peili started doing video installation after that. He took some photos and made the broken glass video very soon after that.[26]

PG: So in your view the 'environment' work of the Pond Association directly influenced Zhang Peili's later work with video?

SL: I think at that time he was starting to find that painting was not enough as a kind of language. He wanted more languages, more media.

PG: When I recorded a conversation with Zhang Peili, he stressed the idea that the Pond Association was about finding a new language—finding something to do as 'art'—and how difficult that was. It's easy to forget that you have to go through a process of learning art as a language.

SL: In the Pond Association we took different steps, we tried different things. We looked for new languages to explore our expressions and tried to understand what art was as we went along. At that time, in 1985, 1986 and 1987, we just wanted something new. So when we found that painting was not enough, we needed more ways in which to express ourselves.

PG: How important do you think the influence of traditional Chinese culture was for the work of the Pond Association? Was it important for you to have a relationship with it and to express a Chinese cultural identity? Is that something you thought about or talked about at the time?

SL: Actually, that's not something we talked about. We really just wanted something new, something that would give art back to people. That's mainly what we talked about: giving art back to ordinary people, not just a small group of people. Ordinary people gave us the opportunity to study art. We wanted to give it back to them. At that time, I think we mostly copied the West. Although when we copied the way we did, it still had a Chinese influence. The Chinese influence came out naturally. We did paintings.…In 1985, we did lots of copies. I liked Salvador Dalí, I liked Andy Warhol. So I did similar things. I think that's the first stage; after that our understanding of the work increased, and we moved on to the next stage. In 1985, 1986 and 1987, it was mainly a copying period. But, naturally, we still had traditional cultural influences.

PG: What do you think those traditional cultural influences were? Can you be specific? Maybe the way you were thinking? Or the way in which you were making the work?

SL: I can't remember if we talked about that or not at the time. But I think the main reason we probably chose *tai chi* was the influence of Chinese culture. We didn't choose a big animal piece. I had made some works related to animals—I did a lot of images of sheep and cows. As a group we didn't choose animals. We didn't choose trees. We chose *tai chi*. I can't remember why.…Oh, I remember now why we chose *tai chi*: because every morning, elderly men, a group of them, did *tai chi* on that street.

PG: So it relates to something that actually took place on that particular street?

SL: Yes, that's why we used *tai chi* figures. That's what we were thinking: when the people arrive in the morning to do their exercises, they would probably think it's a kind of instruction.

PG: So they would make an immediate connection between what they were doing and your work as artists? You chose the *tai chi* theme because you thought ordinary people would identify with it as part of traditional Chinese culture?

SL: Yes. We had a big room for cutting the paper. The project had a sort of free movement to it; we didn't do anything beforehand.…We didn't do sketches. We just did it.

PG: Western avant-garde art often involved attempts to bring art and life together. The hope was that life would then be transformed along the more playful lines of art, that art would change the way people lived their lives. The point I want to make is that this is often an intentionally violent and unsettling action in the West. My reading of a lot, though by no means all, of the Chinese 'avant-garde' art of the 1980s is that when it attempted to bring life and art together, the action wasn't an especially violent one. It often seems to have been more reciprocal, wanting a kind of—as you've said—conversation or dialogue.

SL: Yes, it's a conversation or dialogue. We chose the road because it had a lot of people, especially old men and women, doing morning exercises. They would go to the West Lake and that's the road they would have to travel along. They would also have an instructor to teach them *tai chi*. That's why we wanted to do something that would make them think. It's a kind of instruction, teaching them how to do *tai chi*. Each character had a different movement. Maybe they would think it's an instruction, which someone put on the wall. But actually, it's not. It's an artwork.…That's the point.

PG: How was the work received? You wanted to give art back to ordinary people. So what kind of response did you get from them?

SL: Actually, I don't think we had any response from ordinary people. Maybe ordinary people didn't even notice it. We had a response from the college. After dinner, they went for a walk and they passed by saying: 'Oh, what's that?' First, they probably thought it's a kind of *tai chi* instruction. But they also thought it might not be, because it's so big. The main response was from the college, the students and the teachers.

PG: So they could see that it might be a work of art?

SL: Yes. But for ordinary people at that time, they didn't know that. Now, maybe it's different. But at that time, art was only really serious if it was in a museum or gallery.

PG: That's a key issue, isn't it? The right circumstances have to be in place for something to be seen as a work of 'art.'

SL: Yes. At that time, people thought that art was only in exhibitions and galleries, or in college. Most people wouldn't have realized that this was a kind of art as well. I don't think it would have been seen as art by ordinary people.

PG: How did you feel about this lack of response? You'd tried to bring art and everyday life together, but most people couldn't recognize what you were doing. Once the work had been done and you didn't get a response from the people it was aimed at, did you reflect on what you had done? Did it make you consider carefully what you were going to do next?

SL: I think we knew that we might not get a response.

PG: So you knew in advance?

SL: Yes. We just wanted to make something happen, to do something new.

PG: So, you didn't have an especially long-term view of things at the time?

SL: Well, we just wanted to do something new. Now, a lot of people think our work has a lot of meanings, but actually we were quite simple. We wanted to do something different, to give art back to ordinary people. We wanted to do something to shock the college—'Ha! Who did this?'

PG: So it wasn't so much about the symbolic or metaphorical meaning of the work—it was about the social and institutional impact it might have as something new?

SL: Yes. Ordinary people didn't understand it. But we still targeted the students and teachers in the college. That's why we chose the road near the college and not somewhere else.

PG: What was the name of the road?

SL: Nanshan Road.

PG: What about the piece in the woodland? Was that meant to connect with ordinary people as well?

SL: I think we just wanted something different because the one on the wall only had two dimensions. But when we hung the figures in the trees, it had real space. It's a spatially different form of art.

PG: Was it an attempt to get away from the dominance of painting? That's to say, painting as an illusion. Did you try to create actual spatial relationships instead?

SL: Yes. At that time, we got really interested in real space. We took a lot of photographs, we used lights—very interesting, very happy. Actually, no one saw the artwork hanging in the trees. We just took photographs of it.

PG: So, no one else saw it?

SL: Ordinary people would just think: 'it's woodland'…that it's probably a tourist place. It's not a real forest. It's very close to here—a place named *Wan song lin*.

PG: So you were trying to conduct an experiment in the local environment by inserting something into it which would then alter one's perception of the space. In the case of the *tai chi* piece, it's about connecting with others. But in the case of the woodland piece, it's about inserting something into the space which would then change your perception as artists?

SL: Yes—although we actually did bring some people to see it. I think we still had some sort of conversation with people. At that time, we called upon a group of people and let them walk around. I can't remember—students—perhaps art students? I'm not sure. I think it was students—actually only four or five. It was a kind of beginning of installation in China.

PG: So it's a kind of experiential learning? You brought students along, saying, 'how about this experience?' You invited them to learn from what you were doing.

SL: Maybe. I'm not sure.

PG: Was it also a metaphor for the state of China at the time? China was also changing. It was opening up and reforming economically.

SL: Yes. In China we called this change the 'Open-Door Policy'.[27]

PG: Do you think the artworks we are talking about had some relationship to that…to that lived experience?

SL: Maybe not. We didn't think like that. At the time, we thought purely of art.

PG: So for you and the other members of the Pond Association, it was largely about the formal language of art: about trying to establish or learn this new language, about finding a way to develop a language that could be used as art?

SL: Yes, that's right. We were trying to develop a new language. That's why we wanted to do environment art. We wanted to bring art into the environment. We never did it before. We didn't know how it would work.

PG: Does this have anything to do with the construction of space in traditional Chinese painting? It's very difficult to tell from the published photographs of the work, but when I look at those photographs, I think that there is a certain similarity to the way in which traditional Chinese painting constructs the relationship between the viewer and the viewed. One of the ways that traditional Chinese painting differs from Western painting is that when you look at the image you have a sense that you are immersed in the space rather than looking at the depicted space from a distance. Do you think that had an influence on your work?

SL: Yes. You could probably explain it in that way. Yes, it's a sort of Chinese landscape painting. You put yourself into the painting; you are involved in it.

PG: The Pond Association produced an interesting declaration of intent. It's very poetic. It talks about immersion, about being immersed.

SL: Being immersed in the pond?

PG: Yes.

SL: I think we chose the pond, like being washed in the pond and coming out with a new life, a new language. At that time, we were thinking, it's kind of like going to the pond and being washed and coming out with a new life, like rebirth.

PG: Did being in the Pond Association have that effect in practice? Did it work like that for you? Did it work like that for the others?

SL: Yes. For me, I gained a new understanding of art. We all had a very traditional education in art school. You learned drawing and painting—all these very traditional things. I think from 1985 New Space and *Chi she* we learned to do things differently.

PG: So, if we relate the Pond Association declaration—the idea of immersion, being immersed—to the experimental piece in the woodland, was it about being immersed in a space and coming out of that with a new way of looking at the world?

SL: Yes. That's what we tried to do.

PG: During the mid-1980s, did you have any concerns about being an artist? Did you get into any trouble with the authorities for taking part in *Chi she*?

SL: No, not much trouble. Not really. People just didn't like the work. It was too early for China. No one was able to appreciate it. Even in the college, many teachers…we didn't really get any support from them. They were against it. We just loved it. We didn't really think about the art we did. But at that time some magazines published our work.

PG: So, at the time, in the mid-1980s, you were not at all worried that your work may get you into trouble with the authorities?

SL: No, because we didn't do anything political. It was pure art. No politics, no violence. So we thought it would be okay.

PG: Was that deliberate? Did you exclude politics from your art deliberately?

SL: Yes. We didn't want to worry about that sort of thing. We were pretty sure that we wouldn't get into trouble with the police.

PG: But wasn't it a political act just to do something new like that in China during the mid-1980s?

SL: Yes. Just as I've said, we just wanted to do something new.

PG: Do you think about it as political now, in retrospect?

SL: More personal, not really political. At that time, we talked about it as something more personal. I think Political Pop started a bit later, in the early 1990s.

PG: Do you think that what the Pond Association did in the 1980s has been influential on the work of the present generation of Chinese artists? Do you think you set up the circumstances for the things that are going on now…for them to happen?

SL: I think it was a stage that we had to go through. Yes, we had to go through that stage. I think it was the beginning of having the freedom to express. At that time, we were only taught painting. Usually we did traditional realistic work, and a bit of abstract work, but still in two dimensions. After the Pond Association, I think we had more artistic languages than painting. I think that's the beginning of having media art in China. After that, we had video art, installation—straightaway after that. I think the Pond Association was a beginning, the very beginning. After the Pond Association, we found painting itself was not enough. We needed more languages to express ourselves—new media of expression. I think we had to pass through that period. For me, as well, it's very important. Even though I do paintings, it still influences me. It was the first time I used my emotions to do different things. The Pond Association is for me a sort of history, a long time ago. But for my art life, the Pond Association is still an important experience. The role I acted was very important. It's a short period, but it's the first time I truly expressed myself. The two or three years with Zhang Peili and Geng Jianyi during 1985 New Space and the Pond Association I can say was my best time as an artist, with the group—very sweet, with no concerns about money, just pure art, and a kind of love for art.

Notes

1 Hangzhou is a historically important city in the south-eastern Chinese province of Zhejiang, close to Shanghai. Hangzhou was the capital of China during the Song dynasty (960–1279) and is widely regarded as the birthplace of Chinese *shan-shui* painting. The city is well known for its picturesque landscape settings, such as those surrounding the city's well-known West Lake, which have inspired generations of Chinese painters and poets (Beccaria 2005: 18).

2 For an English translation of Shi's essay, see Wu with Wang (2010: 83–89).

3 This is an edited version of a conversation recorded at the Bernini Restaurant close to the West Lake in Hangzhou on 3 November 2006.

4 The Hangzhou Crafts School was founded before the Cultural Revolution. Teaching at the school was suspended during the Cultural Revolution, but was resumed in 1984, the year of Zhang Peili's graduation from the Zhejiang Academy. The school has since been closed.

5 The Same Generation Painting Association exhibited its work at the National Art Museum in Beijing in 1980.

6 The critic Gao Minglu has referred to the 1985 New Space exhibition as the starting point of rational art in southern China (Gao 1991: 159).

7 Berghuis states that the work of 14 artists was exhibited at the 1985 New Space exhibition (Berghuis 2008: 48).

8 For a Chinese language version of 'The Declaration of the Pond Association,' see Lv (2007). The English language version of the declaration published here was translated from Mandarin Chinese by Xu Sujing and was originally published in support of an article in the journal *Yishu* (Gladston 2008d: 50–60).

9 Köppel-Yang asserts that the 'grey humour' (*huise youmo* 灰色幽默) of paintings by members of the Pond Association is related 'to the paradoxical epigrams of Chan Buddhism' and that this reflects 'a critical awareness of the self and of society' (Köppel-Yang 2003: 61).

10 According to Berghuis, artists belonging to the Pond Association include Bao Jianfei, Geng Jianyi, Guan Ying, Song Ling, Wang Qiang and Zhang Peili (Berghuis 2008: 230). Shi Jiu lists the members as Zhang Peili, Geng Jianyi, Song Ling, Bao Jianfei, Wang Qiang and Wu Ying (Shi 1987).

11 Zhang Peili's video *30x30* (1988) shows the artist smashing a mirror repeatedly and sticking the pieces back together again. It can be understood to represent the relationship between order and disorder as well as the underlying instability of society.

12 These cut-out figures were inscribed with Chinese characters giving the titles of the *tai chi* poses to which they referred; for example, '*jing ji du li*' 金鸡独立 ('golden chicken standing on one leg').

13 *No. 1—Yang Style Tai Chi Series* was prepared between 9am and 6pm, 2 June 1986, in the gymnasium of a middle school in Hangzhou. It was installed at around 2am on the morning of 3 June 1986. According to Zhang Peili, speaking in an unrecorded conversation in Hangzhou on 28 January 2010, *No. 1—Yang Style Tai Chi Series* was restaged at its original location, sometime during 1988, at the behest of the curator and critic Gao Minglu who had

arranged for the event to be filmed by a television crew from Beijing (Plate 25). It is unclear whether the film footage of this second staging has ever been aired within the PRC or elsewhere, or, indeed, whether it is still in existence. The initial staging of the work included figures cut out of sheets of newspaper, while the second staging included figures cut out of sheets of plain paper.

14 A significant number of the artworks produced by 'avant-garde' artists within the PRC during the 1980s make explicit reference to aspects of traditional Chinese culture. See, for example, the work of Xu Bing, Gu Wenda, Wu Shanzhuan and Wang Guangyi.

15 The Zhuhai Symposium, which took place in the provincial town of Zhuhai on the Zhujiang delta in Guangdong province on 15 August 1986, was organized as a result of an initiative by the artist Wang Guangyi. The symposium brought together artists as well as critics and members of China's official arts administration to view a slide show of over 300 artworks from across the PRC and to discuss concepts and trends related to the emerging of the 1985 New Wave art movement. The idea of a national exhibition of modern Chinese art which eventually led to the staging of the China/Avant-Garde exhibition in Beijing in 1989 was discussed for the first time during the symposium.

16 Since the 1990s, Zhang Peili has made a number of video works that involve the appropriation and repetition of scenes from official Chinese films of the 1960s and 1970s. These works include the single-channel video *Happiness* (*Xiyue* 喜悦) (2006). For a brief overview of the video art of Zhang Peili, see Peckham (2008). Also see Peckham (2011).

17 The present author has been unable to identify the author or provenance of this book.

18 The English translation of Shi Jiu's essay 'On New Space and the Pond Society' (1987) mistakenly attributes this book to the Polish filmmaker Krzysztof Kieślowski (Shi 2010: 87).

19 For an English translation, see Wu with Wang (2010: 83–89).

20 The performance *Wrapping Up—King and Queen* was staged privately in Luoyang, Henan, on 2 November 1986. The performance involved Geng and Zhang wrapping themselves tightly from head to foot in newspapers held in place by string. Both the title and the form of the work suggest a connection to sculptural works and drawings by the sculptor Henry Moore.

21 This is an edited version of a conversation recorded at the China Academy of Fine Art in Hangzhou on 23 November 2007.

22 The retrospective exhibition of Rauschenberg's work, which took place at the National Gallery in Beijing between 15 November and 5 December 1985, was the first major exhibition of the work of a Western avant-garde artist to be staged within the PRC. During its run, the exhibition attracted approximately 300,000 visitors and had a major impact on the work of the 1985 generation of Chinese artists. While in China, during the exhibition, Rauschenberg gave a lecture at the Central Academy of Graphic Art in Beijing and participated in discussions with members of the No Name Group.

23 According to Berghuis, this installation was accompanied by a performance titled *After Hours Artist* in which Wang Qiang performed as a living sculpture wearing a suit covered in paint and plaster and with his head wrapped entirely in white cloth (Berghuis 2008: 48). However, this is almost certainly an over-interpretation of a photograph of the making of *The Start of the 2nd Movement of the 5th Symphony in Adagio*, which involved the covering of a suit with plaster while still on the human body.

24 This is an edited version of a conversation recorded at a restaurant on Nanshan Road near the China Academy of Fine Arts in Hangzhou on 23 November 2007. A version of the conversation was previously published in the journal *Yishu*. See Gladston (2008d: 50–60).

25 Here Song Ling may be referring to his participation in the exhibition *Sport in Chinese Art*, which was staged at National Museum in Beijing as part of the International Olympic Art Festival in 1985.

26 Here Song Ling refers to Zhang Peili's video, *30x30* (1988).

27 Here, Song Ling refers to Deng Xiaoping's policy of 'Reform and Opening.'

Xiamen Dada (*Xiamen Dada* 厦门达达)

In 1983, a group of four artists who had recently graduated from university, Huang Yongping 黄永砅, Jiao Yaoming 焦耀明, Xu Chengdou 许成斗 and Yu Xiaogang 余晓刚, and a self-employed art director, Lin Jiahua 林嘉华, came together to stage an exhibition at the Cultural Palace in the city of Xiamen[1] (*Xiamen wenhua guan* 厦门文化馆), titled 'A Modern Art Exhibition of Five Artists' (*Wuren xiandai huazhan* 五人现代画展) (Plate 26).[2] The exhibition, which comprised assemblages as well as paintings—including Huang Yongping's work *Haystack (Duocao* 垛草*)*, which was based on Bastien Lepage's painting *Les Foins* with a plaster mask in place of the peasant woman's face—was a profoundly challenging one within the still culturally conservative context of the PRC at that time (which was still in the midst of the Anti-Spiritual Pollution Campaign) and provoked a strong response both from the public and the local authorities in Xiamen.

Over the next three years, the group that had staged A Modern Art Exhibition of Five Artists came increasingly under the leadership of Huang Yongping who began to explore the relationship between Western Dada and Chinese—principally Daoist and Chan Buddhist—cultural influences as part of his artistic practice. Works produced by Huang at this time include his *Roulette Series* (*Zhuanpan xilie* 转盘系列) (1985) and *Non-expressive Painting* (*Fei biaoda huihua* 非表达绘画) (1985), both of which make use of chance to determine the making of artworks beyond the constraints of established aesthetic taste and a desire for personal self-expression.

In 1986, the development of the group that had staged A Modern Art Exhibition of Five Artists culminated in the staging of two further exhibitions held under the collective title of Xiamen Dada: one titled 'The Xiamen Dada Modern Art Exhibition' (*Xiamen dada xiandai yishu zhan* 厦门达达现代艺术展), which took place at the Cultural Palace in the City of Xiamen between 28 September and 5 October 1986; and another known as 'Events' (*Shijian* 事件), which opened in December 1986 at the Fujian Fine Art Museum (*Fujian meishuguan* 福建美术馆) in Fujian Province (Plates 27, 28 and 29).

On 23 November 1986, following the end of the first of these exhibitions, seven artists under the leadership of Huang Yongping took part in an action known as the *Burning Event* (*Fenshao shijian* 焚烧事件) in Wenhua Gong Square next to the Cultural Palace in the City of Xiamen, during which 60 artworks included in the Xiamen Dada Modern Art Exhibition were publicly incinerated accompanied by slogans daubed on the ground around the fire, among them the statement 'Dada is Dead!' (Plate 30).

A declaration written to accompany the *Burning Event*, titled 'Statement on Burning' (*Fengshou shenming* 焚烧声明) (Huang 2010a), is like the 'Declaration of the Pond Association' of the same year, somewhat elliptical in tone. Nevertheless, it can be interpreted as upholding a resolutely non-desiring stance towards art, which, it suggests, can be arrived at through a calculated act of negation involving the destruction of artworks and the consequent extinguishing of desire. The final passage of the statement asserts that

Artworks are to artists what opium is for men.
Not until art is destroyed will life be peaceful.
Dada is dead! Beware of Fire! (Huang 2010a: 95)[3]

As Yu Xiaogang makes clear in the conversation with members of Xiamen Dada published here, the *Burning Event* is therefore open to interpretation as having been influenced not just by a Western Dadaist intention to negate art through the production of works of anti-art, but also, and perhaps more importantly given the immediate cultural context within which the event took place, by a Buddhist belief in *Nirvana* as the extinguishing of all desire and of individualism, and a sign of the ultimate emptiness of all things.[4]

As a result of the incineration of their work during the *Burning Event*, the four members of Xiamen Dada who subsequently took part in the Events exhibition at the Fujian Art Museum—Huang Yongping, Lin Jiahua, Jiao Yaoming and Yu Xiaogang—were compelled to exhibit a combined work involving various found objects which were distributed around the Fujian Art Museum with accompanying labels. This final public exhibition of work by Xiamen Dada proved too much for the authorities and was closed down on the orders of the local branch of the Ministry of Propaganda only two hours after its opening.[5] A statement relating to the Events exhibition written by Huang Yongping, 'Introduction to the Events Exhibition that took place at the Exhibition Hall of the Fujian Art Museum' (Huang 2010b) was posted in the exhibition hall during the time of the exhibition. This statement claims that the exhibition was an intentional 'assault' on the audience's 'views of "art"' as well as on the 'exhibition hall' as a 'model of the art system.' It also states that the Fujian exhibition was one 'without works of art.'[6]

Besides its various public exhibitions, events and statements, Xiamen Dada is also associated with published writings by Huang Yongping that shed some light on the collective thinking of the group and, in particular, Huang's interest in the relationship between Western Dada and traditional Chinese cultural thought and practice. Among these writings are two essays: 'Xiamen Dada—a Kind of Postmodernism?' (*Xiamen Dada—yizhong houxiandai?* 厦门达达——一种后现代?), which was first published in *Zhongguo meishu bao* in 1986, and 'A Completely Empty Signifier' (*Wanquan kong de nengzhi* 完全空的能指), which was first published in *Meishu zazhi* (Art) in 1989 (Huang 1986: 1; 1989: 30–32, 72). The essays 'Xiamen Dada—a Kind of Postmodernism?' and 'A Completely Empty Signifier' are important in this regard because they make a case for the continued relevance of attitudes associated with Western Dada within the context of the indigenous Chinese artworld of the 1980s. In 'Xiamen Dada—a Kind of Postmodernism?' Huang presents five interrelated lines of argument: first, that modern art produced and exhibited in China between 1983 and 1986 'was obviously very "Dada"' because it had 'turned the art establishment upside down and contributed to the emergence of a new generation'; second, that 'the time to promote the Dada spirit explicitly in China' had therefore 'arrived'; third, that the strain of artistic postmodernism exemplified by Western Dada can be seen to correspond in detail with aspects of traditional Chinese thinking and practice associated with Daoist influenced Chan Buddhism—such as Zhuangzi's notion of 'the ubiquity of the Dao' and a Daoist belief in the 'equality, sameness, and coexistence of everything'; fourth, that works by Western postmodernist artists such as Robert Rauschenberg, John Cage and Joseph Beuys therefore 'embody the essence of Eastern thought—that is, greatness and vastness, nonattachment, and following nature's lead'; and fifth, that Dada can thus be interpreted as a modern 'renaissance' of Chan Buddhism insofar as both uphold 'the impossible reality of reality, as well as extreme doubt and disbelief.'

Although he does not say so explicitly in 'Xiamen Dada—a Kind of Postmodernism?' by mounting this series of arguments, Huang can be interpreted as having put forward what is effectively a deconstructive view of the historical relationship between Western avant-garde art and that of China by undermining the supposedly originary status of the former—a situation which he complicates still further by arguing that, while close in spirit, art and Chan are not equitable with one another and that neither Dada nor Chan Buddhism have any fixed historical standing but are constantly open to reinterpretation within differing historical contexts. Indeed, Huang gives further credence to such a reading by stating explicitly that '[e]verything that hasn't yet appeared will certainly disembark one day—it's just a matter of time before everything comes to China—which will bring about a more complete confusion' and that '[i]n the art world, everything is permitted, but this freedom and this permission are not worth anything in themselves, because having freedom, and even the greatest extent of permission, also means that untruthfulness exists…[t]herefore, one of the main characteristics of a new kind of artwork, artist and public is the blurring of boundaries.'

In his essay 'A Completely Empty Signifier,' Huang then goes on to bolster the arguments set out in 'Xiamen Dada—a Kind of Postmodernism?' by arguing that signifying practices associated with Dada and Chan Buddhism can be interpreted through the use of structuralist theory as revealing the inherent emptiness of linguistic signification insofar as both leave the meaning of linguistic signs open to the meditations of the reader—an argument which Huang illustrates by referring to a passage from volume one of the Buddhist classic the *Collection of Five Lamps* (*Wudeng huiyuan* 五灯会元), in which Buddha holds up a flower as a sign to a group of his followers saying 'I have the eye of the true law, the secret essence of *Nirvana*, the formless form and the ineffable *Dharma* which is not dependent on speech or words; a special transmission beyond all the other teachings.'

Although the exhibitions and events staged by Xiamen Dada were clearly far more provocative in relation to prevailing Chinese cultural mores than those carried out by the Northern Art Group and the Pond Association, it would, however, be a mistake to see such cultural provocations as involving a clearly defined political or critical intent on the part of the group beyond the addressing of localized Chinese concerns related to the production and reception of art. Again, it is conceivable that the group chose not to disclose its collective political position for fear of the consequences of doing so. However, in the absence of any evidence supporting such a view, no unequivocal statement on the subject can be made. Nevertheless, it is possible to view Xiamen Dada's profoundly sceptical vision of linguistic signification—alongside that of the Pond Association—as implicitly critical, intentionally or otherwise, of the CCP's long-standing alignment with the principles of scientific Marxism-Leninism and the associated notion that historical events are subject to objective representation.

A Conversation with members of Xiamen Dada

Xiamen Dada[7]: Lin Jiahua (b. 1953), Huang Yongping (b. 1954), Jiao Yaoming (b. 1957) and Yu Xiaogang (b. 1958)[8]
Paul Gladston: When, where and under what circumstances did Xiamen Dada first come together as a group?

Yu Xiaogang: Most of us graduated from university in either 1981 or 1982. Jiao Yaoming was a student in the sculpture department at the Guangzhou Academy of Fine Arts from 1977 to 1981. I studied in the oil painting department of the Zhejiang Academy of Fine Arts in Hangzhou from 1978 to 1982. And Huang Yongping graduated from the Zhejiang Academy of Fine Arts in 1982. Lin Jiahua didn't go to university. He was an art director. During May 1983, we held an exhibition at the Cultural Palace in the City of Xiamen (*Xiamen wenhua guan* 厦门文化馆), titled A Modern Art Exhibition of Five Artists (*Wuren xiandai huazhan* 五人现代画展). It was through this exhibition that the five members of what was to become Xiamen Dada—Huang Yongping, Lin Jiahua, Jiao Yaoming, Xu Chengdou and me, Yu Xiaogang—first started working together. When our first exhibition opened, there was a remarkable public response.[9] At the time of the exhibition, official art in China was still strongly influenced by socialist-realism from the Soviet Union. The idea of the exhibition was to resist that influence.[10] Later on, the work of the group had nothing to do with this initial idea. Huang Yongping became the leader among us. Members of Xiamen Dada then participated in two further exhibitions: one titled the Xiamen Dada Modern Art Exhibition (*Xiamen dada xiandai yishu zhan* 厦门达达现代艺术展), which took place at the Xiamen Cultural Museum between 28 September and 5 October 1986; and then another known as Events or Attack Museum Event (*Xiji meishuguan shijian* 袭击美术馆事件), which opened in December 1986 at the Fujian Fine Art Museum in Fujian Province. For this exhibition, we collected together a thousand-year-old boat and other antiques which we destroyed before distributing the remains around the museum. The exhibition was closed by the propaganda ministry two hours after its opening. Only four members of Xiamen Dada,

Huang Yongping, Lin Jiahua, Jiao Yaoming and me, Yu Xiaogang, took part in this last exhibition. We were also involved in an action, known as the *Burning Event,* which took place in Wenhua Gong Square (*Wenhua Gong guangchang* 文化宫广场) next to the Xiamen Cultural Museum on 23 November 1986, after the Xiamen Dada Modern Art Exhibition. Some representative work by Xiamen Dada was also included in the China/Avant-Garde exhibition in Beijing in 1989.

PG: When did you first start to use the name Xiamen Dada?

YX: It was in September 1986, before we started organizing the big Xiamen Dada exhibition. I brought forward the name saying: 'Dada, Dada Art, Dada....' Then we met to discuss what we were going to call the new exhibition; finally, we—Lin Jiahua, Huang Yongping, Jiao Yaoming and me—chose the name 'Xiamen Dada.'

PG: Were there other members or close associates of Xiamen Dada apart from the four of you and Xu Chengdou? One source claims that at the time of Xiamen Dada's second exhibition, in late 1986, there were ten members of the group, including Huang Yongping, Jia Tiaran, Jiao Yaoming, Cai Lixiong, Li Yuenian, Li Xiang, Lin Jiahua, Lin Chun and Wu Yanping. The same source also claims that, at the time, Xiamen Dada was jointly led by Huang Yongping and Jia Tiaran (Berghuis 2008: 47). Other sources also identify Lin Chun as a member of the group.

YX: Yes, we did invite some local artists and art students to join with us. Of course, we wanted to expand the Xiamen Dada art group.

PG: When did the activities of Xiamen Dada come to an end?

YX: The group broke up towards the end of the 1980s. In 1989, Huang Yongping went to France to participate in the international survey exhibition Magiciens de la Terre at the Pompidou Centre in Paris.[11] Soon afterwards the events of 4 June 1989 overtook us and Huang Yongping stayed in Paris. Huang Yongping now lives and works as an artist in France. Lin Jiahua currently lives and works as an artist in Xiamen. He owns an advertising company there. Jiao Yaoming lives and works as an artist in Guangzhou, China. And I live and work as an artist in Melbourne, Australia.

PG: When you first got together as a group during the early 1980s, how much did you know about the history of the Western avant-gardes? In particular, how much did you know about the activities of Dada in the West?

Huang Yongping: We had heard of the Western avant-gardes and knew something about them even though China was still quite closed during the early 1980s. Information about the

West came to China on and off, but one had to search for it and put it into some sort of historical order by oneself. We had a good knowledge of Western Dada; for example, the names of its members. We had also begun to touch on Western art theories. The reason we called our group Xiamen Dada had something to do with Western Dada. So, it would be accurate to say that the name of our group was influenced by the West.

PG: To what extent did the events of the Cultural Revolution influence the activities of Xiamen Dada? I'm thinking here, in particular, of the use of big character posters, large-scale paintings and performances during the Cultural Revolution as direct forms of public communication as well as the widespread destruction of traditional culture—for example, the public burning of books—which took place at that time, both of which would appear to resonate strongly with aspects of the work of Xiamen Dada.

Lin Jiahua: You're asking about the influence on our work of the Cultural Revolution and the damage to Chinese culture and society which took place at that time. I think we were greatly affected by those events. We wanted to change things through the art we loved.

HY: Artistic formalities during the Cultural Revolution were quite simplistic, but the essence of it was to damage existing things. It was a release to young people. Life during the Cultural Revolution was a revolutionary life—very political—which is very different from life in China today. Life in China is now much more diverse. The exhibitions we did in 1983 and 1986 were different from those which took place during the Cultural Revolution, that's for sure [laughs]. We were quite young when we formed Xiamen Dada. As Xiaogang just said, we had just graduated from university. At that time, it was very difficult for young graduates to find work within the traditional fine art organizations or institutions. So what we did in forming Xiamen Dada as an unofficial art organization had something to do with the existing social conditions. We often say art is closely related to life. The things we paid attention to changed as life in China changed. As I mentioned before, life before the 1980s was political, but during and after the 1980s, it was different. As a result of the adoption of Deng Xiaoping's policy of opening-up and reform, our life was no longer dominated by politics. So, what we paid attention to also changed.

PG: Artists associated with Dada in the West were highly critical of authority and tradition as well as what they saw as the means-end rationality and inauthenticity of modern life. Their work is characterized by the use of collage-montage techniques which often seek to bring art and life violently together as a means of critically reworking the latter along the more playful lines of the former. Was that also the case with regard to the activities of Xiamen Dada?

YX: We had the idea to work together, but it had nothing to do with violence, or being against anything. We wouldn't deny that Western art influenced us to some extent, but it's more to do with ourselves and the situation we were in. It's not like we tried to copy or interpret someone else's art, especially Western modern art. They, Dada, were also a very small group, just like us. I think we were making art just for fun.

HY: We can't assess the influence of the Western avant-gardes and the Cultural Revolution on the work of Xiamen Dada so mechanically. The reason why our group was called Xiamen Dada had something to do with the influence of the Western Avant-gardes. But it also had something to do with our own experiences and the social background within China at the time. It was very complex. It's unavoidable that when we talk about the historical situation, we do so from current perspectives. But it's better to look at the historical material and leave it in the past. We can have a big discussion now, but there must have been some real circumstances at the time.

PG: Artists associated with Western Dada were often highly politicized. Was Xiamen Dada a politicized group in any sense?

YX: We were initially against the socialist-realist style of art from the Soviet Union, but that had nothing to do with politics. We just wanted to try out other things.

PG: Was that your only frame of reference: a desire to develop new forms of artistic expression? Didn't you see your work as having a critical function in relation to Chinese society and politics?

YX: Jiahua had his own advertising company at the time, the rest of us were art teachers. Jiao Yaoming and I both taught at The Xiamen Academy of Art and Design (*Xiamen yishu yu sheji xueyuan* 厦门艺术与设计学院) from 1982 till 1989. Jiahua's life conditions were better than ours. He was the owner of the first private advertising company in Xiamen. We got a lot of financial support from him. We didn't want to create something big, we shared some ideas and we just wanted to do something for fun—something that was different from what others were doing.

Jiao Yaoming: Other than being against the style of art from the Soviet Union, we didn't have particular purposes or aims when we first started the group. Because of the opening-up and reform policy, we saw a lot of changes. We were rebellious and we wanted to do something to break the existing restrictions on art.

PG: What other things did you do together apart from making art and talking about art?

YX: We were very close friends and we often visited each other when we had time. Actually, when we got together we seldom talked about art.

HY: Though we didn't talk about art that often, we all had the idea of doing an exhibition together. So we talked about that. After our first exhibition together in 1983, we thought it would be good to do bigger exhibitions.

YX: In talking about our work together and the exhibitions, we should mention Xu Chengdou, who passed away in 1999. He was born in Vietnam and lived there for many years before coming back to China. He often invited us to his place to drink coffee, which wasn't that common in China at that time. He liked French art very much and he knew quite a lot about French art. He had a friend who lived in Paris who often sent letters to him with interesting pictures taken from art magazines or other information on European art.

PG: Why did Xu Chengdou come back to live in the PRC?

YX: Xu Chengdou's ancestors were from Xiamen. Although he was born in Vietnam, he loved China and felt that it was his motherland. Another reason he returned to China was because of the Vietnam War.

PG: Were you influenced by the information about European art which was sent to Chengdou?

HY: The information and the pictures sent to Chengdou weren't so important. They didn't have a direct impact on our art-making.

PG: Could you say something about the influence of traditional Chinese cultural thought and practice on the work of Xiamen Dada?

JY: We were influenced quite a lot, I think. Huang Yongping was greatly influenced by traditional Chinese aesthetics and philosophical ideas. We can see the influence of those things on his work during the 1980s; for example, his work, *Wet Method – 'History of Chinese Painting' and 'Concise History of Modern Painting' Washed for Two Minutes in a Washing Machine* (*Zhongguo huihua shi he ziandai huihua jian shi zai xiyiji li jiaoban le liang fen zhong* 中国绘画史和现代绘画简史在洗衣机里搅拌了两分钟) (1987). The way Yongping used the *taijitu* 太极图 was similar to the way in which Duchamp made his art.[12] As for Yu Xiaogang, he knows a lot about traditional Chinese art, for instance, calligraphy. Though he studied oil painting, some of his works used Chinese ink and water colours. At the time, we didn't integrate Chinese and Western aesthetics deliberately. One thing I would like to emphasize is that what we did was actually part of Chinese culture. As for the spirit of Western Dada, it met our needs at the time because we were trying to break away from established tradition.

YX: I think the similarities between traditional Chinese ways of thinking and those of Western Dada are a kind of coincidence.

PG: Writings by Huang Yongping published in China during the mid-1980s, including the essays 'Xiamen Dada—a Kind of Postmodernism?' and 'A Completely Empty Signifier' (Huang 1986: 1; 1989: 30–32, 72), suggest that as a group you were aware of an affinity between the work of the Western avant-gardes, including Dada, and traditional East-Asian cultural thought and practice. The work of the musician John Cage had a significant impact on the development of Huang Yongping's work at this time. Cage openly acknowledged the influence of geomantic divinatory practices associated with the *I Ching* 易经 (*The Book of Changes*)[13] on his approach to musical composition. This, in turn, I think, allowed Yongping to conceive of a contemporary Chinese art that would bring together and play across the boundary between Western and Chinese cultural influences. What I'm interested in here is the idea that by coming to know the work of the Western avant-gardes you were also engaging critically with aspects of traditional East-Asian thought and practice that had previously been mediated/translated by Western artists for their own purposes.

JY: Yes, we were aware of these art-historical facts.

YX: Although, we did wonder at the time how Daoist and Buddhist thinking had been introduced to Western countries.

HY: I read a story about Duchamp somewhere: he was asked whether he was interested in Oriental culture, he answered that it's enough to have European culture. Looking at his work, it's not immediately obvious that he was influenced by Oriental culture. I think there might be some Oriental influences on his work, but he absorbed them so well that you don't notice. As you say, I compared Dadaism and Chan Buddhism and wrote an article about it called 'Xiamen Dada—a Kind of Postmodernism?' which was published in 1986. A Chinese journalist once interviewed John Cage, and told him there was a Dada group in China. He said: 'there's no need.'[14] So I think it's really a matter of personal choice. Everyone has his or her own interpretations. I met Cage at an exhibition in 1992.[15] He was quite old and not so well. Since I couldn't speak English, I didn't talk to him. I think we all have predecessors, either in China or elsewhere, whom we are inspired or influenced by. We respect these predecessors, but sometimes the respect is shown in a disrespectful way. We draw on their experience, but also try to avoid being influenced by them too much. Dadaism is just like a stone which has been thrown somewhere, and picked up by somebody. It doesn't decay and can be used at any time. Each generation uses it to break the silence and interpret things in a new way. So it's not a question of whether one is influenced by Western culture or not. It's something that re-emerges generation after generation.

PG: It's undeniable that there are conceptual and practical similarities between Dada and Daoism, as well as aspects of Chan Buddhism. But they shouldn't be conflated. Even though there are historical links between Dada, Daoism and Buddhism, they are by no means identical with one another. The collage-montage and automatist techniques associated with the Western avant-gardes can be interpreted as deconstructive—that is to say, as ways of performatively demonstrating the inherent instability of linguistic meaning and, therefore, the absence of any single authoritative meaning or all-encompassing metaphysical state of being—while Daoism and Chan Buddhism point towards something similar but are ultimately metaphysical in their outlook. Yongping's essays acknowledge the possibility of the historical mutability of Chan Buddhism and Daoism—that they might now have manifested themselves as an aspect of contemporary Chinese art—but they don't discuss fully the historical differences between the deconstructive tendencies of the Western avant-gardes and the metaphysical tendencies of Daoism/Chan Buddhism.

HY: Western deconstruction and Daoism or Chan Buddhism may appear to have some similarities. But, as you say, it would be a little bit strained to lump them together directly. The origins of these things are quite different. Deconstruction was based on Western metaphysics. Nevertheless, it shouldn't be denied that there are some connections between these different cultural heritages. The connections can be grasped by some individuals. Some people can connect things which seem obscure to others.

YX: As Huang said, Dada is just like a stone. During a particular period of time, the younger generation or some other people may choose to pick up the stone and break the silence, just like Xiamen Dada did. We saw a stone, but we didn't know exactly where that stone came from. We just picked it up. We didn't know where to throw it, or where it would end up.

PG: In other words, it's important not to see cultural influence in too simplistic a way. What you are suggesting is that we should abandon the idea that Xiamen Dada was simply an extension of Western Dada. It's more complex than that. The relay of historical events is more complicated and unstable.

YX: I think your point is appropriate.

HY: Dadaism was mentioned in Japan during the 1920s. Xiamen Dada was founded 60 years later. So it's impossible for Western art historians to include Xiamen Dada directly in the lineage of Western Dadaism. The time gap is just too big. Another point is that while we gave our group the name Xiamen Dada, our ideas were different from Dadaism. In the name of our group…the Dada part was just a symbol.

JY: I'd like to say something too. We were not trying to imitate or copy Dada. In 1986, I made a series of photographic works, titled *Chair* (*Yizi* 椅子), which was about the back of a chair. The back of the chair was arranged in four different ways: straight on to the viewer, sideways, diagonally and lying flat. It's just like our thoughts at the time. There were many different ways to express things. This might be similar to Duchamp or the spirit of Dada.

PG: Was Xiamen Dada influenced at all by its immediate surroundings in Xiamen and the province of Fujian—for example, the landscape or the local culture? Members of the Northern Art Group have been explicit in making a link between their 'rational' approach towards painting and the 'cold' landscapes of northern China where they were based.

HY: Most of the members of Xiamen Dada were not from Xiamen. We were from different places: Yu Xiaogang was originally from Hangzhou; Jiao Yaoming was from Guangzhou; and Huang Yongping and Lin Jiahua were both from Xiamen. Xu Chengdou, was born in Vietnam. Not all of us were rooted in the local culture of Xiamen. The Xiamen in Xiamen Dada was simply a name identifying the location of the group.

YX: We were in Xiamen at the time and we had to give our group a name. That's how we came to call the group Xiamen Dada.

PG: Xiamen Dada is perhaps best known for the action the *Burning Event*: a public bonfire of the group's more conventional artworks that took place on 24 November 1986 after the end of the Xiamen Dada Modern Art Exhibition at the Fujian Fine Art Museum. What was Xiamen Dada aiming to do by carrying out this spectacular sacrificial act? A declaration accompanying the *Burning Event*, titled 'Statement on Burning,' suggests that the event was an attempt to liberate the group from conventional artistic expectations and desires through a calculated act of self-negation. The final passage of the statement asserts that

> Artworks are to artists what opium is for men.
> Not until art is destroyed will life be peaceful.
> Dada is dead! Beware of Fire! (Huang 2010a: 95)[16]

The reference to opium, and by extension the China's involvement in the Opium Wars during the nineteenth century, also suggests a resistance to the debilitating effects of outside cultural and economic influence.

JY: The case of the bonfire of our works should be looked at according to the context at that time. Our intention was to explore new things and to satisfy our curiosity. We didn't think about making any public impact or being written into the history of Chinese fine art. If I had known that in the future there would be organizations wanting to collect our artworks, I wouldn't have allowed us to burn it all [laughs].[17]

YX: To quote a Buddhist term, the bonfire should be considered as *Nirvana*: that is to say an act of self-liberation—the extinguishing of desire, of individualism and a sign of the ultimate emptiness of things. It wasn't an easy thing to do—to burn our works in public. So in a way, what we did even surpassed Dada. We burned everything. They just talked about destroying art—about anti-art—we actually carried it out.

PG: Did you need permission from the authorities to carry out the *Burning Event*? If so, who gave you permission?

YX: By that time we did not need any permission from the authorities to burn our artworks.

PG: Some sources say Xiamen Dada was banned by the authorities after the *Burning Event*. Was Xiamen Dada banned as a result of the *Burning Event*?[18]

YX: We told the local authorities that we were going to burn our artworks. Xiamen Dada was not banned as a result of the *Burning Event*.

PG: What do you think of recent attempts by some Chinese scholars to detach readings of contemporary Chinese art entirely from the use of Western theories and interpretative methodologies?

HY: Could you explain the intellectual framework of the Chinese theorists you mentioned? In what ways are they different from Western theorists? I don't see much difference between them.

PG: Take Gao Minglu for example: recently he has argued that the historical development of contemporary Chinese art should be interpreted without significant reference to Western concepts such as deconstruction and feminism (Yu 2006: 17–35). Other Chinese critics and art historians have also argued that contemporary Chinese art is imbued with some sort of essential Chinese national-cultural spirit which sets it apart from Western modernist and postmodernist art (Li 2003: 70–73). This is very much at odds with mainstream Western attitudes towards cultural identity, which is now widely seen, in relation to post-colonialism and the notion of third space, as hybrid and unstable rather than essential.

HY: The only difference is that Chinese theorists understand Chinese circumstances better.

PG: What sort of influence do you think the work of Xiamen Dada has had on subsequent generations of contemporary Chinese artists?

HY: I think this question should be posed directly to the young artists themselves. Even though there may well be some influences, we might overlook them. Just as I said earlier, we are all influenced by our predecessors. So we may also have had some impact on the next generation. There could be good influences or bad influences. That's normal.

YX: It's difficult for Xiamen Dada to make a strong impact on the work of young artists because we didn't leave many actual things behind. We burned all of our work at the end of the Xiamen Dada Exhibition of Modern Art in November 1986.

PG: So, the work of Xiamen Dada is in some sense unpresentable—just like Duchamp's ready-made *Fountain*, which no longer exists in its original form, it can't actually be shown other than through representation or simulation. But doesn't that state of unpresentability have continuing repercussions for contemporary Chinese art? Like the unpresentability of Duchamp's *Fountain* for later generations of artists in the West and elsewhere, doesn't it continue to raise questions about the function of art and of representation in a modern capitalist, or capitalist-influenced society?

HY: It's not yet time to draw that conclusion....

Notes

1   The city of Xiamen is in Fujian Province on China's southern seaboard. The city of Xiamen proper occupies a position on Xiamen Island at the mouth of the Jiulong River overlooking an excellent natural harbour. In 1957, a large dike was constructed to support a railway line connecting Xiamen island to the mainland. Opposite Xiamen Island, across the city's inner harbour, is the island of Gulangxu, the former site of a European trading settlement which was first occupied by the Portuguese in the sixteenth century and then the Dutch in the seventeenth century. Xiamen was later captured by the British during the Opium War of 1841 before becoming a treaty port in 1842.

2   This exhibition is sometimes referred to as The Five Person Exhibition of Modern Artists (*Xiamen wuren xiandai yishu zuopin zhan*) (Anon. http://www.asiasociety.org). The exhibition comprised paintings as well as installations and constructions, including Huang Yongping's painting *Haystack (Duocao)* which was based on Bastien Lepage's *Les Foins* with a plaster mask in place of the peasant woman's face. One commentator has interpreted *Haystack* not as a critical response to the influence of Soviet socialist realism, as indicated in the conversation with members of Xiamen Dada published here, but as a satire on the tendency of Chinese artists at the time 'to ape Western art without real understanding'(Anon. http://www.asiasociety.org). Berghuis identifies those taking part in The Five Person Exhibition of Modern Artists as Huang Yongping, Jiao Yaoming, Lin Jiahua, Qian Xiaogang and Xu Chengtou (Berghuis 2008: 47).

3   For an alternative English translation of Xiamen Dada's 'Statement on the Burning,' see Fei (2007: 35).

4   Here it is also possible to read intentional or unconscious allusions to China's involvement in the Anglo-Chinese Opium Wars (1839–1842 and 1856–1860). In this light the incineration of modern Westernized art can also be interpreted as a symbolic resistance to the persistence of Western colonialist/imperialist influence.

5   Köppel-Yang states that Xiamen Dada held three exhibitions and three events together. However, she only discusses two exhibitions and one event in any detail: Xiamen Dada's 'first exhibition,' which she says opened on 28 September 1986 at the New Art Gallery of Xiamen City (*Xiamen shi xin yishu guan* 厦门市新艺术馆); *The Burning Event*, which she says took place in November 1986 at the end of the group's first exhibition; and Xiamen Dada's third exhibition, which she says took place at the Museum of Fujian Province (no date given) and was closed by the authorities because of public indignation after only one and a half hours. Köppel-Yang makes the anachronistic claim that this exhibition comprised found objects, installations and objects which were then consumed at *The Burning Event* in November 1986 (Köppel-Yang 2003: 61–62). Berghuis dates *The Burning Event* to October 1986, following a large group exhibition at the Xiamen City Arts Gallery of the Masses (no dates given). Berghuis also states that because *The Burning Event* consumed artworks intended for a group exhibition at a provincial museum in the city of Fuzhou, Fujian Province, the exhibition in question, titled Events, consequently contained scrap materials collected from the streets (Berghuis 2008: 47). Another source states that an exhibition of the work of Xiamen Dada, titled 'Exhibition of Xiamen Dada' (*Xiamen dada xiandai yishu zhan* 厦门达达现代艺术展) took place in September 1986 (no venue given) and that *The Burning Event* took place on 24 November 1986. The same source also refers to an exhibition of the work of Xiamen Dada in December 1986 (Anon. http://www.asiasociety.org).

6   For an English translation of Huang's 'Introduction to the Events Exhibition that took place at the Exhibition Hall of the Fujian Art Museum,' see Wu with Wang (2010: 96).

7   This is an edited version of a conversation recorded at the Rosedale Hotel in Beijing on 21 March 2008; the day after the opening of a major retrospective of the work of Huang Yongping titled 'The House of Oracles' at the Ullens Centre for Contemporary Art in Beijing. The conversation included four members of Xiamen Dada: Huang Yongping, Yu Xiaogang, Lin Jiahua and Jiao Yaoming. A fifth member of the group, Xu Chengdou, who is referred to during the conversation, died in 1999.

8   Köppel-Yang identifies the members of Xiamen Dada as Huang Yongping, Cai Lixiong, Lin Chun and Jiao Yaoming (Köppel-Yang 2008: 61). Another source identifies the members of Xiamen Dada as Huang Yongping, Cha Lixiong, Liu Yiling, Lin Chun and Jiao Yaoming (Anon. http://www.asiasociety.org). A catalogue accompanying the 1985 New Wave exhibition at the Ullens Centre in Beijing identifies the main members of Xiamen Dada as Lin Jiahua, Jiao Yaoming, Yu Xiaogang, Lin Chun and Huang Yong Ping.

9   One source claims that the exhibition was never opened to the public (Anon. http://www. asiasociety.org).

10   Although this exhibition was staged at the height of the Anti-Spiritual Pollution Campaign (1983–1984), it is likely to have been made possible by the unevenness of restrictions on artistic expression at a local level within the PRC at the time.

11   The exhibition Magiciens de la Terre, which was staged at Centre Georges Pompidou and La Grande Halle de la Villette between 18 May and 14 August 1989, was the first major international survey show to include work by contemporary artists from the PRC. The three Chinese artists included in the exhibition were, Huang Yongping, Gu Dexin and Yang Jiechang. The exhibition was organized by the director of the Centre Georges Pompidou,

Jean-Hubert Martin. The Chinese critic Fei Dawei was responsible for the selection and organization of the work of the Chinese artists included in the exhibition.

12   The traditional Chinese symbol the *taijitu* 太极图 (*yin-yang* 阴阳 symbol) depicts the relationship between the primal cosmic forces of *yin* and *yang*—*yang* relating to light and masculinity and *yin* darkness and femininity. The *taijitu* pictures the relationship between *yin* and *yang* as a reciprocal one in which each term remains distinct but in a state of dynamic interaction with the other. By placing Western and Chinese art-historical texts together in a washing machine and washing them until they became a pulpy mass as part of the artwork *Wet Method – 'History of Chinese Painting' and 'Concise History of Modern Painting' Washed for Two Minutes in a Washing Machine*, Huang Yongping can be understood to have played knowingly with this traditional Chinese conception.

13   The *I Ching* (*The Classic of Changes* or *Book of Changes*) or *Zhouyi* 周易, as it is otherwise known, is one of Chinese culture's oldest texts. The book, which upholds the concepts of dynamic balance between opposites and the persistence of change, contains a system of geomantic divination that is still widely used within the PRC. The concepts of dynamic balance between opposites and the persistence of change are conventionally symbolized by the well-known *taijitu* or *yin-yang* symbol. Within the *I Ching* the dynamic interaction between *yin* and *yang* is further subdivided into eight principles known as the *bagua* 八卦, each of which is represented by a symbolic arrangement of lines.

14   This ambiguous assertion suggests that Dadaist attitudes were in some sense already part of vernacular Chinese culture.

15   John Cage died in 1992.

16   For an alternative English translation of Xiamen Dada's 'Statement on the Burning,' see Fei ed. (2007: 35).

17   Xiamen Dada's 'Statement on the Burning' includes the following passage: 'The fact that art collection doesn't exist in China might be a good thing; an artist can therefore do whatever he likes with his works and does not have to be careful with them.'

18   According to at least one source, this resulted in the group being banned from mounting any further public art exhibitions (Anon. http://www.asiasociety.org).

References

Ai, Weiwei and Feng, Boyi eds. (2000), *Fuck Off* (*Bu hezuo fangshi* 不合作方式), Shanghai: Eastlink Gallery.

Andrews, Julia (1994), *Painters and Politics in the People's Republic of China, 1949–1979*, Berkeley: University of California Press.

Anon (n.d.), 'An Exhibition which Twice Took Beijing by Storm', http://www.shigebao.com. Accessed 1 March 2010.

—— (n.d.), 'New Chinese Art Chronologies', http://www.asiasociety.org. Accessed 6 December 2006.

—— (n.d.), http://www.artinfo.com. Accessed 11 January 2010.

—— (n.d.), http://www.todayartmuseum.com. Accessed 11 January 2010.

Beccaria, Marcella (2005), 'Yang Fudong: The Foreigner and the Search for Poetic Truth', in Marcella Beccaria, et al. (eds.), *Yang Fudong*, Milan: Skira, pp. 18–27.

Berghuis, Thomas J. (2006), *Performance Art in China*, Hong Kong: Timezone 8.

Bhabha, Homi K. (1994), *The Location of Culture*, London: Routledge.

Bigsby, C.W.E. (1978), *Dada and Surrealism*, London: Methuen.

Bürger, Peter (1984) [1974], *Theory of the Avant-Garde*, Manchester: Manchester University Press.

Burn, Gordon (2009), *Sex & Violence, Death and Silence: Encounters with Recent Art*, London: Faber & Faber.

Chang, Fangwei ed. (2005), *The Yellow Box: Contemporary Calligraphy and Painting in Taiwan*, Taipei: Taipei Fine Arts Museum.

Chang, Tsong-zung et al. (1989), *The Stars: Ten Years*, Hong Kong: Hanart 2 Gallery.

Chen, Yingde (1987), *Haiwai kan dalu yishu* 海外看大陆艺术 (*Overseas Perspectives on Mainland Art*), Taipei: Artists' Press.

Choucha, Nadi (1991), *Surrealism and the Occult*, Oxford: Mandrake Books.

Clarke, David (2008), 'Revolutions in Vision: Chinese Art and the Experience of Modernity', in Kam Louie (ed.), *The Cambridge Companion to Modern Chinese Culture*, Cambridge: Cambridge University Press.

Clunas, Craig (2009) [1997], *Art in China*, 2nd ed., Oxford: Oxford University Press.

Confucius (1979), *The Analects* (trans. D.C. Lau), London: Penguin Classics.

Danzker, Jo-Anne Birnie (2004), 'Shanghai Modern', in Jo-Anne Birnie Danzker, Ken Lum and Shengtian Zhang (eds.), *Shanghai Modern: 1919–1945*, Munich: Hatje Cantz, pp. 18–72.

Derrida, Jacques (1972), *Margins of Philosophy*, London: Routledge.

—— (1974), *Glas*, Paris: Editions Galilée.

Erickson, Britta (2005), *On the Edge: Contemporary Chinese Artists Encounter the West*, Hong Kong: Timezone 8.

Fei, Dawei ed. (2007), *'85 New-Wave: the Birth of Chinese Contemporary Art*, Beijing: Ullens Centre.

Gao, Minglu (1987), '*Beifang Yishu Tuanti Shuangnian Zhan*' 北方艺术团体双年展('Biennial Exhibition of the Northern Art Group'), *Zhongguo meishu bao* 中国美术报(*Fine Arts in China*), April, p. 98.

——— (1991), *Zhongguo dangdai meishu shi 1985–1986* 中国当代美术史 *1985–1986* (*Chinese Contemporary Fine Arts 1985–1986*), Shanghai: Shanghai People's Press.

——— (2005), *The Wall: Reshaping Contemporary Chinese Art*, Buffalo: Albright-Knox Gallery; Beijing: Today Art Museum.

——— (2007a), *The '85 Movement: An Anthology of Historical Sources*, vols. 1 and 2, Guanxi: Gaunxi Normal University Press.

——— (2007b), *The No Name: A History of A Self-Exiled Avant-Garde*, Guangxi: Guanxi Normal University Press.

Gladston, Paul (2007), 'Overcoming the Anxiety of Displacement: Song Tao and B6's Video Installation *Yard*', in Nicholas Hewitt and Dick Geary (eds.), *Diaspora(s): Movements and Cultures*, Nottingham: Critical, Cultural and Communications Press, pp. 183–195.

——— (2008a), 'A(n) (In)Decisive Act of Disclosure: Reflections on the '85 New-Wave Exhibition at the Ullens Centre for Contemporary Art in Beijing', *Yishu: Journal of Contemporary Chinese Art*, 7:2, pp. 98–104.

——— (2008b), 'Chan-Da-da(o)-De-construction or, The Cultural (Il)Logic of Contemporary Chinese 'Avant-Garde' Art', *Yishu*, 7:4, pp. 63–69.

——— (2008c), 'Something (and Nothing) Beyond the Text', in Robin Peckham (ed.) *Song Kun: Fragments—River Lethe*, Beijing: Timezone 8.

——— (2008d), 'Song Ling in Conversation with Paul Gladston', *Yishu*, 7:6, pp. 50–60.

——— (2009), 'Bloody Animals!: Reinterpreting Acts of Violence Against Animals as Part of Contemporary Chinese Artistic Practice', in Lili Hernández and Sabine Krajewski (eds.), *Crossing Cultural Boundaries: Taboo, Bodies and Identity*, Newcastle-upon-Tyne: Cambridge Scholars, pp. 92–104.

——— (2011a), 'Answering the Question: What is the Chinese Avant-Garde—Zhai Zhenming in Conversation with Paul Gladston', http://www.randian-online.com. Accessed 1 September 2011.

——— (2011b), *Contemporary Art in Shanghai: Conversations with Seven Chinese Artists*, Hong Kong: Timezone 8–Blue Kingfisher.

——— (2011c), 'Low Resolution: Towards an Uncertain Reading of the Art of Zhang Peili', in Robin Peckham and Venus Lau (eds.), *Zhang Peili: Certain Pleasures*, Shanghai: Mingsheng Art Museum, pp. 36–42.

Gombrich, Ernst H. (1979), 'A Plea for Pluralism', in *Ideals and Idols: Essays on Values in History and in Art*, London: Phaidon, pp. 184–188.

Greenberg, Clement (1939), 'Avant-Garde and Kitsch', *Partisan Review*, 6:5, pp. 34–49.

——— (1965), 'Modernist Painting', *Art and Literature*, 4, pp. 193–201

Hou, Hanru (2002), *On the Mid Ground* (ed. Yu Hsaio-Hwei), Hong Kong: Timezone 8.

Huang, Rui (2010) [1979], 'Preface to the First Stars Exhibition (*Xingxing Meizhan* 星星美展)', in Hung Wu and Wang Peggy (eds.), *Contemporary Chinese Art: Primary Documents*, New York: Museum of Modern Art, pp. 7–8.

Huang, Yongping (1986), '*Xiamen Dada—yizhong hou xiandai?*' 厦门达达——一种后现代? ('Xiamen Dada—a Kind of Post-Modernism?'), *Zhongguo meishu bao* 中国美术报(*Fine Arts in China*), 46, p. 1.

——— (1989), '*Wanquan kong de nengzhi*' 完全空的能指('A Completely Empty Signifier'), *Meishu zazhi* 美术杂志(*Art*), 3, pp. 30–32 and 72.

——— (2010a) [1986], 'Statement on Burning', in Hung Wu and Wang Peggy (eds.), *Contemporary Chinese Art: Primary Documents*, New York: Museum of Modern Art, pp. 95–96.

——— (2010b) [1986], 'Introduction to the Events Exhibition that Took Place at the Exhibition Hall of the Fujian Art Museum', in Hung Wu and Wang Peggy (eds.), *Contemporary Chinese Art: Primary Documents*, New York: Museum of Modern Art, p. 96.

Jameson, Fredric (1992), *Postmodernism, or, the Cultural Logic of Late Capitalism*, London: Verso.

Jullien, François (2004), *In Praise of Blandness: Proceeding from Chinese Thought and Aesthetics*, New York: Zone Books.

Köppel-Yang, Martina (2003), *Semiotic Warfare: The Chinese Avant-Garde, 1979–1989—a Semiotic Analysis*, Hong Kong: Timezone 8.

Li, Xianting (1980), '*Guanyu Xingxing meizhan*' 关于星星美展('About the Stars Art Exhibition'), *Meishu zazhi* 美术杂志 (*Art*), 147:3, pp. 8–9.

——— (2010) [1980], 'About the Stars Art Exhibition', in Hung Wu and Wang Peggy (eds.), *Contemporary Chinese Art: Primary Documents*, New York: Museum of Modern Art, pp. 11–13.

Li, Xu (2003), 'Chinese Contemporary Art that has transcended its Identity', in David Chan (ed.), *Beyond Boundaries*, Shanghai: Shanghai Gallery of Art, pp. 70–73.

Li, Zehou (1999) [1981], *The Path of Beauty—A Study of Chinese Aesthetics* (trans. Gong Lizeng), Beijing: Morning Glory Publishers.

Liu, Yuanyuan (2006), '*Kongzi de "da" he "zhunagmei" yu xifang "chonggao" meixue de yitong*' 孔子的"大"和"壮美"与西方"崇高"美学的异同('The Differences and Similarities between Confucian "Giant" and "Magnificence" and the Western "Sublime"'), *Lilun jianshe* 理论建设(*Theory Research*), 4, pp. 69–70.

Louie, Kam (2008), 'Defining Modern Chinese Culture', in Kam Louie (ed.), *The Cambridge Companion to Modern Chinese Culture*, Cambridge: Cambridge University Press, pp. 1–19.

Lü, Peng and Yi, Dan (1991), *Zhongguo xiandai yishu shi, 1979–1989* 中国现代艺术史, 1979–1989 (A History of Modern Chinese Art, 1979–1989), *Changsha: Hunan mei shu chu ban she* 长沙:湖南美术出版社(Hunan Fine Arts Publishing).

Lv, Yintong (2007), 'Recollections of the Pond Association—Interview with Zhang Peili', http://www.mahoo.com.cn. Accessed 1 December 2007.

Lyotard, Jean-François (1984), *The Postmodern Condition: A Report on Knowledge*, Manchester: Manchester University Press.

Mackerras, Colin (2008), *China in Transformation: 1900–1949*, 2nd ed., London: Pearson Education.

Mahon, Alyce (2005), *Surrealism and the Politics of Eros, 1938–1968*, London: Thames and Hudson.

Mainusch, Herbert (2006), 'The Importance of Chinese Philosophy for Western Aesthetics', in Mazhar Hussain and Robert Wilkinson (eds.), *The Pursuit of Comparative Aesthetics: An Interface between the East and West*, Aldershot: Ashgate, pp. 137–143.

Meecham, Pam and Sheldon, Julie (2005), *Modern Art: A Critical Introduction*, 2nd ed., London: Routledge.

Murray, Oswyn (1986), 'Greek Historians', in John Boardman, Jasper Griffin and Oswyn Murray (eds.), *The Oxford History of the Classical World*, Oxford: Oxford University Press, pp. 186–203.

Owens, Craig (1980a), 'The Allegorical Impulse: Towards a Theory of Postmodernism, pt. 1', *October*, 12, pp. 67–86.

—— (1980b), 'The Allegorical Impulse: Towards a Theory of Postmodernism, pt. 2', *October*, 12, pp. 59–80.

Pan, Lynn (2008), *Shanghai Style: Art and Design between the Wars*, Hong Kong: Joint Publishing.

Peckham, Robin (2008), *A Gust of Wind*, Beijing: Boers-Li Gallery.

Peckham Robin and Lau, Venus (eds.) (2011), *Zhang Peili: Certain Pleasures*, Shanghai: Mingsheng Art Museum.

Roberts, Claire (2010). *Friendship in Art: Fou Lei and Huang Binhong*, Hong Kong: Hong Kong University Press.

Shao, Yiyang (2012), 'The International Identity of Chinese Art: Theoretical Debates on Chinese Contemporary Art in the 1990s', in Jason C. Kuo (ed.), *Contemporary Chinese Art and Film: Theory Applied and Resisted*, Washington D.C.: New Academia, pp. 62–77.

Shen, Fuwei (2009), *Cultural Flow between China and Outside World throughout History*, Beijing: Foreign Languages Press.

Shi, Jiu (1987), '*Gunyu xin kongjian he "Chi she"*' 关于新空间和" 池社 ('On New Space and the Pond Association), *Meishu sichao* 美术思潮(*The Trend of Art Thought*), 1, pp. 16–21.

—— (2010) [1987], 'On New Space and the Pond Society', in Hung Wu and Wang Peggy (eds.), *Contemporary Chinese Art: Primary Documents*, New York: Museum of Modern Art, pp. 83–89.

Shu, Qun (1985), '*Beifang yishu qunti de jingshen*' 北方艺术团体的精神('The Spirit of the Northern Art Group'), *Zhongguo meishu bao* 中国美术报(*Fine arts in China*), 18, p. 1.

—— (1987), '*Wei "Beifang yishu qunti" chanshi*' 为北方艺术群体阐释('An Explanation of the Northern Art Group'), *Meishu sichao* 美术思潮(*The Trend of Art Thought*), 1, pp. 36–39.

—— ed. (2009), *Image Dialectic: The Art of Shu Qun (Tuxiang de bianzhengfa: Shu Qun de yishu* 图像的辩证法：舒群的艺术*)*, Shenzhen: OCT Art Terminal.

—— (2010) [1987], 'An Explanation of the Northern Art Group' in Hung Wu and Wang Peggy (eds.), *Contemporary Chinese Art: Primary Documents*, New York: Museum of Modern Art, pp. 79–82.

Smith, Karen (2005), *Nine Lives: The Birth of Avant-garde Art in New China*, Zurich: Scalo.

—— (2006), 'From the Times of Mao Zedong to Today of Wang Guangyi', in *Wang Guangyi: Art and People*, Sichuan: Sichuan Fine Arts Publishing.

Spence, Jonathan (1999), *The Search for Modern China*, 2nd ed., New York: W.W. Norton & Co.

Sullivan, Michael (2001). *Modern Chinese Art: The Khoan and Michael Sullivan Collection*, Oxford: Ashmolean Museum.

Sylvester, David (1980), *Interviews with Francis Bacon, 1962–79*, 2nd revised ed., London: Thames and Hudson.

——— (1987), *Interviews with Francis Bacon: the Brutality of Fact*, 3rd ed., London: Thames and Hudson.

Tang, Xiaobing (2008), *Origins of the Chinese Avant-Garde: the Modern Woodcut Movement*, Berkeley and Los Angeles: University of California Press.

Tong, Dian (2005), *China! New Art and Artists*, Atglen, PA: Schiffer Books.

Ulmer, Gregory L. (1985) [1983], 'The Object of Post-Criticism', in Hal Foster (ed.), *Postmodern Culture*, London: Pluto, pp. 83–110.

Wang, Guangyi (1986a), '*Women zhege shidai xuyao shenmo yang de huihua?*' 我们这个时代需要甚么样的绘画? ('Which Kind of Painting Is Needed in Our Age?'), *Jiangsu huakan* 江苏画刊(*Jiangsu Pictorial*), 4, p. 33.

——— (1986b), '*Women—''85 meishu yundong' de   canyuzhe*'   我们-85美术运动的参与者 ('We—Participants of the ''85 Art Movement'), *Zhongguo meishu bao* 中国美术报(*Fine Arts in China*), 36:September 1986, p. 1.

——— (2010) [1986], 'We—Participants of the ''85 Art Movement', in Hung Wu and Wang Peggy (eds.), *Contemporary Chinese Art: Primary Documents*, New York: Museum of Modern Art, pp. 78–79.

Wang, Keping (2009), *Chinese Way of Thinking*, Shanghai: Shanghai Brilliant Publishing House.

Wang, Yao-t'ing (1995), *Looking at Chinese Painting: A Comprehensive Guide to the Philosophy, Technique and History of Chinese Painting*, Tokyo: Nigensha Publishing.

Whittaker, Richard (2008), *The Conversations: Interviews with Sixteen Contemporary Artists*, Lincoln, NE: Whale and Star, The University of Nebraska Press.

Wimmer, Franz Martin (2004). *Interkulturelle Philosophie*. Vienna: UTB.

Wu, Guanzhong (1979), '*Huihua de xingshi mei*' 绘画的形式美('On the Beauty of Form in Painting'), *Meishu zazhi* 美术杂志(*Art*), 5, pp. 33–35.

——— (1980), '*Guanya chouxiang mei*' 关于抽象美('Concerning the Beauty of the Abstract'), *Meishu zazhi* 美术杂志(*Art*), 10, pp. 37–39.

——— (1981), '*Neirong jueding xingshi*' 内容决定形式('Form is Decided by Content'), *Meishu zazhi* 美术杂志(*Art*), 3, pp. 52–54.

Wu, Hung (2008a), 'A Case of Being "Contemporary": Conditions Spheres and Narratives of Contemporary Chinese Art', in Terry Smith, Okwui Enwezor and Nancy Condee (eds.), *Antinomies of Art and Culture: Modernity, Postmodernity, Contemporaneity*, Durham, NC, and London, UK: Duke University Press.

——— (2008b), *Making History: Wu Hung on Contemporary Art*, Beijing: Timezone 8.

——— with Wang, Peggy (eds.) (2010), *Contemporary Chinese Art: Primary Documents*, New York: The Museum of Modern Art.

Xu, Wenli and Liu, Qing (2010) [1979], 'A Letter to the People' (*Dui ren minde yifeng xin* 一封信给人), in Hung Wu and Wang Peggy (eds.), *Contemporary Chinese Art: Primary Documents*, New York: Museum of Modern Art, pp. 8–10.

Yan, Li (2008), '*Zhaoyu wenge he wode chungzhang*' 文革和我的成长('My Bitter Experience of the Cultural Revolution and My Upbringing'), in Yan Li (ed.), *Jia shi guoshi shidaishi* 家事国

事时代事(*Family, Country and Historical Period*), Hong Kong: *Tianyuan Shuwu* 田原书屋 (Garden Bookstore).

Yang, Luo (2008), '*Bijiao xifang jie gou he Zhuangzhi*' 比较西方后解构和庄子('Compare Western Deconstruction and Zhuangzhi'), http://wenku.baidu.com. Accessed 1 September 2010.

Yu, Christina (2006), 'Curating Chinese Art in the Twenty-first Century: An Interview with Gao Minglu', *Yishu*, 5:1, pp. 17–35.

Zhang, Dainan (2002), *Key Concepts in Chinese Philosophy* (trans. Edmund Ryden), New Haven: Yale University Press.

Zhang, Xueying (2008), 'Thirty Years of Chinese Contemporary Art', *China Today*, 4 April.

Zhu, Qingsheng (1986), '*Fanhui yishu de ren*' 返回到人民的艺术 ('Return Art to the People'), *Meishu zazhi* 美术杂志(*Art*),11, p.56.

Zhu, Zhu (2007a), 'Origin Point: The Star Star Group', in Zhu Zhu (ed.), *Origin Point*, Hong Kong: Visual Art Publications.

Index

I

I Ching (*The Book of Changes*) 28, 169, 175
i-ching 12, 32, 33, 96, 99, 105, 126
Impressionism 13, 71
Inside Out: New Chinese Art (exhibition) 29

J

Jaspers, Karl *109*
Jia, Tiaran 165
Jiang, Feng 44, 79, 117
Jiang, Zhaoke 13
Jiangsu huakan (*Jiangsu Pictorial*) (journal)
    23, 86, 95, 113, 118
Jiao, Yaoming 161, 162, 164, 165, 167, 171,
    173, 174
    Untitled (1986) **161**
Jilin Architecture and Engineering
    College 111
Jilin Art Academy 85, 95, 118
Jintian (*Today*) (journal) 42, 69, 75

K

Ka, Sang 88, 90, 111, 118, 119
    Paintings exhibited at the Northern Art
        Group Biennale (1987) **113**
    Boating on Songhua River (*Songhua he*
        shanghuai chuan) (1984 or 1985) **113**
Kant, Immanuel 92, 116
Kitsch 93, 104
Kollwitz, Käthe 46
Köppel-Yang, Martina 30, 53
Kuhn, Thomas 86, 116
Kuomintang (KMT) 14, 15, 80
Kwok, Mang-ho 42

L

Laozi 86, 87, 109, 140
Lei, Feng 64, 65, 80
Leone, Sergio 136
Lepage, Bastien 161, 173
Li, Keran 33
Li, Shuang 41, 49, 70, 77
Li, Xiang 165

Li, Xianting 41, 45, 85, 89
Li, Yuenian 165
Liberate Your Thinking and Search for the
    Truth in the Facts (directive) 18, 35
Li-jiao 72
Lin, Biao 67, 80
Lin, Chun 165, 174
Lin, Fengmian 13, 17
Lin, Jiahua 161, 162, 164, 165, 166, 171,
    173, 174
    Untitled (1986) **161**
Lin, Tianmiao 27
Lingnan School *14*
Linhai xueyuan (*Linhai Academy*) 62
Literati 27, 46, 64, 79, 87, 108, 110
Liu, Qing 42, 43, 44, 46, 57
Liu, Suola 50
Liu, Xun 43, 79
Liu. Yan 85, 89, 98, 116, 118
London, Jack *53, 109*
Lü, Peng 23
Lu, Xun 71, 81
Luo, Zhongli 20, 102
    Father (*Fuqin*) 20, 21, 100, 101, 102, 104
Luxun Academy of Fine Arts 111, 116, 119
Lyotard, Jean-François 92, 93

M

Ma, Desheng 41, 45, 49, 52, 54, 70, 77
    Untitled (1979) **45**
Madam Mao 66, 67
Magiciens de la Terre (exhibition) 27, 28,
    165, 174
Mang, Ke 42, 43, 53
Mao, Lizi. 41, 49, 70
Mao, Zedong 3, 15, 17, 18, 22, 31, 33, 35, 44, 46,
    51, 57, 61, 64, 76, 79, 81, 94, 117, 135
Marcel, Duchamp 74, 168, 169, 170, 173
Marx, Karl 92
Marxist-Leninism 33, 164
May Fourth Movement 12, 15, 19, 23, 33
Meishu zazhi (*Art*) (journal) 23, 117,
    137, 162

Q

Qi, Baishi 61, 79

qianwei (avant-garde) 30, 32

Qing dynasty 51

Qu, Leilei 41, 45, 46, 49, 52, 54, 61, 77, 80, 81
    Dance (Wu) (1979) **45**

Qu, Xiaosong 50, 77

R

rational analysis 94

Rational Painting 87, 88, 96, 1010, 102, 103,
    105, 108, 111, 118, 125

Rauschenberg, Robert 141, 156, 163

reconstructive memory 4

Red Guards 16, 33, 46, 52, 59, 66, 67, 77

Reform and Opening 3, 18, 23, 44, 85, 157

Ren, Bonian 61, 79

Ren, Jian 85, 89, 116

Renmin jiefangjun (People's Liberation
    Army) 63

Rivera, Diego 15

Rolland, Romain *109*

Rousseau, Jean-Jacques *109*

Rural Realism 20, 86, 91

S

Sanyu (Chang Yu) 13

Sartre, Jean-Paul 137, 143
    Being and Nothingness 109

Scar Art 20, 59, 127, 128

Scar Literature 20, 59

Schlöndorff, Volker 136

Second National Exhibition of Young Art 21

Second Sino–Japanese War 11, 15

self-surveillance/self-discipline 31

Shakespeare, William 99

Shanghai Biennale 29

shan-shui 14, 23, 107, 126, 155

Shao, Fei 70, 77

Shu, Qun 85, 86, 87, 89, 90, 95, 97, 98, 99,
    111, 112, 113, 116, 117, 118, 119, 135
    Absolute Principle (Juedui yuanzi)
        (1985–1989) **87**, 100, 103

*Identity Voice—Rigorous Religious
    Dialogue (Xiangzheng de zhixu xilie)*
    (1985) **107**

shui-mo 17, 34

Sichuan Academy of Fine Arts 20

Sichuan School of Painting 20

Six Announcements 42

Social Darwinism 12

Socialist-realism 3, 15, 17, 25, 30, 41, 56, 86,
    117, 164

Song, Dong 27

Song dynasty 33, 79, 106, 107, 155

Song, Kun 29

Song, Ling 123, 124, 126, 127, 130, 133, 141,
    146, 155, 157

Soviet Union 15, 24, 53, 63, 117, 164, 167

Stars (*Xingxing*) *3, 21, 22, 23, 36, 37, 39–81,
    85, 127, 179*
    Exhibition of the Stars (1979) **41**, 76, 78
    Second official exhibition (1980) **44**
    Stars protest march **43**

Storm Society (*Juelanshe*) 13

Su tuo (Purge Trotsky) 63

sublime (*chonggao)* 92

sublimity and magnificence (*Da)* 86

Sun, Yat-sen 11, 14
    suit 64

Surrealism 71, 104

Sylvester, David 7

T

Tagore, Rabindranath 101, 118

*tai chi 123, 128, 132, 133, 147, 148, 149, 150,
    152, 155*

Taijitu 168, 175

Tan, Dun 77

Tan suo (Explore) (journal) 69

Tan, Wanchun 61

Tang, Song 26

Tangshan earthquake 68, 69, 81

The Day of the Jackal (cinema film) 136

The Wall: Reshaping Contemporary Chinese
    Art (exhibition) 29